Mastering JBoss Drools 6

Discover the power of Drools 6 and Business Rules for
developing complex scenarios in your applications

Mauricio Salatino

Mariano De Maio

Esteban Aliverti

BIRMINGHAM - MUMBAI

Mastering JBoss Drools 6

Copyright © 2016 Packt Publishing

First published: March 2016

Production reference: 1220316

Published by Packt Publishing Ltd.
Livery Place
35 Livery Street
Birmingham B3 2PB, UK.

ISBN 978-1-78328-862-5

www.packtpub.com

Credits

Authors
Mauricio Salatino

Mariano De Maio

Esteban Aliverti

Reviewer
Mario Fusco

Commissioning Editor
Anthony Albuquerque

Acquisition Editor
Llewellyn Rozario

Content Development Editor
Prashanth G Rao

Technical Editor
Danish Shaikh

Copy Editor
Vibha Shukla

Project Coordinator
Bijal Patel

Proofreader
Safis Editing

Indexer
Monica Ajmera Mehta

Graphics
Disha Haria

Production Coordinator
Nilesh Mohite

Cover Work
Nilesh Mohite

About the Authors

Mauricio Salatino is a Senior software engineer at JBoss/RedHat. Mauricio works full time as a Drools and jBPM Core Developer and is in charge of developing the new generation Business Process Management Suite, along with contributing to the evolution of Drools and jBPM. Mauricio is the author of three *Packt Publishing* books about jBPM: *jBPM6 Developer Guide*, *jBPM5 Developer Guide*, and *jBPM Developer Guide*. Mauricio is based in London, UK, and in his spare time he likes to meet community members of different open source projects to build interesting projects.

Mariano De Maio is an IT consultant and software developer with over eleven years of experience in Java and open source frameworks. He has been working with Drools and jBPM for the last six years and has collaborated with the Drools and jBPM projects several items, including Infinispan's persistence modules, extensions to the jBPM APIs, and different add-ons to the tooling functionality. In 2013, he wrote *jBPM6 Developer Guide* for *Packt Publishing*, along with *Mauricio Salatino* and *Esteban Aliverti*. In 2015, he co-founded jWoop, http://www.jwoop.com, which is a company that provides consultancy and training around the world. He has participated in international conferences, such as Decision Camp and other Decision Management webinars. Mariano is based in Buenos Aires, where he is happily married to his wife, Tamara, and takes care of his beautiful daughter, Sofia. In his free time, he likes to work on contributions to the open source projects he is using. He also runs his personal blog, http://marianbuenosayres.wordpress.com, about jBPM, Drools, and Decision Management. You can find him through the official Drools IRC channel #drools at irc.freenode.net, under the nickname mariano or mariano84.

Esteban Aliverti is a software engineer and a former Drools/JBPM consultant. He is also a fervent open source promoter and developer with meaningful contributions to the JBoss Drools and JBPM frameworks for the past six years. He is the coauthor of *jBPM5 Developer Guide* and *jBPM6 Developer Guide* by *Packt Publishing* and was awarded the JBoss' Community Recognition Award in 2012 and 2013.

About the Reviewer

Mario Fusco is a senior software engineer at Red Hat. He was born in Napoli, Italy. He works on the development of the core of Drools, the open source JBoss rule engine. He has huge experience as a Java developer, having been involved in (and often leading) many enterprise level projects in several industries, ranging from media companies to the financial sector.

Among his interests, there are also functional programming and Domain Specific Languages. By leveraging these two passions, he has created the open source library lambdaj with the purpose of providing an internal Java DSL for manipulating collections and allowing a bit of functional programming in Java before the introduction of lambda expressions.

He is the co-author of *Java 8 in Action*, published by Manning, and a technical speaker at several conferences both international, such as Devoxx and JavaOne, and local, such as Voxxed Days and Codemotion. He is also a co-lead of the Java User Group of Milano, Italy, and the leader of the program committee at both Voxxed Days Zurich and Voxxed Days Ticino.

www.PacktPub.com

eBooks, discount offers, and more

Did you know that Packt offers eBook versions of every book published, with PDF and ePub files available? You can upgrade to the eBook version at www.PacktPub.com and as a print book customer, you are entitled to a discount on the eBook copy. Get in touch with us at customercare@packtpub.com for more details.

At www.PacktPub.com, you can also read a collection of free technical articles, sign up for a range of free newsletters and receive exclusive discounts and offers on Packt books and eBooks.

https://www2.packtpub.com/books/subscription/packtlib

Do you need instant solutions to your IT questions? PacktLib is Packt's online digital book library. Here, you can search, access, and read Packt's entire library of books.

Why subscribe?

- Fully searchable across every book published by Packt
- Copy and paste, print, and bookmark content
- On demand and accessible via a web browser

Table of Contents

Preface   **vii**

Chapter 1: Rules Declarative Nature   **1**

What are rules?   **2**
Rules basic structure   2
Declarative approach   3
Imperative versus Declarative implementation   3
Why do we use rules?   **5**
Rules independence   5
Rule execution chaining   6
    Atomicity of rules   7
    Ordering of rules   7
Rule execution life cycle   8
    Collaboration with Rules   9
    Involving more people with Rules using a BRMS   11
Letting the rule engine do its job   12
    Rule engine algorithm   13
When should we use rules?   **14**
Complex scenario, simple rules   14
Ever-changing scenarios   15
Example–eShop system   16
When not to use a rule engine   **17**
Summary   **18**

Chapter 2: Writing and Executing Rules   **19**

Setting up our environment   **20**
Creating our first Drools project   **21**
Writing and executing our first rule   **24**
Using CDI to bootstrap the Rule Engine   28
The Rule language   **30**

Organizing our projects	**35**
Summary	**40**
Chapter 3: Drools Runtime	**41**
Understanding the Drools runtime instances	**41**
KieModule & KieContainer	44
Loading rules from the classpath	45
Loading rules using Maven artifacts (Kie-CI)	48
KieModule configurations (KieBases, KieSessions & StatelessKieSessions)	**49**
KieScanner	**53**
Artifacts version resolution	54
Dealing with unexpected issues and errors	57
Putting it all together	57
Summary	**60**
Chapter 4: Improving Our Rule Syntax	**61**
Adding external interactions with global variables	**61**
Modifying the data in the working memory	**62**
The insert keyword	63
The modify and update keywords	64
The delete/retract keywords	65
Rule attributes	**66**
Example – controlling which rules will fire	67
Example – splitting rule groups with agenda group	70
Other types of rule groups	72
Rule dates management	73
Controlling loops in rules	**74**
Lock-on-active	76
Model properties execution control	77
Declared types	78
Property-reactive beans	79
Special Drools operations	**81**
Boolean and numeric operations	82
Regex operations – matches	83
Collection operations – contains and memberOf	83
Working memory breakdown: the from clause	**84**
Collect from objects	86
Accumulate keyword	87
Advanced conditional elements	91
NOT keyword	92
EXISTS and FORALL keywords	92

Drools syntactic sugar   **94**
Nested accessors   94
Inline casts   95
Null-safe operators   95
Decorating our objects in memory   **95**
Adding traits with the don keyword   97
Removing traits with the shed keyword   97
Logical insertion of elements   **98**
Handling deviations of our rules   99
Deviations to our deviations   100
Rule inheritance   **102**
Conditional named consequences   102
Summary   **103**

Chapter 5: Understanding KIE Sessions   **105**
Stateless and stateful Kie Sessions   **106**
Stateless Kie Sessions   106
Stateful Kie Sessions   109
Kie runtime components   **110**
Globals   110
Globals as a way to parameterize the condition of a pattern   111
Globals as a way to introduce new information into a session in the LHS   114
Globals as a way to collect information from a session   116
Globals as a way to interact with external systems in the RHS   117
Channels   118
Queries   120
On-demand queries   121
Live queries   122
Event Listeners   123
Kie Base components   **125**
Functions   125
Custom operators   127
Custom accumulate functions   134
Summary   **138**

Chapter 6: Complex Event Processing   **139**
What is complex event processing?   **139**
What are events and complex events?   140
Declaring CEP-based Rules   **141**
Semantics of events   142
Declaring time-based-events in Drools   143
Temporal operators   144

Event-driven architecture   **148**
Split event sources with entry points   149
Sliding windows   150
  Length-based sliding windows   150
  Time-based sliding windows   151
  Declared sliding windows   152
Running CEP-based Scenarios   **153**
Stream processing configuration   153
Continuous versus Discrete rule firing   154
Testing with the session clock   155
Drools CEP limitations   **156**
Summary   **158**
Chapter 7: Human-Readable Rules   **159**
Domain Specific Languages   **160**
The Dictionary file   160
  Adding constraints to patterns   162
Rules files   163
DSL troubleshooting   164
A simple scenario   165
Decision tables   **167**
What is a decision table?   168
Decision tables structure   168
  RuleSet section   169
  RuleTable section   171
Coming back to our scenario   173
Decision table troubleshooting   175
Enhanced decision tables   176
Rule templates   **178**
Rule template structure   178
Working with rule templates   180
  Spreadsheet data source   181
  Array data source   182
  Objects data source   183
  SQL result set data source   184
PMML   **185**
PMML in Drools   186
Customer classification decision tree example   188
  Header   189
  DataDictionary   189
  Model   190
PMML troubleshooting   191
PMML limitations   191
Summary   **192**

Chapter 8: Rules' Testing and Troubleshooting   193

Create loosely coupled DRLs   194
Prefer KieHelper over a KieContainer classpath   194
Benefits of using globals   195
Debugging the left-hand side of a rule   196
   Left-hand side troubleshooting   197
     Compilation errors   197
     Runtime errors   198
     Rules not being triggered   200
   Event listeners   204
   Drools logs   207
   Create simpler versions of a rule   207
Debugging the right-hand side of a rule   208
   Right-hand side troubleshooting   209
     Compilation errors   209
     Runtime errors   210
   Right-hand side good practices   211
   Dumping the generated Java classes   212
Reporting a bug in Drools   213
Summary   213

Chapter 9: Introduction to PHREAK   215

Introducing PHREAK   216
   Object Type Nodes   218
   Alpha Nodes   220
     Alpha Node sharing   221
     Constraint JIT compilation   223
   Beta Nodes   223
     Beta Node sharing   225
     Or between patterns   228
Special nodes in the network   229
   The Not Node   230
   The Exists Node   231
   The Accumulate Node   233
   The From Node   234
Queries and backward-chaining   236
   Unification   237
   Positional arguments   240
   Backward reasoning in Drools   241
   The Query Element Node   244
PHREAK improvements over RETE   245
   Delayed rule evaluation   245
   Set-oriented propagation   245
   Network segmentation   246

Phreak Inspector	**246**
Summary	**247**
Chapter 10: Integrating Rules and Processes	**249**
jBPM – the process engine	**250**
Simple business process example	**252**
Kie Session advanced configurations	255
Kie Session event listeners	255
Kie Session Work Items	255
Understanding our process execution	260
Drools and jBPM: integration patterns	**263**
Accessing the process engine from our rules	264
Process instances as facts	265
BPMN2 Business Rule Tasks	267
Persistence and transactions	**270**
How is state persisted?	270
JPA implementation	272
Infinispan implementation	274
Extending persisted data	276
Transaction management	278
Summary	**279**
Chapter 11: Integrating Drools with our Apps	**281**
Architecture considerations	**282**
Asynchronous versus Synchronous Design	282
Integrating with the rest of an application	**284**
Embedding Drools into our application	284
Knowledge as a Service	286
CDI integration	**288**
Spring integration	**288**
Introducing Spring Framework	289
Kie Spring Config example	289
Camel integration	**290**
Integrating the Apache Camel framework	290
Creating our Kie endpoints	290
Kie Execution Server	**292**
Configuring Kie Server	293
Default exposed Kie Server endpoints	294
Kie Workbench	**296**
Drools and beyond: extending our functionality	**299**
Summary	**301**
Index	**303**

Preface

Mastering JBoss Drools 6 was written to provide a comprehensive guide that helps you understand the main principles used by the Drools project to build smarter applications, using the power of business rules. This book covers important topics such as the drools rule syntax, Drools runtime configurations, internal mechanisms of the rule engine, and different ways of writing rules using domain-specific languages, integration patterns, and tooling descriptions. All these topics are covered with a technical perspective that will help developers adopt these technologies. The book is also targeted at topics that are not always covered by business rule systems, such as business processes, complex event processing, and tooling extension capabilities that are introduced to demonstrate the power of mixing different business knowledge descriptions into one smarter, adaptive platform.

What this book covers

Chapter 1, Rules Declarative Nature, talks about what the reader will need to understand about rules to apply them to a project of their own. In short, it will cover the main structure of rules and why said structure is so useful for solving complex problems, along with some of the problems usually solved using rules. Also, we'll explain how rules adjust within the development life cycle.

Chapter 2, Writing and Executing Rules, concentrates on creating a project with rules defined in a simple text file in order to understand both the basic components of rules and all the parts involved in a Drools rule project. This chapter also covers the basics of installing the necessary libraries to work with Drools in a project.

Chapter 3, Drools Runtime, concentrates on the KIE modules (Knowledge Is Everything modules) that are needed to create a rule environment and how to use them to create a rule runtime. All the different ways of creating a runtime for rules are introduced in this chapter.

Chapter 4, Improving Our Rule Syntax, teaches the concepts we need to understand the basic technical syntax used to define Business Rules in Drools. This chapter concentrates on learning about rule attributes, such as `salience`, `lock-on-active`, `agenda-groups`, and so on, which give a lot more control over which rules are to be fired and when. Also, we'll learn about the `from` clause of rules, which allows for different sources of data for evaluating our rule conditions.

Chapter 5, Understanding KIE Sessions, starts with an introduction to the different types of session supported by Drools. It then covers many of the different components that can be added to the session to make it register, alter, or change our rules execution, such as global variables, channels, event listeners, operators, and accumulate functions.

Chapter 6, Complex Event Processing, gives a brief introduction to the **Complex Event Processing (CEP)** concept and how Drools allows us to work with complex events. It covers features such as events, type declarations, temporal operators, sliding windows, and other components of Drools for detecting and managing complex events.

Chapter 7, Human Readable Rules, explains human readable ways to define our rules, such as **Domain Specific Language (DSL)**, Decision Tables, and Templates. They allow the user to create a mapping between the rule language (highly technical) and the specific language that domain experts can easily understand. These mappings will allow business users to be able to define and modify rules without much knowledge of the technical aspects of Drools.

Chapter 8, Rules Testing and Troubleshooting, explains what the different challenges of testing Drools' rules are. It gives an overview of the possible errors and problematic scenarios we may find when testing our application. A set of good practices and techniques to identify and mitigate these problems is also provided in this chapter.

Chapter 9, Introduction to PHREAK, is an introduction to the underlying algorithm Drools uses for the evaluation of business rule assets. It provides an overview of how a Knowledge Base is converted into a PHREAK network composed of specialized nodes that perform different kinds of task, such as classification, constraint evaluation, and join operations. This chapter provides concrete examples on how rules are compiled and evaluated, covering some of the most used patterns and operators in PHREAK.

Chapter 10, Integrating Rules and Processes, goes into detail about the workflow aspect of rules. Specifically, it covers how rules can invoke processes and vice versa. In this chapter, we will also cover the aspects required for implementing a persistent Kie Session, to be used (and reused) both for Rules and for Processes execution.

Chapter 11, Integrating Drools with our Apps, shows integration with the Spring and Camel frameworks, in order to integrate Drools in more complex applications. It also shows us how to make changes to our rules while the application runs and how to make services to invoke rules remotely, using a component called Kie Execution Server.

What you need for this book

This is a developer guide, so the thing you will find most useful when you read this book is a computer beside you, where you can try the examples and open, compile, and test the provided projects. The main idea behind the book is to get you up to speed in the development of applications or tooling that use Drools 6 and for this reason the book spends a lot of time with code examples and unit tests to run. Good programming skills are required to easily understand the examples presented in this book. Most of the chapters complement the covered topics with a set of executable Maven projects. A basic understanding of Maven, Java, and JUnit is required.

Who this book is for

This book is for Java developers and architects who need to have a deep understanding of how Business Rule frameworks behave in real-life implementations. The book assumes that you know the Java language well and also have experience with some widely used frameworks, such as Hibernate. You should also know the basics of relational databases and Maven-based applications.

Conventions

In this book, you will find a number of text styles that distinguish between different kinds of information. Here are some examples of these styles and an explanation of their meaning.

Code words in text, database table names, folder names, filenames, file extensions, pathnames, dummy URLs, user input, and Twitter handles are shown as follows: "We can include other contexts through the use of the `import` directive."

A block of code is set as follows:

```
rule "Classify Item - Low price"
    when
        $i: Item(cost < 10.00)
    then
        insert(new IsLowRangeItem($i));
end
```

When we wish to draw your attention to a particular part of a code block, the relevant lines or items are set in bold:

```
rule "Classify Item - Low price"
    when
        $i: Item(cost < 10.00)
    then
        insert(new IsLowRangeItem($i));
end
```

Any command-line input or output is written as follows:

```
# mvn -B archetype:generate
    -DarchetypeGroupId=org.apache.maven.archetypes
    -DgroupId=org.drools.devguide
    -DartifactId=myfirst-drools-project
```

New terms and **important words** are shown in bold. Words that you see on the screen, for example, in menus or dialog boxes, appear in the text like this: "Clicking the **Next** button moves you to the next screen."

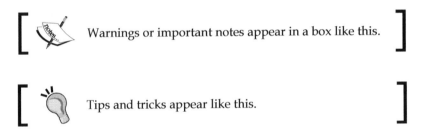

Warnings or important notes appear in a box like this.

Tips and tricks appear like this.

Reader feedback

Feedback from our readers is always welcome. Let us know what you think about this book—what you liked or disliked. Reader feedback is important for us as it helps us develop titles that you will really get the most out of.

To send us general feedback, simply e-mail feedback@packtpub.com, and mention the book's title in the subject of your message.

If there is a topic that you have expertise in and you are interested in either writing or contributing to a book, see our author guide at www.packtpub.com/authors.

Customer support

Now that you are the proud owner of a Packt book, we have a number of things to help you to get the most from your purchase.

Downloading the example code

You can download the example code files for this book from your account at http://www.packtpub.com. If you purchased this book elsewhere, you can visit http://www.packtpub.com/support and register to have the files e-mailed directly to you.

You can download the code files by following these steps:

1. Log in or register to our website using your e-mail address and password.
2. Hover the mouse pointer on the **SUPPORT** tab at the top.
3. Click on **Code Downloads & Errata**.
4. Enter the name of the book in the **Search** box.
5. Select the book for which you're looking to download the code files.
6. Choose from the drop-down menu where you purchased this book from.
7. Click on **Code Download**.

Once the file is downloaded, please make sure that you unzip or extract the folder using the latest version of:

- WinRAR / 7-Zip for Windows
- Zipeg / iZip / UnRarX for Mac
- 7-Zip / PeaZip for Linux

Errata

Although we have taken every care to ensure the accuracy of our content, mistakes do happen. If you find a mistake in one of our books—maybe a mistake in the text or the code—we would be grateful if you could report this to us. By doing so, you can save other readers from frustration and help us improve subsequent versions of this book. If you find any errata, please report them by visiting http://www.packtpub.com/submit-errata, selecting your book, clicking on the **Errata Submission Form** link, and entering the details of your errata. Once your errata are verified, your submission will be accepted and the errata will be uploaded to our website or added to any list of existing errata under the Errata section of that title.

To view the previously submitted errata, go to `https://www.packtpub.com/books/content/support` and enter the name of the book in the search field. The required information will appear under the **Errata** section.

Piracy

Piracy of copyrighted material on the Internet is an ongoing problem across all media. At Packt, we take the protection of our copyright and licenses very seriously. If you come across any illegal copies of our works in any form on the Internet, please provide us with the location address or website name immediately so that we can pursue a remedy.

Please contact us at `copyright@packtpub.com` with a link to the suspected pirated material.

We appreciate your help in protecting our authors and our ability to bring you valuable content.

Questions

If you have a problem with any aspect of this book, you can contact us at `questions@packtpub.com`, and we will do our best to address the problem.

1
Rules Declarative Nature

We developers have always had to deal with the complex problems in software development and they're not going to get any simpler in the future. Systems such as fraud detection software, shopping carts, activity monitors, credit and finance applications, and generally any type of systems that take isolated pieces of data and make a decision based on this information is a very common thing nowadays. Not only is there a necessity to correlate all this data, but also do it as fast as possible for more data each time, and be able to update the correlation mechanisms in a quick manner.

Great expectations spring from this sort of system, of which one of the most trending right now is the Internet of Things. As more and more devices and pieces of software interconnect, a great necessity arises for the systems that allow complex situations to be detected in a simple collaborative way by more and more people outside the development cycle, and be able to react quickly upon detection of these situations. Traditional programming has strived to adjust to this ever-changing pace of adaptation, through agile methodologies and continuous delivery. However, when it comes to the task of actually creating the software that has to detect complex situations and react to them by making a decision, the necessity for a new paradigm for development arises and that's where **business rules** and **Drools** come to our aid.

In this chapter, we will cover a detailed explanation of business rules:

- The definition and structure of business rules
- The importance of business rules to the development life cycle
- The uses of technologies such as Drools and its tooling for the developers and everyone in an organization

What are rules?

Our everyday life is driven by rules. Every time we stop at a red light while driving, we do so as we're following a rule that says we should stop when the light turns red. We all also know the rule that states that when we are of a specific age, we are allowed to take a test to get a driving license.

Even if we don't follow these rules, like the daredevil developers we all are, we're still bound by the rules of nature; if you don't breathe in oxygen, you asphyxiate. If you jump, you're going to touch the ground eventually as the rules of physics determine that gravity will pull you down. Some of these rules (like gravity) have been studied so much that they can be expressed as simple mathematical equations. However, for our everyday rules that we consider common sense, we use a simpler structure: for a group of conditions that we detect, we take specific actions.

These sort of structures are very important for organizations as they have to deal increasingly with complex scenarios. These scenarios are composed of a large number of individual simple decisions, which work together to provide a complex evaluation of the full picture. This complex evaluation starts with simple assessments used to determine the nature of our environment that we will call inferences. These inferences might be crossed with other pieces of data or more inferences until a complex view of the domain can be achieved, understood, and actions can be taken for the benefit of the organization's goals.

These implied decisions were, for a long time, a part of the systems of an organization through very static structures. Starting with the mainframe applications, evolving over time as services, web applications, and middleware solutions, these solutions always had a high coupling with the rest of the system. business rules, on the other hand, allows for a specific, easy-to-read, and split structure to be used to define these decisions in a way that make sense to different groups in an organization—and not just the development areas—and can be quickly implemented and updated automatically.

Rules basic structure

Depending on the specific syntax of each rule engine, the syntax might vary a bit. Nonetheless, there are primal structures that are common to all the rule engines and they look something similar to the following:

```
when a condition is found to be true,
then an action is executed
```

We can add as much syntax sugar on top of this as we can think of; however, this basic structure is what lies underneath it all: a list of conditions and actions. A **condition** is basically a constraint or filter. These filters will look at the information available in a domain to try and find data that meets the defined criteria. Once a group of data is obtained matching the condition, an **action** or **consequence** is scheduled to be executed, taking the matching data as a parameter.

A condition always works like a query; it narrows data from a specific domain by specific filters. This means that a rule will make sense in a specific domain: If your rules are designed to filter apples and the only data you feed these rules are oranges, the rules will never find their conditions to be true.

As simple as this structure might be, it is the basis of all the business rules that we will see in this book. Thanks to this structure, business rule systems provide a great advantage over the conventional code for defining complex scenarios. Over the next sections, we will explain these advantages.

Declarative approach

The business rules are based on a programming paradigm called **Declarative Programming**. This paradigm sustains that you can express the logic of a program without having to explicitly describe the flow of instructions that must be followed. Since the condition works as a filter, whenever data is introduced to the rule engine that matches a condition, a rule or group of rules is determined to be executed.

This means that the control of the flow is neither determined by the order of the rules nor by the order of the incoming data, but by the conditions the rules declare. This declarative approach allows any number of rules to be written without having to worry about any specific place where they need to be written.

Imperative versus Declarative implementation

Imperative programming is the name we give to our everyday programming paradigm. This type of programming is used by languages such as Java, C#, Perl, and many others. It is defined by the control of the sequence flow of instructions, we explicitly inform when each code instruction should be executed.

The declarative approach, on the other hand, doesn't allow a direct control of the sequence flow to the developer, instead it lets the data guide the rule that should be executed. At first, this might seem hard to grasp or be considered as a useful trait for a language. However, we're about to see how Drools allows a very useful union between declarative implementations based on Drools rules and imperative implementations based on Java.

Of course, these Drools-based rules will have to be run on a Java application, where the sequence flow of the steps to be executed is determined by the code. In order to achieve this, the Drools rule engine transforms the business rules into execution trees, as shown in the following image:

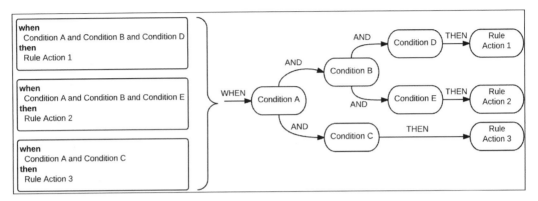

As you can see in the preceding image, each rule condition is split in small blocks, connected and reused within a tree structure. Each time data is fed to the rule engine, it will be evaluated in a tree similar to this one and reach an action node, where they will be marked as data ready for executing a specific rule.

This transformation from business rules to execution tree is possible as the Business Rule structures are excellent for representing themselves as data. This means that the very code of the rules can be quickly transformed into very performing execution structures and also updated and changed during runtime. This happens because every condition can be easily added, moved, or deleted by changing the tree structure.

 It is worth mentioning that, however, the previous image is just an example. The actual decision tree that is generated is a more complex topic, which we will cover in the following chapters. The previous image is just to show the objective of the decision tree.

In the next section, we will discuss the reasons these structures are very useful for performance, collaboration, and maintenance of complex systems.

Why do we use rules?

At this point, you might be still a bit puzzled about why rules are something useful. If we think of it, in terms of one rule or a few, we might consider it better to do it directly on the imperative code like Java, for example. As developers, we're used to break down the requirements into a list of steps to be followed and having to give away that control can be something intimidating.

However, the main strength behind business rules doesn't come from one rule or a small group of rules, it comes from a large, ever-changing group of rules that define a system so complex that it would require extensive work to maintain it if we did it with regular code.

Many rules can work together to define complex systems as the growth of the business rules code base happens organically. Whether we need to implement new requirements, modify existing ones, replace parameters, or change the structure of our system behaviour in new unexpected ways, the only thing we will need to do with the rules is implement new rules that now apply and remove the ones that don't apply anymore. This is possible as business rules work on the following principles:

- They're independent
- They can be easily updated
- Each rule controls minimal amount of information needed
- They allow more people of different backgrounds to collaborate

Rules independence

A Business Rule, all by itself, can't do much. The biggest strength of a business rule-based system is created by having a lot of rules interacting with each other. This interaction, however, is not something the rule should directly know most of the time. That's what we mean when we say rules should be independent. Each rule should be able to detect a particular set of circumstances and act upon it without needing anything other than the data of its domain.

When we think about it, this is the usual way the rules exist once we start formalizing them. Take any law book that you can find and you will see them represented as a group of rules, each one in the form of a clause. Most of them just present a scenario and any specific action or interpretation of that scenario. Most of these clauses won't mention any other clauses. There are a few that do; however, they tend to be the exception. There is a reason for it to be this way and it is to make the rules easier to understand, define, and make them less prone to misinterpretation.

The same principle applies when we define business rules for an organization. Each rule should try not to depend on any other specific rule. Instead, rules should depend only on the data provided by the domain. This allows a rule to be able to make sense by itself, without having to create any other explanation besides the content of the business rule.

However, sometimes rules do depend on others in an indirect way. The assumptions we make on one rule can be used in the conditions of another one. These data creations, through assumptions that a Business Rule engine can make, are called inferences and they are of great use to extend the usability of our rules.

Rule execution chaining

As we mentioned in the previous section, a good Business Rule is an independent entity, depending on nothing but the domain data to make sense. This doesn't mean that each rule should work on completely different data structures. Otherwise, you might end up with very complex rules that would be hard to maintain.

If a rule is too complex, it can be divided into smaller rules; however, even in said case, the independence of rules is still important and you shouldn't have to explicitly invoke rules from each other. That would imply control of the sequence flow and we've already stated that declarative programming doesn't allow this.

Instead, we can split complexity by defining the rules that make assumptions about the base domain and add information to the domain. These assumptions are called **inferences**. Later on, other rules can use this new information, regardless of how it is determined, as a part of their conditions. Let's see the following example to completely understand this splitting of rules:

- When we get a signal from a fire alarm, we infer that there is a fire
- When there is a fire, we call the fire department
- When the fire department is present, we let them in to do their work

Each one of these three rules can be condensed into a single, more complex rule: when we get a signal from a fire alarm, we call the fire department and let them in to do their work. However, by splitting the rules into simpler components, we can easily extend the abilities of our rule engine. We could reuse the first inference that we make—about there being a fire—to trigger other actions such as activating the emergency sprinklers, disabling the elevators, or calling our insurance company.

When a rule no longer makes sense, we can remove it from the rule engine. If a new rule is required, we can create it and take advantage of the already available inferred data. As the sequence flow will be controlled by the engine, we don't have to worry about the order in which things are going to be executed or where the new rules fit among the rest of the existing rules.

Atomicity of rules

As we can create more rules that take advantage of already established inferences, the simpler our rules are, the more extensible they become. Therefore, another principle of good rule writing establishes that we should try to make our rules as simple as possible to the point that they cannot be divided into anything smaller, which could still be considered a rule. This principle is called **Rule Atomicity**.

The atomic rules are simple to understand. They are usually designed with minimal amount of conditions to take an action or infer the occurrence of a situation. As they are independent, they still make sense by themselves. Rule atomicity, rule independence, and inference capabilities together make business rules the simplest component that we can use to define the behaviour of any of our systems. Simplicity allows a clear understanding of why the decisions are made in the system, making rules self-explanatory and allowing us to keep a track of every rule that intervened in a specific decision. This is the reason why laws have been the building blocks of the society's internal regulations for thousands of years.

Ordering of rules

We've already mentioned that rules don't follow one specific order. Sequence flow is determined by the rule engine, which means the rule engine will have to decide, based on the available data from the domain, which rules should fire and in what order. This means the order in which the rules are defined is not important, only the data in their condition is required to match a specific rule.

There are ways of ordering rules that are competing for execution under the same conditions being met in the domain. This ordering works as a second-level prioritizing for rules, with the data in the domain model being the first one needed to determine a rule to be activated. These ordering mechanisms, which we will discuss later in more technical chapters, should be for special cases only. Exceptions to the common way we define rules instead of the norm. If we find ourselves controlling every single rule and the order in which it should fire, we should rethink of the way we're writing our rule definitions.

This is something difficult to absorb by the developers first getting a glance at declarative programming. Nonetheless, it provides a lot of improvements in the way that we can accelerate both our runtime and development efforts mainly based on the fact that if the order doesn't matter, we can add rules wherever we prefer:

- Collaboration between rules becomes simpler to manage
- Conflict avoidance is simpler
- More people can work on the development of rules, which makes inclusion of other areas a very real possibility

Rule execution life cycle

The rule engine optimizes the evaluation of conditions and makes sure that we determine the rules to fire in the fastest way possible. However, the rule engine doesn't execute our business rules immediately at a condition's detection unless we specify so. When we reach a point where we find a rule evaluation to be true for a group of data, the rule and the triggering data are added to a list. This is a part of an explicit rule life cycle, where we have a clear splitting between rule evaluation and rule execution. Rule evaluation adds rule actions and the data that has triggered them to a component that we will call the **Agenda**. Rule execution is done on command. The moment we notify the rule engine, it should fire all the rules that we have in the said agenda.

As we stated earlier, we don't control the rules that are going to be fired. It's the engine's responsibility to determine this based on the business rules that we create and the data that we feed to the engine. However, once the engine determines the business rules that it should fire, we have the control over the time when they should be fired. This is done through a method invocation to the rule engine.

Once the rules are fired, each rule that matches in the agenda will be executed. Rule execution might modify the data in our domain and if these modifications cause some rule to match with the new data, new rule matches can be added to the agenda or if these modifications cause a match to no longer be true, it will be cancelled. This full cycle will continue until no more rules are available in the Agenda for the available data or the rule engine execution is forced to stop. The following diagram shows how this workflow is executed:

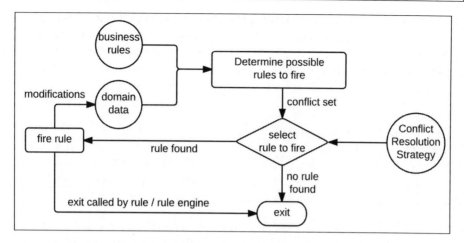

This execution life cycle will continue firing all the rules that the rule engine has decided to add to the Agenda based on the rule definitions and the domain data we feed to it. Some rules might not fire and some rules might fire multiple times.

During the following chapters, we will learn how to control the rules that should fire; however, we will always maintain the principles for Business Rule writing that we already established—independence and atomicity. The more we learn about the configuration of the rule engine, the more we will trust it to do its job. For the moment, it will be a leap of faith; however, with every step, we will learn how to control the rule engine until we can be 100% sure that it will do exactly what we expect of it.

Collaboration with Rules

As the sequence flow is beyond our direct control when creating business rules, one main advantage we have is that we don't have to worry about the code placing. As all rules are independent and the sequence flow is determined by the engine at runtime, it doesn't matter where we place the rule.

With common, imperative programming languages such as Java, each instruction will happen at a specific moment in the program execution and finding said specific point in the code, where we need to add our modifications, involves reviewing the whole set of code. Entire design patterns have been created around managing this limitation in ways that we can collaborate between developers while working on the same system. Every major design pattern works on splitting the code base in groups such as modules, methods, and classes to manage these collaborations between developers with ease.

However, the main limitation with the imperative code is that once the system has been designed, we cannot break beyond the limit that we used to split our code base easily. We are forced to foresee the probable changes that might be added in the future when we create the design—something which can be very difficult to achieve. If we fail to do so and many developers have to modify the same code sections due to the different requirements, their code will be prone to conflicts.

This limitation can be avoided by declarative programming because the specific order of the rules doesn't matter. Collaborations between different people defining different aspects of a same domain module can be done without conflicts as a good place to add another Business Rule is anywhere between the existing business rules. The output execution will be relatively same, regardless of the order.

Let's take a look at the following pseudo code section comparison between the Imperative and Declarative code. When we have to add any modifications to an imperative block of code, we cannot just do it at any place. There are specific places to add a specific correction and if you place them in a different spot, it either doesn't work as expected or is not as performing as it could be, you can the comparison as shown as follows:

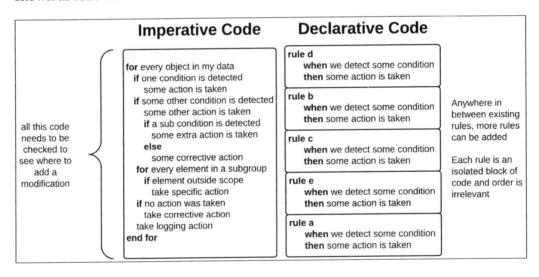

The business rules, on the other hand, define each rule as an isolated block of code. People could add work in any part without any problem. This makes application development with business rules easier in collaborative environments as it is far less prone to conflict problems, as shown in the following image:

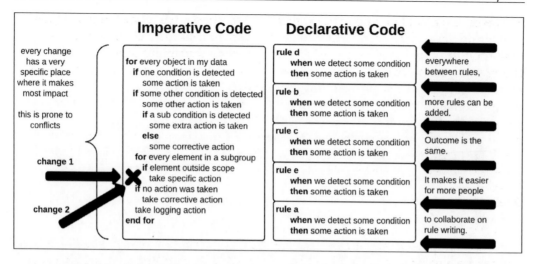

Having less chance for conflict, we can concentrate our time and energies on the solution that we are trying to build instead of worrying about merging the solutions between different components or within a same component.

The increased possibility of having more points on which to add code without conflicts opens the door to have more people involved in the development life cycle. This can help speed up the development and update of our software solutions dramatically.

Involving more people with Rules using a BRMS

Thanks to the increased collaboration business rules provides us during the development time, we can have an increased amount of people working on defining the decisions for our systems. The immediately subsequent bottleneck that we usually face at this point is finding more people who understand how to write the rules.

Writing rules is, at least in the beginning, a technical task. It requires a certain level of knowledge about how to define conditions and actions—topics that we will cover in detail in the next chapters—and getting more people to learn how to write these rules takes a little time.

Even if we get technical people to learn how to write rules quickly, it is usually not enough. It's not due to a technical limitation but mostly due to the people who hold the practical knowledge that we need to write as business rules not being the most available or tech-savvy group of people. It could be the case, of course, and you may have probably found one of the best groups to work with Business Rule-based systems. However, for most of the cases, they will have the practical knowledge but not the time or desire to learn how to write technical rules.

For these groups of business experts, there are platforms that allow them to access rule writing in a more user-friendly way. These platforms are a composition of user-friendly editors, with versioning and publishing capabilities, called **Business Rule Management Systems (BRMS)**. Basically, business experts will be able to create rules using the same everyday language that they are familiar with and use for thinking definitions for decisions. You will learn more about these user-friendly ways of writing rules in *Chapter 5, Human Readable Rules*. For now, let's just mention that we can define business rules in a natural language using editors that allow business experts to work directly on the rules in a very similar speed to how technical experts define business rules.

The following is a small screenshot where we can see one of these editors in the KIE Workbench, a Drools based BRMS:

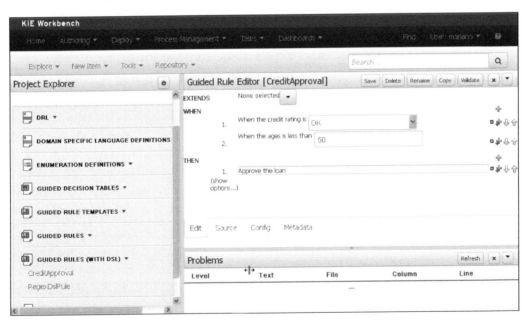

Letting the rule engine do its job

So far, we've covered an introductory explanation about the structure of business rules. Whenever we had to explain how the rules were executed, we simply said that the rule engine will take care of it. When we use business rules, we trust a rule engine to determine the rules that should fire, based on the domain data that we send to it. We will, at this stage, try to define how the rule engine will define the rules that should be fired and when.

In the previous sections, we saw a brief display about how rules can be translated to execution trees, where decisions are taken based on the data, following a declarative paradigm approach. In this section, we will try to explain how this structure helps in creating the most performing execution possible based on our rule definitions.

Rule engine algorithm

The rule engine transforms the business rules that we define to an executable decision tree through a specific algorithm. The performance of the execution tree will depend on the optimization mechanisms the algorithm can generate. The Drools 6 framework defines its own algorithm focused on higher performance. This algorithm is called PHREAK and was created by Mark Proctor. It is based on a series of optimizations and redesigns of a pre-existing algorithm called RETE, created by Charles Forgy. PHREAK is one of the most efficient and performing algorithms implemented as open source to the date.

In the generated execution tree, every condition in our rules will be transformed to a node in the tree and how the different conditions connect to each other in our rules will determine the way these nodes will be connected. As we add data to our rule engine, it will be evaluated in batches, flowing through the network using the most optimized paths possible. The execution tree finishes when the data reaches a leaf, which represents a rule to be fired. These rules are added to a list, where a command will be called to fire all the rules or a subgroup of rules.

Due to this continuous live evaluation of the condition of rules, this rule engine bases its performance on having all the data for rule evaluation available in the memory. The details about how the algorithm builds a decision tree will be introduced later in this book.

Each time we add more data to the rule engine, it is introduced through the root of the execution tree. Every optimization on this execution tree works according to the following two main focus points:

- It will try to break down all the conditions to the smallest amount of units in order to be able to reuse the execution tree as much as possible
- It will try to make only one operation to go to the next level below, until it reaches a false evaluation of a condition or a leaf node, where a rule is marked for execution

Every piece of data is evaluated in the most-performing way possible. The optimizations of these evaluations are the main focus of the rule engine. In the following chapters, we will discuss how to make rules that take advantage of each of these advantages in order to make our business rules as fast as possible.

When should we use rules?

The business rules are very powerful components. They introduce a large number of changes in the way we define our business logic. They allow us to handle the complexity, performance, and maintenance of our systems in order to accomplish a lot in a very little time.

These improvements are of great value for any project and business rules can be implemented and added to any type of project that you might find out there. Nonetheless, we want to remark these projects that would benefit the most on introducing business rules to their technological stack. These projects have one or more of the following characteristics:

- They define a very complex scenario that is difficult to fully define even for business experts
- They don't have a known or well-defined algorithmic solution
- They have volatile requirements and need to be updated very often
- They need to make decisions fast, usually based on partial amounts of data

Complex scenario, simple rules

Every once in a while, we find systems—or parts of systems—where small relations among components start having more importance the more we investigate them. At first, they might seem innocuous components that take very little decisions based on small relations between two or three sources of data. As we start investigating them further, these relations take on more and more importance. Eventually, we might find the relationship between the parts produces more collective behaviors that even the business experts were unaware could happen; however, this still make sense. These kinds of systems are called **Complex Systems** and they are one of the places where business rules provides a great aid.

Complex scenarios are usually defined by small statements. The full picture, involving every single composition, aggregation or abstraction of data needed to completely define the scenario, is usually something beyond our initial grasp. Therefore, it is common that such systems start being defined through partial explanations. Each small relation in the system gets defined as a different requirement. When we analyze each one of these requirements, on splitting them into their most basic elements, we find ourselves defining business rules.

Each Business Rule helps in defining every small component of a complex scenario. As more and more rules are added to the system, more and more of these relations can be handled in a simple-to-read way. Each rule then becomes a self-explanatory manual for each small decision that the system takes when executing our complex scenario.

The examples of complex applications can be very varied, as follows:

- **Fraud detection systems**: Usually they take information from every transaction done within a central service and investigate the correlations between them to determine situations that are unlikely to come from an honest and legal use of the system. Things such as unusual credit card operations, large amounts of activity in usually stable accounts, and unexpected parameters in transactions are usually the things searched by these systems.

- **Customized retail coupons for returning clients**: In all kinds of commercial activities, client fidelity is always valued. A usual strategy to maximize it is through special coupon generation based on the client's shopping habits. To accomplish the right coupon, a complex system needs to evaluate the purchase history of the client, frame the client in a specific demographic subgroup, and select the best offer available for this subgroup. All these things need to be done based on the complex relations between different purchases and their tendencies.

- **Credit scoring software**: Credit scoring is a numerical expression based on a level analysis of a person's credit files to represent the person's credit worth. Every debt, credit, purchase, or relation can be a valid source of data to determine the scoring of a person. The complexity of this scenario comes from having to correlate, weigh, and return a specific score for a person based on the correlation of all these sources of data.

Ever-changing scenarios

Even when we don't have a complex scenario in our hands, we might still benefit a great deal from defining our application's logic using business rules. If the elements involved in making a particular decision tend to change very frequently, business rules can be a good solution for managing such volatility in the behaviour of a system.

The business rules are represented in the rule engine as a data tree. In the same way that we can modify the elements of a list, we can remove or add a Business Rule from a rule engine. This can be achieved without having to restart our application or reinstalling any components. Internal mechanisms provided by the Drools 6 framework can be used to update the rule definitions automatically from external sources. The tooling provided by Drools 6 is also prepared to provide update mechanisms for the business rules from user-friendly editors. The complete architecture of the Drools 6 API is based on making this as adaptive as possible.

If we find a system where the requirements might change very frequently, even in a daily or hourly frequency, business rules may be the best fit for such requirements due to its update capabilities, regardless of the complexity of the system.

Example–eShop system

Along the rest of the book, we will work on a set of decision services based on business rules with a common domain: an eShop application. Practise is a crucial component of learning about a new framework and in order to make it simple in order to go into detail on the rule engine as fast as possible, we will define a basic model shared between most of our examples.

To start with, we will define the model of our eShop system. This model will contain all the different things that are relevant to make decisions about our application. Some of these objects are as shown in the following:

- **Product**: Our shop will sell different kinds of items. Each kind will be represented by a product object, containing the details about the specific item.

- **Stock**: This is the amount of each product that we have in storage.

- **Provider**: Our products come from different providers. Each one of them can provide the eShop with specific kinds of products in a specific capacity for delivery.

- **Provider Request**: When we run low or out of a specific product, we will have to create a request for our providers to fill our stock.

- **Client**: The shop has clients that will have preferences for specific products, pending and completed orders, specific demographic information, payment preferences, and any type of data that we can obtain from their navigation on our eShop.

- **Order**: When a client likes one or more products in our eShop, they can order them to be delivered. The orders have different status, depending on whether the client received it successfully or not. They also have information about its specific products and their quantity.

- **Discount**: The eShop offers different types of discounts, depending on the type of purchase.

- **Sales channel**: The eShop that we will emulate can work with multiple sites and each one of them is treated as a different sales channel. Each sales channel will have its own specific target audience, which is determined by the clients who use it.

As we need more types of objects to define the reality of our eShop, we will define more classes to extend the understanding of our world. Once we start correlating all these pieces of domain data together, we will be able to detect all types of situations and act upon them in the benefit of both our eShop and its clients. Some of the things that we will be able to do are shown in the following:

- Defining the best sales channel for a specific kind of product by correlating products with each sales channel and comparing them with the rest of them. Based on this information, we can create custom discounts for the products in these channels.

- Defining the client preferences for specific products. Based on this information, we can offer them discount tickets tailored for their specific tastes.

- Determine the average consumption of specific products and compare them with our stock. In case of necessity, we can automatically trigger provider requests.

- Based on how many orders we have in process for specific providers, we can ask for a discount on the price.

- We can analyze the different purchases that our clients make in our eShops. If, at some point, the purchases go beyond what we consider normal, we can take a series of actions, from a simple warning to providing direct human support for a specific purchase.

These are just a few things that we could do with business rules for such domains. As we find more situations with specific requirements to be fulfilled, we will learn new techniques to write our rules and configure our runtime. Each new necessity will guide us to define new components in order to get the most out of the Drools 6 framework.

When not to use a rule engine

Every project, in one way or another, can benefit from using business rules. They are highly performing, easy to change, and self-explanatory software components. However, there are a group of conditions that a project might have that would make use of business rules a bit of overkill. Some of the characteristics that make a project benefit the least from business rules are shown in the following:

- There are very few, self-contained rules involved in the project: If the business rules identified in the requirement gathering are very simple and span about one or two objects at most, we don't need a rule engine to run them. A good rule of thumb is that if we can write the business rules that we need as the pseudo code in less than a page and with less than two nested if-then clauses, we might not need a rule engine at this particular time.

- The business logic doesn't change often: If changing rules at runtime is not going to be needed but the logic is still complex, a rule engine might still be a good idea. However, if the complexity behind the rules is not that high and we can assume it will remain that way for a long time, we might not need a rule engine.

- A very strict control of the execution flow is crucial for the application: As we stated before, a sequence-flow control is not provided when we execute our business rules. If the business logic behind the business rules depends a lot on a strict set of steps that need to be executed sequentially, business rules might not be the right fit. However, if it does change frequently, perhaps a business process would be worth considering.

It is still a responsibility of the project team to determine whether business rules might be a good fit even if these conditions are met. After all, our experience can lead us to think that the amount of rules has a big chance of growing in the future or there might be situations where the rules will eventually need to change more frequently. Each project has its own unique characteristics and it might be that a project with no need for business rules right now cannot be thought without them in the future.

Summary

The business rules is a very strange concept to deal with on our first encounter as traditional developers, and the purpose of this first chapter was to present how they fit in our everyday application development and why they can help us define better systems.

We've seen what rules are, defined their structure, and covered their practical uses. We've also covered a few examples of projects where rules are useful—and some other examples where they might be not necessary. We've also introduced our eShop project, which will guide us through the next few chapters in order to establish all the benefits Drools 6 provides, from Business Rule writing to Rule Engine configuration.

In the next chapter, we will start writing our first business rules and take our first steps in defining our rule-based projects.

Writing and Executing Rules

2

The best way to learn something new is by trying it out. For this reason, in this chapter, we are going to cut to the chase to write and execute our first rules. We will also cover the most important points about the rule language and how to effectively write rules that mean something to your domain. This chapter will use the eShop model introduced in the previous chapter to demonstrate a set of scenarios where rules can be applied.

Before we start coding, in the first half of this chapter, you will learn how to set up all the standard tools required to work with Drools and the examples provided with this book. We will be creating a project from scratch, therefore, you can use this chapter as a reference to start your applications from the ground up. The second half of the chapter will cover the introduction to the DRL language and how we recommend to organize your projects when you are using rules or other knowledge assets such as business processes.

Briefing this up, this chapter we will cover the following topics:

- Setting up our environment
- Creating our first Drools project
- Writing and executing our first rule
- Discussing the DRL rule language
- Organizing our projects

Setting up our environment

In order to start working with rules, there are a couple of things that we need to consider. First of all, we will be relying on Maven to provide the structure for our projects. I strongly recommend you read about Maven if you are not familiar with it as most of the Drools and jBPM infrastructure is nowadays aligned with Maven, therefore, you will feel much more comfortable when you know how it works. I recommend the following link from the Maven project website if you are completely new to the subject:

```
https://maven.apache.org/guides/getting-started/index.html
```

This is not a strong requirement for Drools; however, it is a recommended way to use it. Most of the integration with the project tooling and other modules relies on Maven serving as the standard for project structure and project life cycle and dependency management.

In order to get started, we need to make sure that we have the following software installed on our computer:

- Java 8 JDK, notice that Drools doesn't require JDK 8, yet all the book examples were created using that. To avoid problems with the examples, we recommend using this version.
- Maven 3.1.x or newer version to compile, test, and package our projects.
- GIT 1.9.x or newer version for source version control.

We will be using Git to get the project examples from our repository hosted on Bitbucket. If you are not familiar with Git, we recommend you to take a look at their official documentation at `http://git-scm.com/docs`.

In order to get a copy of the examples in our local environment, we will clone the remote repository by executing the following command in the terminal:

```
>git clone https://bitbucket.org/drools-6-developer-guide/drools6-dev-guide.git
```

Depending on the platform (operating system) that you are running, you can use a Git client to interact with the remote repositories. Feel free to look at the different alternatives for your operating system, here is a list provided by the Git project at `http://git-scm.com/downloads/guis`.

Now, you have a copy of all the examples of this book in your local environment. To make sure that everything is correctly set up, go to the `drools6-dev-guide/` directory and run the following command:

```
> mvn clean install
```

This command tells Maven to clean all the previously compiled classes and packaged resources and remove them from our projects to start a fresh compilation process. In order to compile all the Java classes, Maven needs to make sure that it has all the third-party dependencies required by this projects. In our case, Drools is one of the third-party libraries that will need to be downloaded by Maven if we don't have it locally. However, this will not only compile the Java classes, but also run all the tests defined in the projects and package every project if, and only if, all the tests are successful.

This process of downloading, compiling, and running the tests might take some time the first time you run it in your local environment. This is mostly due to the initial downloads and unless you are using nightly builds (SNAPSHOTS), it should only happen the first time you run the command. Notice that the repository hosting the examples doesn't host any third-party libraries, not even Drools.

If you are behind a proxy, read the Maven guide to set up your proxy configurations at `https://maven.apache.org/guides/mini/guide-proxies.html`.

If this command ends with **BUILD SUCCESS**, we are good to go. It should look similar to the following:

```
[INFO] ------------------------------------------------------------------------
[INFO] BUILD SUCCESS
[INFO] ------------------------------------------------------------------------
[INFO] Total time: 7.068 s
[INFO] Finished at: 2016-02-03T18:14:47+00:00
[INFO] Final Memory: 25M/327M
[INFO] ------------------------------------------------------------------------
```

Now, we know that the JDK and Maven are working correctly, we are ready to move forward and create our first Drools project.

Creating our first Drools project

As mentioned in the previous section, we will use Maven to provide us with the project structure. For this, Maven provides the concept of archetypes, which are project templates that we can use to bootstrap our projects. Most of the IDEs provide a way to use these archetypes in order to create and initialize our projects. Check for your IDE if you need to download a Maven plugin or if Maven support is already bundled. If you want to do this via the command line, we can run the following command:

```
mvn -B archetype:generate
  -DarchetypeGroupId=org.apache.maven.archetypes
  -DgroupId=org.drools.devguide
  -DartifactId=myfirst-drools-project
```

I recommend you to run this command in the `drools6-dev-guide/chapter-02/` directory. This will enable Maven to inherit all the configuration from the parent project configuration defined in `drools6-dev-guide/pom.xml`. If you do this, your project will know the version of Drools that all the other examples in the book are using, avoiding you to define these versions in the following sections.

Notice that you can change the values for `DgroupId`, which represents the logical group your application belongs to and `DartifactId`, which represents the name of your specific Maven module. This command will create a `myfirst-drools-project` `directory` in the directory.

Once we run this command, a new project structure will be ready for us to use. This structure looks similar to the following image:

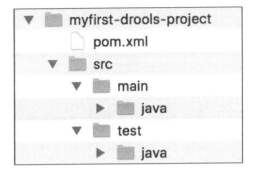

Here, some important things are as follows:

- `pom.xml`: This contains the project definition and first-level dependencies. I strongly recommend you to open this file and take a look at it. You need to become familiar with how to change this file to include new dependencies and project configurations.
- `src/main/java`: This contains our Java classes that need to be compiled.
- `src/test/java`: This contains our test classes that need to be compiled and executed during the test phase.
- `src/main/resources`: We need to create this directory when we need it (or your IDE might need to create this one). It will contain all the static resources that don't need to be compiled; however, it needs to be packaged along with our compiled classes.
- `src/test/resources`: We will need to create this directory when we need it (or your IDE might need to create this one). It will contain all the static test resources that don't need to be compiled; however, they are required by our test classes.

This basic structure serves as a starting point for any Java project, no matter which frameworks are you going to use in it. In order to use Drools in this project, we will need to define the framework dependencies in the pom.xml file. The following dependencies (in the dependencies tag) needs to be added to use Drools in our project:

```xml
<project xsi:schemaLocation="http://maven.apache.org/POM/4.0.0
                    http://maven.apache.org/xsd/maven-4.0.0.xsd"
         xmlns="http://maven.apache.org/POM/4.0.0"
         xmlns:xsi="http://www.w3.org/2001/XMLSchema-instance">
  <modelVersion>4.0.0</modelVersion>
  <parent>
      <groupId>org.drools.devguide</groupId>
      <artifactId>chapter-02</artifactId>
      <version>1.0</version>
  </parent>
  <artifactId>myfirst-drools-project</artifactId>

  <dependencies>
    <dependency>
      <groupId>org.kie</groupId>
      <artifactId>kie-api</artifactId>
    </dependency>
    <dependency>
      <groupId>org.drools</groupId>
      <artifactId>drools-core</artifactId>
    </dependency>
    <dependency>
      <groupId>org.drools</groupId>
      <artifactId>drools-compiler</artifactId>
    </dependency>
  </dependencies>
</project>
```

The first org.kie:kie-api dependency contains all the public interfaces exposed by the KIE Platform, which is composed by Drools, jBPM, and OptaPlanner. Next, we include the org.drools:drools-core artifact, which contains the Drools rule engine implementation. Finally, we will include the org.drools:drools-compiler artifact that contains the algorithm to translate the rules written in different resources (text files, spreadsheets, your own types, and so on) to executable rules. This artifact is required only because we are compiling our rules in the project. It is possible to separate the rules compilation from the rules execution to remove this dependency from our project; however, for the sake of simplicity, we are going to compile our rules in the same project.

In order to start writing rules about our own domain, we will also need to add a dependency to it. The dependency defined for the domain model provided by the book examples is as follows:

```
<dependencies>
  (... Drools dependencies here ... )
  <dependency>
    <groupId>org.drools.devguide</groupId>
    <artifactId>model</artifactId>
  </dependency>
</dependencies>
```

In this way, we can add any dependency that we want and directly start writing the rules using the classes provided in this third-party library as we will see in the next section.

There is one last thing that we need to do in order to complete our project configuration, define a file in the `chapter-02/myfirst-drools-project/src/main/resources/META-INF/` directory called `kmodule.xml`. This file will be used to configure how to load the rules defined in the project in the rule engine. For now, the content of `kmodule.xml` will be quite simple as we will be using all the default configurations. The following is an example of an empty `kmodule.xml`:

```
<kmodule xmlns:xsi="http://www.w3.org/2001/XMLSchema-instance"
         xmlns="http://jboss.org/kie/6.0.0/kmodule">
</kmodule>
```

We will take a look at how to customize this file with more fine-grained settings in *Chapter 3, Drools Runtime*. This file will be picked up when we instantiate a Rule Engine session automatically to figure out what needs to be loaded.

We are now set up and ready to write and execute our first rule.

Writing and executing our first rule

Now that we have our project structure ready, we can write our first rule. For that, we will create a new empty text file. This will be a static resource, therefore, we need to place it in the `src/main/resources` directory. This text file needs to have the `.drl` extension so that it can be picked up as a rule file. In the `.drl` files, we will write as many rules as we want. Now, we will start easy with just one rule.

Let's write our first rule to classify the items based on what they cost us. Our `rules.drl` text file will look similar to the following:

```
package myfirstproject.rules
import org.drools.devguide.eshop.model.Item;
```

```
import org.drools.devguide.eshop.model.Item.Category;
rule "Classify Item - Low Range"
    when
        $i: Item(cost < 200)
    then
        $i.setCategory(Category.LOW_RANGE);
end
```

This rule checks for each item that costs less than 200 USD and automatically tags it with a category, in this case, LOW_RANGE. For our shop, it makes sense to differentiate our items in different ranges so that we can apply different discounts and marketing strategies for them. This classification process can be done automatically using rules, which centralize the point where we have this business definition of what LOW_RANGE, MID_RANGE or HIGH_RANGE items they are.

In general, these files will be structured as follow:

- **Package definition**: This is the same as in Java, we will declare a package for our rules

- **Imports section**: We need to import all the classes that we are going to use in of our rules

- **(Optional) declared types and events**: We will look at this in more detail in *Chapter 4, Improving our Rule Syntax*

- **Rules**: (1..N)/Queries (1..N)

Before analyzing further, let's try to execute the rule and see what happens. In order to execute and test our new rule, we need to create a Java class, where we bootstrap the Rule Engine and provide the required information for it to work. We can just create an empty class with a main method, bootstrap the engine, and start using it right away.

In order to do this, we just create an App.java class for this example and place it in the src/main/java/ directory so that it can be compiled by Maven. For this example, we have created the org/drools6/book directory that follows the standard Java package structure, as follows:

```
package org.drools6.book;
import ...

public class App {
  public static void main( String[] args ) {
    System.out.println( "Bootstrapping the Rule Engine ..." );
    //1) Bootstrapping a Rule Engine Session
    KieServices ks = KieServices.Factory.get();
    KieContainer kContainer = ks.getKieClasspathContainer();
```

```
KieSession kSession =  kContainer.newKieSession();

Item item = new Item("A", 123.0,234.0);
System.out.println( "Item Category: " + item.getCategory());
//2) Provide information to the Rule Engine Context
kSession.insert(item);
//3) Execute the rules that are matching
int fired = kSession.fireAllRules();
System.out.println( "Number of Rules executed = " + fired );
System.out.println( "Item Category: " + item.getCategory());
    }
}
```

As you can see in the previous example, there are three main stages, as shown in the following:

- **Bootstrapping the Rule Engine session**: We will look at what `KieServices`, `KieContainer`, and KieSession's main responsibilities are in *Chapter 3, Drools Runtime*. For now, we need to know that `KieSession` represents a running instance of the Rule Engine with a specific configuration and set of rules. It holds the evaluation algorithm used to match the rules against our domain objects.

- **Letting the Rule Engine know about our data**: We are responsible for providing all the information to the engine so that it can operate on it. In order to do this, we use the `insert()` method on `KieSession`. We can also remove the information from the Rule Engine context using the `delete()` method or update the information using the `modify()` method. We will look at the `KieSession` operations in *Chapter 3, Drools Runtime*.

- If the information that we provided matches with one or more defined rules, we will get **Matches**. Calling the `fireAllRules()` method will execute these matches. We will learn more about Matches in *Chapter 3, Drools Runtime*.

- You will need to compile the project in order to execute this class and you can do this by executing from the terminal or your IDE, as follows:

    ```
    > mvn clean install
    ```

This will compile and package your project, look for the **Build Success** output in the terminal. After executing this line, you will find the `/target` directory containing a `myfirst-drools-project-1.0.0.jar` jar file that you can use to execute the previously compiled class using the following line:

```
mvn exec:java -Dexec.mainClass="org.drools6.book.App"
```

You will see the following output on the terminal:

user$ mvn exec:java -Dexec.mainClass="org.drools6.book.App"

[INFO] Scanning for projects...

[INFO]

[INFO] ---

[INFO] Building myfirst-drools-project 1.0.0

[INFO] ---

[INFO]

[INFO] --- exec-maven-plugin:1.4.0:java (default-cli) @ myfirstproject ---

Bootstrapping the Rule Engine ...

...

Item Category: NA

Number of Rules executed = 1

Item Category: LOW_RANGE

[INFO] ---

[INFO] BUILD SUCCESS

[INFO] ---

[INFO] Total time: 2.945 s

[INFO] Finished at: 2015-04-02T09:55:08+01:00

[INFO] Final Memory: 20M/257M

[INFO] ---

As you can see, the rule was executed as the category of the item was changed accordingly with what the rule says. I would encourage you to change the cost of the item to effectively see that the rule will not be executed if the cost is over the value defined in the rule. You can also add more items with different costs to `KieSession` and see what happens.

Using CDI to bootstrap the Rule Engine

The **Contexs and Dependency Injection (CDI)** `http://www.cdi-spec.org` is a set of standardized APIs defined to provide our applications with these features, while it allows us to choose the context and dependency injection container that we want. CDI is now becoming a part of the Java SE specification and its adoption is growing every year. For this reason and due to the Drools Project added a lot of support for the CDI environment, this section briefly shows how to simplify our Hello World example that we wrote in the previous section.

In order to use CDI in our projects, we need to add a couple of dependencies to our project, as follows:

```
<dependencies>
  ...
  <dependency>
    <groupId>javax.enterprise</groupId>
    <artifactId>cdi-api</artifactId>
  </dependency>
  <dependency>
    <groupId>org.jboss.weld.se</groupId>
    <artifactId>weld-se-core</artifactId>
  </dependency>
</dependencies>
```

The `javax.enterprise:cdi-api` artifact contains all the interfaces defined in the CDI specification and `org.jboss.weld.se:weld-se-core` is the container that we are going to use, which implements the CDI interfaces. By adding these dependencies, we will be able to `@Inject` our `KieSessions` and the Weld container will take care of bootstrapping the Rule Engine for us.

CDI works based on the principle of convention over configuration and it introduced the need to add a new file in `src/main/resources/META-INF/` called `beans.xml`, which will be used to configure how the container has the access to our beans in the projects and some other configurations. Notice the similarity with the `kmodule.xml` file that we introduced earlier. This is an example content of an empty `beans.xml` file, which is used by the CDI containers to know the jars that need to be parsed and made available to the container to `@Inject` beans, as follows:

```
<beans xmlns="http://java.sun.com/xml/ns/javaee"
       xmlns:xsi="http://www.w3.org/2001/XMLSchema-instance"
       xsi:schemaLocation="http://java.sun.com/xml/ns/javaee
           http://java.sun.com/xml/ns/javaee/beans_1_0.xsd">
</beans>
```

As soon as we have the dependencies to the container and the `beans.xml` file, the container can scan the class path (meaning our project and its dependencies) and look for beans to inject, we can start using these features in our application.

The following class represents the same simple example that creates a default `KieSession` with our first rule and then interacts with it.

The following code snippet initializes `KieSession` via CDI and interacts with it, as follows:

```java
public class App {
    @Inject
    @KSession
    KieSession kSession;

    public void go(PrintStream out){
        Item item = new Item("A", 123.0,234.0);
        out.println( "Item Category: " + item.getCategory());
        kSession.insert(item);
        int fired = kSession.fireAllRules();
        out.println( "Number of Rules executed = " + fired );
        out.println( "Item Category: " + item.getCategory());
    }

    public static void main( String[] args )
    {
        // Bootstraping the WELD CDI container
        Weld w = new Weld();
        WeldContainer wc = w.initialize();
        App bean = wc.instance().select(App.class).get();
        bean.go(System.out);
        w.shutdown();
    }
}
```

Notice that the `main(...)` method is now bootstrapping the Weld container and for this reason, our bean (App) can inject any bean. In this case, the `@KSession` annotation is in charge of bootstrapping the engine and creating a fresh instance for us to use. We will look at the annotations provided by the CDI extension in *Chapter 3, Drools Runtime*.

Consider this as another very valid option to interact with the Drools Rule Engine. If you are working with a Java EE container such as WildFly AS (`http://www.wildfly.org`), which is constructed on top of a core that is purely based on CDI, this way of working will be the way to go.

For this example, we are using WELD, which is the reference CDI implementation at `http://weld.cdi-spec.org`. Notice that you can use any other CDI implementation, such as Apache Open Web Beans at `http://openwebbeans.apache.org`.

Now, in order to understand how the rule is being applied and executed, we should clearly understand the language that we are using to write the rules called **Drools Rule Language (DRL)**. The following section covers a more detailed view of this language. The next chapter will cover the execution side in more detail, explaining what is going on when we bootstrap the rule engine session and how to configure it for different purposes.

The Rule language

Now that we have executed our first rule, it is time to learn a little bit more about the language that we use to define them. In order to do this, we will start by analyzing the rule that we wrote previously and then we will start creating more advanced rules.

All the rules and examples contained in this section can be found in the `chapter-02/chapter-02-kjar/` project. We will use this project throughout the rest of the chapter to store different rules.

As it was mentioned in the first chapter, the rule structure is composed of the conditions and consequence, as follows:

```
rule "name"
when
     (Conditions) - also called Left Hand Side of the Rule (LHS)
then
     (Actions/Consequence) - also called Right Hand Side of the Rule
(RHS)
end
```

The `Conditions` (LHS) of the rule are written following the DRL language, which for the sake of simplicity, will not be entirely explained in here. We will be looking at the most common usage of the DRL language throughout the book examples. We will try to cover as much of the language as possible. You can always refer to the official documentation for a complete and detailed explanation of its structure at `http://docs.jboss.org/drools/release/6.3.0.Final/drools-docs/html_single/index.html#DroolsLanguageReferenceChapter`.

The LHS of the rule is composed by conditional elements, which serve as the filters to define the conditions that need to be met for the rule to evaluate true. This conditional element filter facts, which in our case are the object instances as we are working in Java.

If you take a look at our first rule LHS, the condition expressed is quite simple, as shown in the following:

```
rule "Classify Item - Low Range"
    when
        $i: Item(cost < 200)
    then
        $i.setCategory(Category.LOW_RANGE);
end
```

The line in the Left Hand Side of the rule can be separated in the following three sections:

- The Item(...) filter for the item object type. This filter will pick up all the item objects that we insert into our session and filter them for processing.

- The cost < 200 filter will take a look in the item objects and make sure that the field **cost** contains a value under 200.

- The $i represents a variable binding, which is used to later reference the matched object. Notice that we are using the $ symbol to name the variables so that we can easily identify them in contrast with the object fields. Consider this as good practice.

To summarize, we are filtering based on Objects and their properties. It is important to understand that we will be filtering the Object instances that matches with these conditions. For each item instance that evaluates to true to all the conditions, the rule engine will create a match.

A little bit more complex rule could be to categorize our customers by the size of the order that they make. A big difference between this new rule and the previous one is that now the rule will need to evaluate orders and customers. Take a look at how the rule looks:

```
//File classify-customer-rules.drl

rule "Classify Customer by order size"
    when
        $o: Order( orderLines.size >= 5, $customer: customer )
        $c: Customer(this == $customer, category == Customer.Category.
NA)
```

```
        then
            ;
        modify($c){
            setCategory(Customer.Category.SILVER)
        };
    end
```

In this rule, we are evaluating the orders with more than five order lines, which means five different items. Then, we look for the customer associated to this order and set this customer category. The relationship between the customer and order is achieved by binding the customer reference in the Order object to a variable called `$customer` and comparing Customer that we are evaluating against that reference by doing the following: `Customer(this == $customer…)`. The order of the conditional elements is only defined by the bindings that we need. In this case, we are picking `Order.getCustomer()` to match the customer fact. However, we can do it the other way around as well and it will work in the same way, as shown in the following:

```
    $c: Customer(category == Customer.Category.NA)
    $o: Order( orderLines.size >= 5, customer == $c )
```

An important thing to understand at this point is that `Customer()` and `Order()` need to be facts, in other words, they need to be explicitly inserted to `KieSession` using the `insert()` method. While `Order.getCustomer()` is not a fact, it is an object in a fact.

For this rule to evaluate true, we need an `Order` and `Customer` object instances that make all these conditions true. Between the `Order(..)` and `Customer(...)` filters, there is an implicit AND, therefore, the rule can be read When there is an order with more than 20 items AND a customer that is associated to that order, Then. This is also equivalent and valid in the DRL language, as follows:

```
    $o: Order( orderLines.size >= 5, $customer: customer )
    and
    $c: Customer(this == $customer, category == Customer.Category.NA)
```

You may also have noticed the `modify($c);` sentence on the right-hand side of the rule. This `modify()` method is another operation provided by the Rule Engine to make sure that the engine knows that a fact has been changed and the change needs to be notified to other rules that might be looking to match these changes. In this case, we are letting the engine know about the modification of the category of the customer. If you omit `modify($c)`, no other rule will know about the change in the category, which means that rules that depend on already categorized items will not be matched. For this reason, you will notice that we are also updating the item fact when the category is set in the rules located in the `classify-item-rules.drl` file.

Now that our rules have become more complex, it is important to notice the fact that we are clearly separating the business definition from our application code. We are extracting the definition of how to categorize customers to these rules and we will be able to update this definition if the business definition changes without modifying the rest of the application. This is one of the core concepts of using business rules.

Now, based on this categorization, we can create different types of coupons for different customers, allowing us to treat each of our customers differently, based on their loyalty and previous orders:

```
coupons-creation.drl:
rule "Create Coupons for Silver Customers"
    when
        $o: Order( $customer: customer )
        $c: Customer(this == $customer, category == Category.SILVER)
    then
        insert(new Coupon($c, $o, Coupon.CouponType.POINTS));
end
```

Like the previous example, here, the rule is filtering by `Orders` and `Customers`; however, as you can see in the rule RHS, we are creating a new Object of the `Coupon` type and making it available to the Rule Engine using the `insert()` method. This means that as soon as this rule gets executed by the Rule Engine, it will trigger any other rule that is expecting Coupons. Here the things become a little bit more interesting. We saw how the rules can generate new data and chain different rules together as soon as we make the new data available to the Rule Engine.

If you feel the need to experiment, we encourage you to write a rule in the `coupons-creation.drl` file to match the created coupon and see what happens.

Now let's make things a little bit more complex, let's imagine that we want to check an order with two or more items that only contain HIGH_RANGE items and we want to apply some discounts to these specific orders.

In order to write a rule that check for this situation, we will also need to evaluate the `OrderLine` objects (we will need to add this import as well). This can be translated to adding more filters to our rules. Now, we will need to put constraints on the Order object, OrderLines and Item associated. The following UML diagram shows the relationships among these objects:

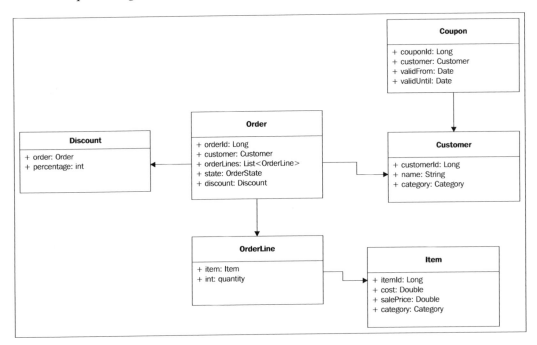

The following rule file expresses the previously introduced rule for discounts:

```
rule "High Range Order - 10% Discount"
    when
        $o: Order( $lines : orderLines.size >= 2, discount == null )
        forall( OrderLine( this memberOf $lines,  $item : item)
                Item(this == $item, category == Item.Category.HIGH_
RANGE)
        )
    then

modify($o){
setDiscount(new Discount(10.0))
};
end
```

We have three different object filters for `Order()`, `OrderLine()`, and `Item()`. Notice that this rule also depends on having our items classified; however, there is no explicit relationship between this rule and our first rule that categorize our items. One new thing introduced by this rule is the conditional element `forall`, which makes sure that all `OrderLines` and the associated items of the order are categorized as `HIGH_RANGE` items. If there is at least one item with a different category set associated with the current order, this rule will not get activated and fired. In the same way as earlier, we are updating the order so that if another rule is looking at the discount applied, the information is available to the engine.

You can find these rules in the `chapter-02/chapter-02-kjar/src/resources/` directory. In the following section, we will analyze a little bit of these project structures and tests provided to execute these rules.

We will be covering more of the DRL language in this book, but feel free to access the following official documentation if you need a detailed explanation of each of the DRL constructs:

`http://docs.jboss.org/drools/release/6.3.0.Final/drools-docs/html_single/index.html#DroolsLanguageReferenceChapter`

As you will see in the previous link, there is no way to include a detailed explanation about the constructs in a book; however, we will make sure to cover the most common ones using examples.

Organizing our projects

The more complex our rules become, the more important it is to have tests for them and keep them organized as much as possible. In this section, we will discuss how we organized our example projects for keeping our rules, their tests, and related classes in a structure that can be easily maintained.

We recommend this way of structuring the projects so that each of them keeps a very well-defined scope, set of dependencies, and they can be tested independently. You should keep all the application infrastructural code (user interfaces, system integration, services, and so on) in separate Maven modules as well, therefore, the infrastructure can be maintained in separate cycles from the business knowledge that tends to be updated more frequently by the business needs.

The example repository contains a high-level parent project that is composed by each individual chapter modules. Each individual chapter contains the following three main modules:

- `-kjar`: This will contain our business assets such as rules, business processes, and so on

- `-tests`: We will include all the tests here
- `-extras` (optional): This module usually contains classes to extend the Drools and jBPM functionality, such as custom evaluators for rules, work item handlers for business processes, and so on

The `-kjar` and `-tests` modules are considered to be knowledge projects as they contain the rules, definitions, and tests to ensure that the defined knowledge is behaving correctly. As you can see in the following image, the `*-test` project will depend on the domain model project from your application. It might also depend on the service layer to execute operations; however, as good practice, these services can be mocked. From the application perspective, it is most likely that the Services and User Interfaces modules end up having dependencies to knowledge-related projects. If the knowledge-related projects are only defining the core business logic, the services from your application will end up using them in order to make decisions internally. From the user interface's perspective, we can also define knowledge projects to assist the user at the UI level, as shown in the following diagram:

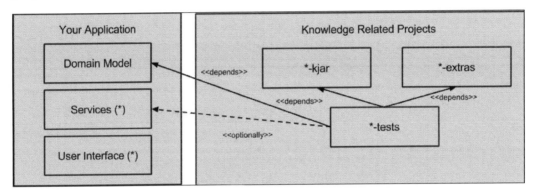

At this point, don't worry about this structure, it will become more clear when we move forward on the next chapters. Now, if you take a look at the `chapter-02-test/` project, you will find that we need to define some extra dependencies for the testing frameworks that we will be using, as follows:

```
<dependency>
  <groupId>junit</groupId>
  <artifactId>junit</artifactId>
  <scope>test</scope>
</dependency>
<dependency>
  <groupId>org.hamcrest</groupId>
```

```
    <artifactId>hamcrest-library</artifactId>
    <scope>test</scope>
</dependency>
<dependency>
    <groupId>org.mockito</groupId>
    <artifactId>mockito-core</artifactId>
    <scope>test</scope>
</dependency>
```

After adding these dependencies to our projects, we can create our first JUnit test to make sure that our rules are working as expected. Notice that we have defined several rules in different rule files throughout this chapter, and for now, we are going to load all of them in the same `KieSession`. This means that when we insert information in the engine, all the rules will be evaluated and probably fired.

The first test that we will look into is the one in the `ClassifyItemsTest.java` class and it is located in the `src/tests/java/org/drools/devguide/chapter-02` directory in the `chapter-02/chapter-02-test` project, as follows:

```
public class ClassifyItemsTest extends BaseTest {
    @Test
    public void simpleClassification() {
        KieSession kSession = createDefaultSession();
        Item item = new Item("A", 123.0, 234.0);
        kSession.insert(item);
        int fired = kSession.fireAllRules();
        assertThat(1, is(fired));
        assertThat(Category.LOW_RANGE, is(item.getCategory()));
    }
}
```

This test shows how to make sure that our item is categorized correctly. We encourage you to open the `classify-item-rules.drl` file, look at the other rules, and write tests to make sure that other categories are also being processed correctly.

When we compile this project using Maven (clean install), these tests will be executed, assuring us that our items are classified accordingly. If we use a continuous build system (such as Jenkins CI at `https://jenkins-ci.org`), we will get notified as soon as a rule changes and one of these tests breaks. Allowing us to review whether the test needs to be changed or the change introduced in the rules is breaking some other policies that are already defined in the system.

Another test class called `OrderDiscountTest.java`, is located in the same package as the previous one. Lets see the code for this as follows:

```
@Test
public void highRangeOrderDiscountTest() {
  KieSession kSession = createDefaultSession();
  Order o = ModelFactory.getOrderWithFiveHighRangeItems();

  kSession.insert(o.getCustomer());
  kSession.insert(o.getOrderLines().get(0));
  kSession.insert(o.getOrderLines().get(1));
  kSession.insert(o.getOrderLines().get(2));
  kSession.insert(o.getOrderLines().get(3));
  kSession.insert(o.getOrderLines().get(4));
  kSession.insert(o.getOrderLines().get(0).getItem());
  kSession.insert(o.getOrderLines().get(1).getItem());
  kSession.insert(o.getOrderLines().get(2).getItem());
  kSession.insert(o.getOrderLines().get(3).getItem());
  kSession.insert(o.getOrderLines().get(4).getItem());
  kSession.insert(o);

  int fired = kSession.fireAllRules();

  // We have 5 Items that are categorized -> 5 rules were fired
  // We have 1 Customer that needs to be categorized -> 1 rule fired
  // We have just one order with all HIGH RAnge items -> 1 rule fired
  // One Coupon is created for the SILVER Customer -> 1 rule fired
  assertThat(8, is(fired));
  assertThat(o.getCustomer().getCategory(), is(Category.SILVER));
  assertThat(o.getDiscount(), not(nullValue()));
  assertThat(o.getDiscount().getPercentage(), is(10.0));
  assertThat(o.getOrderLines().get(0).getItem().getCategory(),
    is(Item.Category.HIGH_RANGE));
  ..

  // The Coupon Object was created by the Rule Engine so we need to
    get it from the KieSession
  Collection<Coupon> coupons =
                  getFactsFromSession(kSession, Coupon.class);
  assertThat(1, is(coupons.size()));

}
```

A common requirement for these tests is to consume our domain models, which can contain complex structures and a lot of data. Usually, we end up having helpers to retrieve these information from a data store such as a database or we can create local instances for the sake of the tests.

For these tests, we are using the ModelFactory helper, which initialize different orders, customers, and items for us. Feel free to review the different methods of this factory to understand the information that is being initialized there. We encourage you to create more methods in the ModelFactory class to provide more data for your tests.

This test loads all the rules (in no particular order) that we defined so far in the following DRL files:

- classify-customer-rules.drl
- classify-item-rules.drl
- coupons-creation.drl
- order-discount-rules.drl

After KieSession is created by the helper method createDefaultSession(), ModelFactory provides us with an order that gives us access to OrderLines, Customer, and Items. In order to enable the Rule Engine to work and match these objects with the previously defined rules, we need to insert each of them using the insert() method. As you may have noticed, this could become a problem quite easily if we need to insert all the objects separately. There are a couple of alternatives to solve this issue and we will cover them in the following chapters. For now, we need to know if we have rules that filter facts by type. We need to make these facts available to the Engine.

Now, after inserting all the facts to KieSession, the evaluations are done by the engine and matches are created. It is important to understand that not all matches need to be executed on the fireAllRules() call, some of them might be cancelled and new matches can also be created during execution. We will analyze a detailed rules-execution flow in *Chapter 3, Drools Runtime*. For now, we need to understand why we have eight rules fired in the test and in order to do this, we need to do some simple math.

We know that one rule will be fired per item that needs to be categorized. In this test, we have five Items, therefore, we have five rules fired there. We don't know the order in which these rules will be fired; however, we know that they will be fired before a rule that depends on this categorization. The same happens with the customer, therefore, one more rule fired. Again, we don't know or care about the order in which the items and customers are categorized. Finally, one rule is fired for the Coupon creation and one rule is fired to apply the discount to the order. As we mentioned earlier, the firing order is not important, the results are, and for this reason, the test checks whether the objects have being changed as expected. At the end of the test, we cannot check the Coupon object as we didn't have any reference from it. The Coupon object was created by the Rule Engine internally, and for us to get hold of it, we can use the `getFactsFromSession`(`kSession`, `Coupon.class`) helper method, which will get all the Coupon objects that were inserted as facts in `KieSession`.

If you had written more rules about coupons, customers, orders, and so on, these tests might fail. If you did so, make sure to update the tests so that they keep passing.

Summary

In this chapter, we covered the basics to start a Drools project from scratch. This is extremely important, therefore, you can get started with a very basic project that uses Drools. All the other examples in the book are using this structure, which is also recommended as a way of working for your own projects. We have created our first rule, analyzed the basics of the execution, and tested it using JUnit. The section about CDI introduced how Drools 6 can be used in CDI-enabled contexts, leveraging all the integration provided by the framework.

In the next chapter, we are going to look at the KieContainer, KieServices, and KieSession and how they work internally. We will also analyze the rules-execution flow in detail so that we can understand how the rules behave.

3
Drools Runtime

In the previous chapter, we covered how to start a project from scratch, write some rules, and execute them. Now, we need to understand how the Drools internal components work together, their main responsibilities, and their configurations. Knowing this, we will be able to fine-tune the engine and the surrounding services to our specific needs. We will see how Drools can be used in different contexts and ways so that you can decide which fits the best for your projects. This chapter will cover the following topics:

- Understanding the Drools runtime instances
- Common configurations
- Loading dynamic changes using KieScanner

Understanding the Drools runtime instances

Drools allows us to create instances of the Rule Engine in different ways, so that we can choose which fits better to the problem that we are trying to solve. Each Rule Engine instance is an encapsulated context, where the rules that we define will be evaluated against the data that we provide to this particular instance. Historically, Rule Engines were seen as big and monolithic processes that run them in a server and we can send data to it to be processed. Drools, on the other hand, allows us to locally spawn lightweight instances to our application. It is common to have multiple instances dealing with different rules and data than just one big instance.

In order to spawn a new instance of the rule engine, we need to understand the following concepts:

- KieServices
- KieContainer
- KieModule
- KieBase
- KieSession

By using these five concepts, we will be able to define how each instance is configured and rules that will be available to each of them. In cases where we need to create multiple rule engines, it is important to understand what exactly happens under the hood to avoid unnecessary bottleneck and performance issues.

It is important also to understand that these five concepts are extended versions of what was provided in the previous versions of Drools. Notice that the **Knowledge is Everything (KIE)** prefix that indicates the fact that now we are not only dealing with Rule Engine instances, but with more ways of defining and executing business knowledge in general.

We will start by looking at the KieServices class that gives us access to all these other concepts by providing a registry of services where we can find helpers for different purposes. In the future versions of Drools, more services may be included to fulfill different use cases. For now, we need to know how to get hold of a KieServices instance, and we do that by using the following static `KieServices.Factory.get()` method:

```
KieServices ks = KieServices.Factory.get();
```

Using the KieServices, we can access a number of factories, services, and utility methods used along with Rule Engine instances. We will use KieServices to create a new instance of KieContainer, which defines the scope of the rules that will be used to create new instances of the Rule Engine. A KieContainer can host a KieModule and its dependencies. It means that a hierarchical structure of KieModules can be loaded into an instance of the KieContainer.

The relations among these concepts are depicted in the following diagram:

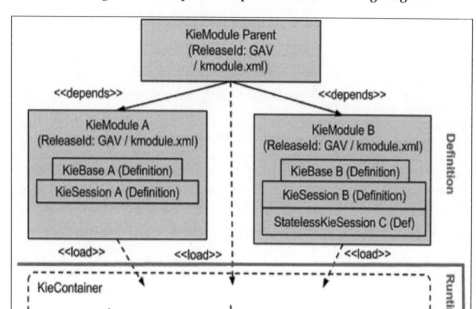

In Drools 6, everything is created around KieModules. Each KieModule contains business assets (business rules, business processes, decision tables, and so on) related to a certain area or domain. These KieModules can include other KieModules, allowing us to compose a top-level KieModule, containing several assets from different domains.

A KieModule is a standard Java-Maven project containing the rules, business process and other assets among its resources. A special file called kmodule.xml (in the META-INF/ directory) that defines the internal configuration about how to group and consume these particular assets must also be present in it.

As we can see in the previous diagram, KieContainer will allow us to instantiate a KieModule in order to create one or multiple instances of the Rule Engine. These instances can be all configured to have the same rules in it or a completely different setup. The previous diagram also shows how to decide which KieModule to load; for example, we can decide to load **KieModule A** as we are just going to use the Rules defined in it or we can load **KieModule Parent**, which depends on **KieModule A** and **KieModule B**, therefore, every configuration in these modules will be loaded.

The following section will go deep into the KieModule and KieContainer specifics. In the beginning, this might sound confusing as there are too many options, however, that's exactly the reason behind the flexibility that Drools provides to configure and instantiate the Rule Engine. Towards the end of this book, we expect you to be an intermediate Drools user that can configure and tune the engine to your specific needs.

KieModule & KieContainer

Once we get hold of the KieServices, we can create new KieContainers. Internally, the KieContainer has references to all the business assets (rules, processes, spreadsheets, PMML documents, and so on) that will be loaded when we create new Rule Engine instances. As it was depicted in the previous section, a KieContainer can spawn multiple Rule Engine instances with different configurations and hosting different rule sets, depending on what our application requires.

In Drools 6, we can choose between two options to define the scope of the resources and configurations that will be included in an instance of KieContainer, as shown in the following:

- Based on the classpath
- Using Maven dependency resolution techniques (KIE-CI)

The first option will look at all the business assets in the application classpath and allow us to load them in different instances of the rule engine. The second option will delegate the responsibility of finding out predefined artifacts and their transitive dependencies into Maven to find out all the resources that need to be included.

Let's look at these two options in detail. First, we will start by looking at how the classpath is being scanned and rules are picked up. The best way for us to understand how this works is to take a look at the projects provided in this chapter.

This chapter provides the following five projects to demonstrate the different setups that can be used for our KieModules:

- **chapter-03-classpath-tests**: This project provides tests showing the classpath resolution strategy to create KieContainers.

- **chapter-03-maven-tests**: This project provides tests showing how to leverage the power of Maven to resolve the KieModules as Maven artifacts.

- **chapter-03-kjar-simple-discounts**: This is a KieModule containing a set of rules for simple discounts.

- **chapter-03-kjar-premium-discounts**: This is another KieModule containing a set of rules for premium discounts.

- **chapter-03-kjar-parent**: This is a KieModule that contains a reference to the previous KieModules. It doesn't include any asset internally, but it makes references to the simple and premium discounts so that they can be referenced together.

The next two sections will cover the following two alternatives:

- Loading rules from the classpath
- Loading rules using Maven artifacts (using Kie-CI)

Loading rules from the classpath

For this section, we will be using the `chapter-03-classpath-tests` project, therefore, we recommend you to open this project in your IDE to review the provided tests together, while we discuss the different options that we have to set up our Rule Engine instances.

The first test in the `KieContainerClassPathTests` class (located in `src/test/java/`) called `loadingRulesFromClassPath()` demonstrates how a new KieContainer can be created by scanning the current application classpath. In this case, we are bootstrapping Drools in a JUnit Test and Maven takes care of setting up the classpath for us based on the definitions in the `pom.xml` file. If we are not using Maven to run the application (or the Unit Test), Drools will scan the application classpath, no matter how it is defined. For this example, as we are in a Maven project, all the dependencies defined for the project and the dependencies defined with the **test** scope will be added to the classpath before running the test.

If we take a look at the `pom.xml` file (located in the root of `project /chapter-03/chapter-03-tests/pom.xml`), we will notice that there are three dependencies to projects that contain the `kmodule.xml` file, as follows:

```xml
<!-- Start dependencies for the other KieModules -->
<dependency>
<groupId>org.drools.devguide</groupId>
<artifactId>chapter-03-kjar-simple-discounts</artifactId>
<version>${project.version}</version>
<scope>test</scope>
</dependency>
```

```
<dependency>
<groupId>org.drools.devguide</groupId>
<artifactId>chapter-03-kjar-premium-discounts</artifactId>
<version>${project.version}</version>
<scope>test</scope>
</dependency>
<dependency>
<groupId>org.drools.devguide</groupId>
<artifactId>chapter-03-kjar-parent</artifactId>
<version>${project.version}</version>
<scope>test</scope>
</dependency>
<!-- End dependencies for the other KieModules -->
```

When we create a new KieContainer based on the classpath, all the available jars will be scanned. In order to create a new KieContainer, we use the **KieServices (ks)** to provide us with a new instance of the KieContainer, as follows:

```
KieContainer kContainer = ks.newKieClasspathContainer();
```

Drools will scan all the jars in the classpath looking for the kmodule.xml file in the META-INF/ directory. When found, this file will load the provided configurations to make them available to use in our applications. For this particular example that we are reviewing, four kmodule.xml files will be found: the three in the dependencies defined in the pom.xml file and the one included in the project itself (in the src/ test/resources/META-INF/ directory). All the configurations in each of the kmodule.xml files will be loaded and made available to the KieContainer, ready to be used. Also, notice that there is a DRL file called classpath-discount-rules.drl in the src/test/resources/rules/cp/discount directory:

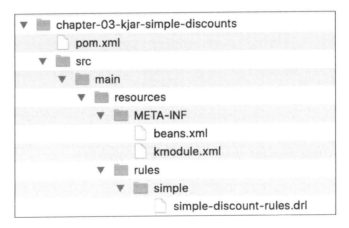

Now, our KieContainer has loaded all these configurations and we can start using them right away. Going back to our loadingRulesFromClassPath() test, which shows how the rules can be loaded from the classpath, as follows:

```
...
KieServices ks = KieServices.Factory.get();
KieContainer kContainer = ks.newKieClasspathContainer();

// Let's verify that all the resources are loaded correctly
Results results = kContainer.verify();
// We can iterate the results
results.getMessages().stream()
        .forEach((message) -> {
          System.out.println(">> Message ( "+message.getLevel()+" ): "
        +message.getText());
          });
// If there is an Error we need to stop and correct it
assertThat(false, is(results.hasMessages(Message.Level.ERROR)));

//Here we make sure that all the KieBases and KieSessions
//  that we are expecting are loaded.
kContainer.getKieBaseNames().stream().map((kieBase) -> {
          System.out.println(">> Loading KieBase: "+ kieBase );
          return kieBase;
        }).forEach((kieBase) -> {
          kContainer.getKieSessionNamesInKieBase(kieBase).stream().
forEach((kieSession) -> {
              System.out.println("\t >> Containing KieSession: "+
kieSession );
            });
        });
```

As we can see, the verify() method will allow us to make sure that our business assets are correct and are loaded correctly in the KieContainer instance. If the verify() method returns Results containing errors, we should stop and correct these errors before moving forward. Notice that the Message object returned by the results.getMessages() method also contains the line and column in the file where the problem is. If everything is okay, we can move forward and check whether all the KieBases and KieSessions that we are expecting to use are loaded. For this test, we are only printing them out, however, making assertions is recommended here.

As mentioned earlier, the kmodule.xml file contains what will be made available to the KieContainer, therefore, let's take a look at the kmodule.xml file content to understand a little bit more of what is loaded when we create a KieContainer classpath.

Briefing up, this simple test demonstrates how all the KieModules are loaded in the container based on a classpath scanning. Make sure that you run this test to verify the results and understand why the different configurations are loaded.

Let's quickly take a look at the second approach before looking at the `kmodule.xml` configurations in detail.

Loading rules using Maven artifacts (Kie-CI)

As we saw in the previous section, all the KieModules that are found in the classpath of the application will be loaded in the KieContainer. There are some cases where we don't want that to happen. Maybe because we don't have these jars locally to the application or we want to decouple our application dependencies from the business rules artifact dependencies, therefore, it is clear what is required for the application to run and what are the **Knowledge Artifacts** that will provide the business logic.

If we now open the `chapter-03-maven-tests` project and look at the `pom.xml` file, we will notice a huge difference. There is no KieModule dependency in this `pom.xml` file, however, a new dependency was added to a `kie-ci` module, as follows:

```
<dependency>
  <groupId>org.kie</groupId>
  <artifactId>kie-ci</artifactId>

  <scope>test</scope>
</dependency>
```

This new dependency will enable Drools to use the Maven mechanism to resolve artifacts that are outside of the application classpath. Let's take a look at the tests in the `KieContainerMavenTests` class. We will see that now we can use the KieServices to create a new container in a different way, as shown in the following:

```
KieContainer kContainer = ks.newKieContainer(ks.newReleaseId(
    "org.drools.devguide", "chapter-03-kjar-simple-discounts",
    "1.0.0"));
```

Notice that now, instead of adding the dependency to our project/application, we are letting the KieContainer resolve an artifact that we are providing based on `GroupId`, `ArtifactId`, and `Version` (also referred as GAV). As you can see, the `newKieContainer()` method is expecting a `ReleaseId` object, which is also created using a helper method of the `KieServices`.

The Drools API allows us to not only use this `ReleaseId` specific version of the KieModule, but also upgrade it to a newer version, should it be necessary, through the `updateToVersion()` method. This method will recreate the KieContainer to become an access point to the KieBases and KieSessions of a newer version of the KieModule.

Using this mechanism, the container will only load the configurations from this artifact and all its dependencies. If you execute these tests, you will see that each of the individual tests is only loading the `kmodule.xml` configuration contained in the artifact that is being requested at the time of the KieContainer creation.

It is time to look at the content of the `kmodule.xml` file, which allows us to configure our KieBases and KieSessions to define exactly how the rule engine instances will be created for us to use in our applications.

KieModule configurations (KieBases, KieSessions & StatelessKieSessions)

The `kmodule.xml` file is used to customize the KieModule configurations. In this file, we can define how the rules are grouped together in different KieBases that can be loaded for different purposes. It also allows us to define more fine-grained configurations for the rule engine instance that will be created.

In this section, we will cover the basic configurations for KieBases, KieSessions, and StatelessKieSessions. In the end, we will also review a mechanism that we can use to include other KieBases from other KieModules in our KieModule.

Let's start simple with the `kmodule.xml` file defined in the `chapter-03-classpath-tests/src/test/resources/META-INF/` directory, as follows:

```xml
<?xml version="1.0" encoding="UTF-8"?>
<kmodule xmlns:xsi="http://www.w3.org/2001/XMLSchema-instance"
        xmlns="http://jboss.org/kie/6.0.0/kmodule">
    <kbase name="rules.cp.discount">
        <ksession name="rules.cp.discount.session" type="stateful"/>
    </kbase>
</kmodule>
```

Using the concepts of KieBase and KieSession, we can define the granularity of how the rules will need to be loaded. A KieBase represents a compiled version of a set of assets, and a KieSession represents an instance of the rule engine containing the rules in the KieBase. For this reason, it makes sense to have multiple sessions defined with different configurations for the same KieBase. In other words, we can use the same rules, but have a session configured in a different way for different needs.

In this case, we are defining a KieBase called `rules.cp.discount`. Notice that the `name` attribute of the KieBase is the same as the directory structure that we are using under the `/src/test/resources/` directory, where the rules are stored. In the KieBase, we are defining a KieSession called `rules.cp.discount.session`. This KieSession will represent the Rule Engine instance containing all the rules defined in the KieBase. In Drools 6, similar to the previous versions of Drools, there are two types of KieSessions (previously called KnowledgeSession): Stateful and Stateless.

The stateful KieSession allows us to keep the state between several interactions with the Rule Engine. In Drools 6, Stateful Knowledge Sessions were renamed to KieSessions, as there are the most common type of session, the name was kept short. In contrast, StatelessKieSession only allows us to interact once, take the results out, and no state is stored for the next interaction. We will see more about KieSessions in *Chapter 5, Understanding KIE Sessions*.

If you take a look at the tests, for example, `loadingRulesFromDependencyParentKieModule()` in the `KieContainerClasspathTests` class, you will notice that we are using a (Stateful) KieSession as we insert a set of facts, then call the `fireAllRules()` method, and then we keep inserting more facts and call `fireAllRules()` again. Between the two calls to the `fireAllRules()` method, the state (meaning the facts and the rules evaluations) are kept. There will be cases where the second set of facts triggers new rules in conjunction with the first set of facts, as follows:

```
...
KieSession kieSession = kContainer.newKieSession("rules.discount.
all");
Customer customer = new Customer();
customer.setCustomerId(1L);
customer.setCategory(Customer.Category.SILVER);

Order order = new Order();
order.setCustomer(customer);

kieSession.insert(customer);
kieSession.insert(order);

int fired = kieSession.fireAllRules();

assertThat(1, is(fired));
assertThat(10.0, is(order.getDiscount().getPercentage()));

Customer customerGold = new Customer();
customerGold.setCustomerId(2L);
```

```
customerGold.setCategory(Customer.Category.GOLD);

Order orderGold = new Order();
orderGold.setCustomer(customerGold);

kieSession.insert(customerGold);
kieSession.insert(orderGold);

fired = kieSession.fireAllRules();

assertThat(1, is(fired));
assertThat(20.0, is(orderGold.getDiscount().getPercentage()));
```

As you can see, the Silver Order and `customer` are still in the KieSession when we insert the Gold Customer and Order. In the next chapter, you will learn how to write more complex rules that, for example, evaluate two orders and their relationships. In such cases, more than one rule can be fired.

Now, we can take a look at the `statelessSessionTest()` test, which shows the interaction against a StatelessKieSession in contrast to a KieSession (which is Stateful). Notice that we need to define the session as stateless in the `kmodule.xml` file, as follows:

```
<ksession name="rules.simple.sl.discount" type="stateless"/>
```

Now we can get a new StatelessKieSession from our kContainer, as shown in the following:

```
...
StatelessKieSession statelessKieSession =
        kContainer.newStatelessKieSession("rules.simple.sl.discount");

Customer customer = new Customer();
customer.setCategory(Customer.Category.SILVER);

Order order = new Order();
order.setCustomer(customer);

Command newInsertOrder = ks.getCommands().newInsert(order,
"orderOut");
Command newInsertCustomer = ks.getCommands().newInsert(customer);
Command newFireAllRules = ks.getCommands().
newFireAllRules("outFired");

List<Command> cmds = new ArrayList<Command>();
cmds.add(newInsertOrder);
```

```
cmds.add(newInsertCustomer);
cmds.add(newFireAllRules);

ExecutionResults execResults = statelessKieSession
                    .execute(ks.getCommands().
newBatchExecution(cmds));

order = (Order)execResults.getValue("orderOut");
int fired = (Integer)execResults.getValue("outFired");

assertThat(1, is(fired));
assertThat(10.0, is(order.getDiscount().getPercentage()));
```

Notice that now we need to use the `newStatelessKieSession()` method to create a new StatelessKieSession. In this type of session, we don't have the `insert()` or `fireAllRules()` methods, instead we have the `execute()` method that allows us to send a command or a set of commands to be executed. From this execution, you can get the `ExecutionResults` object that will contain all the results that we will want to collect after the rule execution. After the interaction (execute and get the results), there is no state hold in the StatelessKieSession and if we call the `execute()` method again, all the rules will be evaluated only against the facts that we send for this interaction.

Finally, if we want to aggregate KieModules, we can use the includes option in the KieBases configuration. You can take a look at `chapter-03-kjar-parent/src/main/resources/kmodule.xml`, as follows:

```xml
<kmodule xmlns:xsi="http://www.w3.org/2001/XMLSchema-instance"
        xmlns="http://jboss.org/kie/6.0.0/kmodule">
    <kbase name="discount" default="true" includes="rules.premium,
    rules.simple">
        <ksession name="rules.discount.all" type="stateful"/>
    </kbase>
</kmodule>
```

As we can see, the `includes` property of the kbase tag is making reference to other KieBases defined in other modules. If these KieBases are available at the initialization time, they will be included and now the KieSession called `rules.discount.all` will contain all the resources defined in these two KieBases.

Just for the sake of completeness, here is the full schema for the `kmodule.xml` file:

https://github.com/droolsjbpm/droolsjbpm-knowledge/blob/master/kie-api/src/main/resources/org/kie/api/kmodule.xsd

We will be using most of the options provided to configure our KieBases and KieSession in the book. Now, it is time to look at one of the most required features provided by Drools to dynamically load changes that we make in our business assets. The second half of this chapter will cover the KieScanner and how to use it in our applications.

KieScanner

If there is a universal truth about applications, it is that business rules will change over time. The criteria used to apply a discount, or even the amount of the discount itself, we are using today will—without any doubt—have to be modified tomorrow. We, as the architects and developers of these applications, have to be prepared for this.

Drools provides us with a way to mitigate this issue already. The separation that Drools introduces between the applications and the business logic allows us to decouple the changes happening in the business logic—which are usually frequent—from the changes happening in the application's infrastructure or UI, which are not so frequent.

Regardless of all the advantages provided by this separation, there is still one major problem that remains: every time our business logic (rules) changes, any KieContainer that referenced it has to be notified.

We already saw how a KieContainer can be manually updated when a new version of a KieModule is deployed, one of the limitations of this approach is that we have to manually notify each of the applications that depend on the modified KieModule. What if there were a way to automatically let out the applications to be notified when a KieModule that they depend on gets updated? Fortunately for us, Drools provides this mechanism out of the box, its name is KieScanner.

In order to use KieScanner in our application, the `org.kie::kie-ci` artifact must be added to the application's classpath.

The KieScanner component in Drools is nothing but a wrapper around a KieContainer that can be configured to automatically detect changes in the resources that the container depends on. There is a catch though, the resources referenced by the KieContainer being monitored must be KieJars residing in a Maven repository. By default, kie-ci will use Maven's `settings.xml` in the `.m2` folder of the user's home. This behavior can be overridden using the `-Dkie.maven.settings.custom` system property, as follows:

```
KieServices ks = KieServices.Factory.get();
```

```
KieContainer kieContainer = ks.newKieContainer(
    ks.newReleaseId("group.test","artifact-test", "1.0"));
KieScanner scanner = ks.newKieScanner(kieContainer);
```

As we can see, a KieScanner can be instantiated—just like most of the Drools 6 components—from the KieServices class. After KieScanner is instantiated, we have two options, we could either configure it to poll for new versions of the underlying KieJars on every fixed amount of milliseconds or we can manually force it to check for new versions on demand, as follows:

```
//Manually run a check for new versions
scanner.scanNow();
//Configure the scanner to check for new versions every 10 seconds
scanner.start(10_000);
```

If the `start()` method was used to start the KieScanner, the antagonic `stop()` method can be used to stop the polling mechanism.

When a new version of a KieJar is found by KieScanner, an incremental build resources is triggered. From this moment, all the new KieBases and KieSessions created from the KieContainer being wrapped will use the new version of the resources. It is important to mention that any pre-existing KieBase and KieSession will also be updated to the latest version of the resources found by the KieScanner.

At first, it is easy to think that an incremental build of a KieContainer could be useful for adding, modifying, or removing rules from it; however, the truth is that a more complex modification of the resources such as new type of declarations, modification on existing type declarations, addition of global variables and/or functions, and pretty much everything you could think of are also allowed to happen when a KieContainer is rebuilt.

Artifacts version resolution

The way KieScanner checks for new versions of the KieJars being monitored is according to Maven's rules for artifact versions: the newest version is always the one with the greatest version number, unless the version is a SNAPSHOT. If two artifacts have the same `GroupId`, `ArtifactId` and `Version`, the timestamp of each artifact is compared in order to determine which one is the newest. KieScanner only checks for versions in the KieJar that are compatible with the one defined in the KieContainer being wrapped. In other words, if the KieContainer is using version 1.0 of a particular KieJar, the corresponding KieScanner will check for new versions of the underlying KieJar that are compatible with 1.0.

The following tables show what compatible version means in the context of different KieContainer versions and the versions of a newly deployed KieJar in Maven repository:

KieContainer version: 1.0		
New KieJar version	**KieScanner triggers?**	**Reason**
0.9	No	0.9 is a different (lower) version than 1.0 (the version that the KieContainer is using).
1.0-SNAPSHOT	No	1.0-SNAPSHOT is considered a different version than 1.0 (the version that the KieContainer is using).
1.0	Yes	1.0 is the same version defined in KieContainer. The newly deployed version has a bigger timestamp than the one the KieContainer is using.
1.1	No	1.1 is a different (higher) version than 1.0 (the version that the KieContainer is using).

As we can see in the preceding table, KieScanner is only triggered when a new (according to its timestamp) version of the KieJar being monitored is detected in the Maven repository. As far as KieScanner concerns, SNAPSHOT versions are treated in the same way as the final ones. The following table shows the behavior of SNAPSHOT KieJar versions:

KieContainer version: 1.0-SNAPSHOT		
New KieJar version	**KieScanner triggers?**	**Reason**
0.9	No	0.9 is a different (lower) version than 1.0-SNAPSHOT (the version that the KieContainer is using).
1.0-SNAPSHOT	Yes	1.0-SNAPSHOT is the same version defined in KieContainer. The newly deployed version has a bigger timestamp than the one the KieContainer is using.
1.0	No	1.0 is considered a different version than 1.0-SNAPSHOT (the version that the KieContainer is using).
1.1	No	Same as the previous case.

A KieScanner can be defined to use a fixed KieJar version (that is, 1.0 or 1.0-SNAPSHOT), but it could also be configured to use Maven's LATEST or RELEASE magic version name or even a range. These special version definitions are useful when we want to keep our KieContainers updated with the latest version—or a range of them—of a KieJar irrespective of its specific version number:

KieContainer version: LATEST/RELEASE (original KieJar version: 0.9)		
New KieJar version	**KieScanner triggers?**	**Reason**
0.9	Yes	0.9 is the same version defined in KieContainer. The newly deployed version has a bigger timestamp than the one the KieContainer is using.
1.0-SNAPSHOT	No	KieScanner treats the LATEST version as RELEASE. Snapshot versions are not used when specifying these magic version names. Consider using ranges if you want SNAPSHOTS to be used.
1.0	Yes	1.0 is a different (higher) version than 0.9 (the version that the KieContainer is using).
1.1	Yes	Same as the previous case.

As noted in the preceding table, KieScanner differs from Maven's specification and treats LATEST magic version name in the same way that it treats the RELEASE: SNAPSHOT versions are being taken into account when using any of these magic version names.

Just like LATEST and RELEASE, magic version names are supported by KieScanner as well as the ranges (more about Maven versions and ranges can be found here: `https://docs.oracle.com/middleware/1212/core/MAVEN/maven_version.htm#MAVEN8903`). A version range allows us to specify a range of valid versions for the KieJar being used by the KieContainer being wrapped by a KieScanner. Ranges support both open and closed-ended ranges.

KieContainer version: (0.9), (original KieJar version: 0.9)		
New KieJar version	**KieScanner triggers?**	**Reason**
0.9	Yes	0.9 is the same version defined in the KieContainer. The newly deployed version has a bigger timestamp than the one the KieContainer is using.
1.0-SNAPSHOT	Yes	1.0-SNAPSHOT is a different (higher) version than 0.9 (the version that the KieContainer is currently using).

KieContainer version: (0.9), (original KieJar version: 0.9)		
New KieJar version	**KieScanner triggers?**	**Reason**
1.0	Yes	1.0 is a different (higher) version than 1.0-SNAPSHOT (the version that the KieContainer is currently using).
1.1	Yes	1.1 is a different (higher) version than 1.0 (the version that the KieContainer is currently using).

In the preceding example, an open-ended version (**[0.9,]**) is specified in the KieContainer. The range is basically saying that the KieContainer allows any version higher than 0.9, including SNAPSHOT versions too.

Dealing with unexpected issues and errors

So far, we have covered how and when a KieContainer is updated when it is used in conjunction with a KieScanner; however, there is an important question that is still open: what happens if there is an error while upgrading a KieContainer to a newer version?

First thing we need to understand is the kind of errors could occur while upgrading the version of a KieJar. Generally speaking, we are talking about the compilation errors in the new version of the KieJar such as the following:

- Syntax errors
- Adding rules with duplicated names
- Removing globals that are still being used, and so on.

KieScanner treats the whole process of a KieJar as an atomic action. When the upgrade of a KieContainer fails for any reason, the entire process is rolledback and the KieContainer remains in its original form. Any error generated during the upgrade process will be silently discarded.

Putting it all together

After the rather long introduction of KieScanner, it's time to put it all together in a unit test that we can play with.

In the `chapter-03/chapter-03-tests` project, there is a `KieScannerTest.java` test class. This class contains a `kieContainerUpdateKieJarTest` JUnit test. This test shows how a KieScanner can be used to update the KieJar that a KieContainer is using. The test also shows how, after the underlying KieContainer is updated, a previously created KieSession is automatically updated to the latest version of the KieJar being used by the KieContainer.

The test starts by creating two SILVER Customers (customerA and customerB) and an Order for each of them (orderA and orderB). The idea behind this unit test is to create a KieJar with a single rule that will apply a discount to Orders from SILVER Customers. The first version of the KieJar will give SILVER Customers a 10% discount on their Orders. The second version—the test will programmatically create and deploy a new version of the KieJar—will give SILVER Customers a discount of 25% instead:

```
ReleaseId releaseId = ks.newReleaseId(groupId, artifactId, version);
InternalKieModule originalKJar = createKieJar(ks, releaseId,
    createDiscountRuleForSilverCustomers(10.0));
```

The preceding lines (this is an extract of the code that you will find in the unit test) programmatically creates a KieJar with a single rule to apply 10% discount on SILVER Customers Orders:

```
repository.deployArtifact(releaseId, originalKJar, createKPom
    (fileManager, releaseId));
KieContainer kieContainer = ks.newKieContainer(releaseId);
KieScanner scanner = ks.newKieScanner(kieContainer);
```

Once the KieJar is created, it is deployed to a local Maven repository and a KieContainer is then created from it. The code excerpt also shows how the KieContainer is wrapped using a KieScanner. In real-life scenarios, we should start the KieScanner using its start method; however, given that we require our unit test to be deterministic, we don't want the KieScanner checking for updates in an asynchronous way. Instead of this, the test will use KieScanner's `scanNow` method when required, as follows:

```
KieSession ksession = kieContainer.newKieSession();
this.calculateAndAssertDiscount(customerA, orderA, ksession, 10.0);
```

From the generated KieContainer, we will create a new KieSession; the
`calculateAndAssertDiscount` helper method is used to insert `customerA` and
`orderA` in the KieSession and assert that the generated discount is `10.0`, as shown in
the following:

```
InternalKieModule newKJar = createKieJar(ks, releaseId,
createDiscountRuleForSilverCustomers(25.0));
repository.deployArtifact(releaseId, newKJar, createKPom(fileManager,
releaseId));
```

The next step is to create a different version of the same KieJar (same group ID,
artifact ID, and version) this time, having a rule that will give 25% discount to
SILVER Customers. Just like before, this KieJar is deployed in Maven's repository,
overriding its previous version.

It's important to note that the KieContainer will not notice this change. The
KieContainer was built using the previous version of the KieJar and will not
update its content until explicitly told (either by the use of a KieScanner or by the
`KieContainer.updateToVersion` method).

```
scanner.scanNow();
this.calculateAndAssertDiscount(customerB, orderB, ksession, 25.0);
```

In the preceding code, we can see how the test is explicitly telling the KieScanner to
scan the monitored KieContainer and check for updates on the underlying KieJar.
Note that, in contrast to `KieScanner.start`, `KieScanner.scanNow` is synchronous.
After it returns, the KieContainer will be updated to the latest version of the KieJar
detected by the scanner.

When the KieContainer gets updated to the latest version of the KieJar being used,
any previously created KieBase—and thus, KieSession—will also be updated. The
test demonstrates this behavior by inserting `customerB` and `orderB` in the same
session that was previously used for `customerA` and `orderA`. The result, this time,
will be different though. The KieSession will now contain the version of the rule that
gives 25% discount instead of 10% and that is what the test is actually asserting.

Summary

In this chapter, we covered the main classes that we will be using to bootstrap, configure, and manage our Rule Engine instances. The first half of the chapter covered how different approaches can be used to define the rules that will be available to each rule engine instance. We also took a look at how Drools can load everything from the classpath and how the KIE-CI module can be used to delegate the KieModules resolution into Maven. We also covered how important the hierarchical structures of KieModules are and how they can be used to group different set of rules so that they can be loaded in the same container, to be used together. The second half of the chapter covered how to update our business knowledge (rules, processes, and so on) using the KieScanner to update the modified assets. This is a quite common requirement due the fact that we need to be able to update the business knowledge quickly so that we can adapt and deal with real-life business changes.

In the next chapter, we will cover more advanced rule structures in order to be able to provide more complex solutions to more complex business needs. We will continue developing our eShop scenario into a more complex application.

4
Improving Our Rule Syntax

In the previous chapters, we've seen how to configure our environment in order to run our first Drools-based rules, written in the DRL language. We've played with the basic structure of rules and how to configure an environment for them to run, however, we've barely seen the surface of the **Drools rule language** (**DRL**) capacity. Like an iceberg, there's much more to it than what you see at first.

In this chapter, we'll discuss the DRL language, its syntax and possibilities, and examples from our eShop case in detail. We will cover the following topics:

- Discussing the different ways in which the rules can read and modify the data, along with their understanding of the world

- Configuring the rules using attributes, global variables, and many other features required to use the rules to its full potential

- Discussing how the execution of Drools rules can be controlled by many different mechanisms

Adding external interactions with global variables

Interactions between our code and the business rules are mainly done by the rules that we define and the data that we feed in our running rule engine. In order to interact with data that is not in the Rule Engine context, Drools allows quite a variety of communication mechanisms to the other parts of our code and even to other systems. One of the most used tools for this are called global variables.

Global variables are defined in the DRL code in a similar way that we would define a variable in regular Java code. The syntax to follow is the global keyword, followed by the type of data, and then by the variable name:

```
global EShopConfigService configService;
```

Global variables can be a lot of things such as external services, lists of cached data, parameter values for our rule configurations, and anything that we might define in a Java code and we wish to have as a configurable component from our runtime.

In our DRL code examples (which we can find in the chapter-04-kjar project in the code bundle), we can find an example of how to define a service to configure our eShop example, called EShopConfigService. We will use it for demonstrative purposes only; however, if we replaced it with real interactions with external systems, such as a **Data Access Object** or a **Web Service** stub, the interconnectivity possibilities for business rules are endless. More about globals and the way they can be used in Drools can be found in the next chapter.

Modifying the data in the working memory

In the previous chapters, we've already seen the basic structure for a business rule: conditions and actions. When a specific set of conditions defined in a rule are met, we trigger specific actions defined in that rule. So far, these actions have only been basic modifications of Java beans or system logs. However, the Drools rule language allows us to do much more.

When a rule becomes too complex or it comprises of multiple complex conditions, defining them in one single rule might not be the best way to go. In imperative programming (such as Java and C++), we would break down a method or function, which is complex, into many smaller, simpler methods. In Drools, we should follow a similar structure defining multiple, simpler rules that work together.

Due to the nature of declarative programming that the DRL language follows, we cannot *call* one rule from another one, therefore, this splitting has to be done differently. To be able to split our rules into simpler ones, the actions of a rule requires to add or modify data so that other rules will re-evaluate themselves against the data and see if they should trigger their actions or not.

The insert keyword

In the `then` part of our rules, new information might be inferred by a rule. More data can be made available to the working memory for further evaluations against all the rules using the `insert` keyword, as follows:

```
rule "Classify Customer - Gold"
    when
        $c: Customer( category == Customer.Category.GOLD )
    then
        insert(new IsGoldCustomer($c));
end

rule "Classify Item - Low price"
    when
        $i: Item(cost < 10.00)
    then
        insert(new IsLowRangeItem($i));
end

rule "Suggest gift"
    when
        IsGoldCustomer($c: customer)
        IsLowRangeItem($i: item)
    then
        System.out.println("Suggest giving a gift of item "+$i.
getName()+" to customer +"$c.getName());
end
```

In the previous example (which we can find in the `chapter-04/chapter-04-kjar/src/main/resources/chapter04/workingMemoryModif/classify-item-rules.drl` file in the code bundle), we can see a simple example of inserting and breaking down a rule into multiple ones. We can just check whether a client has a gold category and we have a low-cost product, and make a suggestion for the gift product all in the same rule. However, we're breaking down the rule in three parts and inserting new model elements (`IsGoldCustomer` and `IsLowRangeItem`) to let another rule make the main decision for us based on these two elements.

By breaking down the rule in smaller sections, having some rules in charge of determining what a gold customer is and other rules in charge of what to do with them, we can define a gold customer in many different ways. Later on, all the rules have to rely on the `IsGoldCustomer` fact and any extra condition to determine what to do.

The modify and update keywords

We can also take the already existing data, which might have triggered the condition of a rule, and notify the engine should re-evaluate it. This can be done using the `modify` keyword, as follows:

```
rule "Categorize Customer - Gold"
  when
    $c: Customer( category == Customer.Category.NA )
    $o: Order(customer == $c, orderLines.size() > 10)
  then
    modify($c){setCategory(Customer.Category.GOLD);}
end
```

This rule is modifying the Customer object to set it to gold category. After this modification, the engine will be notified that this object needs to be re-evaluated for all rules in the engine. This means that if we insert a Customer with no category and an Order on its name with over 10 items, it will not only set the corresponding category, but also trigger any rule that depends on this condition.

Another word that you can use instead of modify in the consequence of the rule is the update keyword. The update keyword does not take a code block as the modify keyword. Instead, it just receives a variable so that the modifications have to be done beforehand to the variable. The following code example would replace the modify keyword in the previous code section, as follows:

```
$c.setCategory(Customer.Category.GOLD);
update($c);
```

However, the use of update is discouraged in favor of modify blocks as they allow to syntactically group the fact's execution that should trigger rule re-evaluations.

As you can see, the modification of the working memory is essential to split a rule into multiple ones as all the rules will be triggered depending—at first—on the data that the engine has available. By modifying the data, the engine can continue triggering rules until no more rules match the available data. If we don't modify/update the data, the engine will not be able to see the changes that you may do in a fact and this object won't trigger any more rules than the ones that had already matched before the change.

The delete/retract keywords

Also, we might let the engine know it should re-evaluate rules as one element of data, which was present in the working memory, is no longer there. This could cancel future rules, which weren't evaluated yet, or trigger other rules, as follows:

```
rule "Init current date"
    when
    then insert(new Date());
end

rule "Expire coupons"
    when
        $now: Date()
        $cp: Coupon( validUntil before $now )
    then
        delete($cp);
end

rule "Execute coupon"
    when
        $o: Order()
        $cp: Coupon(order == $o)
    then
        System.out.println("We have a coupon for this order!");
end
```

In the previous rule, we first make sure that we have a current-date object available for comparison with the `Init current date` rule (which, as its condition is empty, will evaluate to true). After that, if we have an expired coupon in the working memory, the second rule will remove it. Even if we add an order with this associated coupon, the second rule will not be triggered because even after matching, the execution of the first rule will cancel it.

The delete and retract keyword are both valid to remove the objects from the working memory—though the retract keyword is deprecated. Their syntax is equivalent and they are mutually exchangeable in the DRL code.

As you can see, changing the working memory in the rules means that, when we call fireAllRules on our KieSession, not only the rules that matched the data at that moment will fire, but also new rules might be triggered and fired or cancelled during the rule execution.

This is both a very powerful tool as it allows us to control the execution of rules without explicitly calling them and dangerous as, without any control, it could quite easily lead to infinite loops. We will see this problem and how to avoid it in the next section.

Rule attributes

Drools rules are data-driven. This means that the only way to activate a rule is by adding data to the engine that matches the conditions of that rule. However, there are multiple circumstances where we will want some rules with matching situations to be filtered out. One of this filtering mechanism is called rule attributes.

Rule attributes are extra features that we add to our rules to modify their behavior in a specific way. There are many rule attributes (of which, we'll explain the most used ones and some of their possible combinations) and each one modifies the way we filter rules execution in a different way, as follows:

```
rule "simple attribute example"
enabled false
    when Customer()
    then System.out.println("we have a customer");
end
```

If the `enabled` attribute is set to false, the rule will be evaluated, however, it won't be executed. It is perhaps the simplest example of a rule attribute shown here to see that the rule attributes are written before the `when` part of a rule. However, even if that's their syntactic position, they come second to the conditions of the rule. This means that if the conditions of the rule don't find a match for the working memory, attributes won't even play a part in the execution. However, when a rule set of conditions matches a group of objects in the working memory, rule attributes will come as an extra component to decide whether this match should fire now, later, or not at all.

The following subsections will show some of the most commonly used rule attributes and how they influence the execution of our rules is shown as follows

- Deciding the rule matches that will fire and the rule matches that won't fire
- Splitting our rules in groups, which might be valid or invalid in different situations
- Controlling other special situations in which rules might or might not be valid

Example – controlling which rules will fire

When we define rules, the rule that matches the data with its conditions first will be the first in the list of rules to fire. This means that the order of the execution of rules is not deterministic. However, sometimes, we might need some rules to take precedence over the rest. For example, in our example about classifying items of rules, we saw in the previous chapter that we might have a specific subcategory in a special set of values between the mid range and we might want the cases where this rule finds a match to take precedence over the common mid-range classifying, as follows:

```
rule "Classify Item - Mid Range"
    when $i: Item(
      cost > 200 && cost < 500,
      category == Category.NA )
    then
        $i.setCategory(Item.Category.MID_RANGE);
        update($i);
end
rule "Classify Item - Mid/High Range (special)"
    when
        $i: Item( cost > 300 && cost < 400,
        category == Category.NA )
    then
        $i.setCategory(
           Item.Category.SPECIAL_MIDHIGH_RANGE);
        update($i);
end
```

In this example, if we add an item with the cost being 350, the first rule might be evaluated before the second one. If we want the second rule to take precedence, we can set a higher priority to it using the salience rule attribute. The higher the salience, the higher the priority of the rule is, as shown in the following:

```
rule "Classify Item - Mid/High Range (special)"
salience 10
    when
        $i: Item( cost > 300 && cost < 400 )
    then
        $i.setCategory(
           Item.Category.SPECIAL_MIDHIGH_RANGE);
        update($i);
end
```

By default, all rules have an implicit salience attribute of 0 and you can assign positive or negative values to the salience attribute in order to execute them before or after the rest of the rules. Please take into account that rule attributes will only be evaluated after the rule conditions have matched with a group of data in the working memory, therefore, if the rule was not going to be triggered with the existing data, it won't be triggered regardless of how high or low the salience value is set.

 Note that in Drools 6, rules have an implicit relative salience by default that prioritizes the rules that appear earlier in the same DRL file. There's no relative implicit salience between rules in different DRL files though.

There is a catch in the rule that we rewrote here, we stopped checking for the category attribute being set to NA. We did this on purpose in order to explain a common problem when getting started with Drools rules. As you can see, the rule consequence is updating the item and setting a category for it. Once update is called, the object will be re-evaluated for all the rules, including this one. This means that the item will be re-evaluated for this rule and if it still matches its condition (the cost being between 300 and 400), it will trigger the rule multiple times.

This sort of infinite loops can be managed in different ways. In the earlier versions, we checked whether, in the condition of the rule, the category was still NA. Once we modified the category, updating the object would trigger a re-evaluation of the rule, however, as it no longer has an NA category, it wouldn't match the condition. This is the preferred way to do things when possible, however, if checking for a condition of this type becomes too complex, a rule attribute exists to let the engine know that a specific rule should not re-evaluate itself after it modifies the working memory. This attribute is the no-loop attribute, as shown in the following:

```
rule "Classify Item - Mid/High Range (special)"
no-loop
salience 10
    when
        $i: Item( cost > 300 && cost < 400 )
    then
        $i.setCategory(
            Item.Category.SPECIAL_MIDHIGH_RANGE);
        update($i);
end
```

You can test what happens when this attribute is removed in the RuleAttributesTest class of the chapter-04-tests project in the code bundle. The infinite loop is stopped through this attribute as it is this very rule that retriggers itself over and over again.

One other rule attribute that is very simple is the enabled rule attribute. It receives a boolean parameter to let the engine know whether the rule should be executed or not. If false, the rule is not evaluated, as follows:

```
rule "Classify Item - Mid/High Range (special)"
enabled true
no-loop
salience 10
    when
        $i: Item( cost > 300 && cost < 400 )
    then
        $i.setCategory(
            Item.Category.SPECIAL_MIDHIGH_RANGE);
        update($i);
end
```

This might seem like a weird rule attribute. Why would we want to use a rule attribute to disable a rule? You could just comment it out or delete the rule. In order to understand why it exists, we need to understand that rule attributes, even if they are written before the conditions of a rule, are always evaluated after the conditions of a rule. This means that they can use the data from the condition to decide the boolean value of the enabled attribute, integer value of the salience attribute, or any other attribute value that we might define in the future.

Given this information, we're going to rewrite our rule with two different uses of variable values for rule attributes, we're going to set the salience value based on the item's cost from the condition and we're going to set whether the rule is enabled or not based on a boolean method from a global variable, as follows:

```
global EShopConfigService configService;
...
rule "Classify Item - Mid/High Range (special)"
no-loop
salience ($i.getCost())
enabled(configService.isMidHighCategoryEnabled())
    when
        $i: Item( cost > 300 && cost < 400 )
    then
        $i.setCategory(
            Item.Category.SPECIAL_MIDHIGH_RANGE);
        update($i);
end
```

As you can see in the previous example, we're defining the salience of the rule based on a variable numeric value (specifically, the cost of the item detected in the condition), and we're setting the enabled attribute based on the return value of a boolean method in the global variable. As long as the condition is written in parentheses and Java code, the engine is capable of understanding them.

Example – splitting rule groups with agenda group

Now that we've understood the structure of rule attributes and played a bit with the simplest three attributes that are available, it is time to continue stepping up our rule game by going into even more complex rule attributes. The next set that we're going to see are the ones used to define groupings of rules.

Rules should not be microcontrolled in such a way that we say exactly which rule will fire next, however, this doesn't mean that we should let the engine run every single rule we define all at the same time. Even if we create a moderate-size rule-based project, we are going to see our rules fall in different categories. In our eShop example, some rules are going to be for data input validation, some are going to validate promotions that apply to the existing purchases, some will apply different taxes to our purchase invoice, and so on and so forth. Each rule makes sense to be applied at a different time. Drools provides grouping mechanisms for our rules to be able to activate a group of rules each time. These groups are also defined through rule attributes.

It might seem against the declarative approach, however, it is still controlled by the data fed to our rule engine. The fundamental difference between trying to control one rule against a group of rules is that the group is still managed by the rule engine. The declarative approach still applies, but only for a subset of all the rules that we defined.

The most used type of grouping for rules is defined with the agenda-group rule attribute. This rule attribute defines a key, which can be activated by a code in the KieSession and changed as required as many times as it makes sense in our case, as shown in the following:

```
rule "Promotion: more than 10 pencils get 10% discount"
    agenda-group "promotions"
    when
        OrderLine(item.name == "pencil", quantity > 10)
    then
        insert(new Discount(0.10));
end
```

The previous rule defines a rule under the `"promotions"` grouping. This particular group should have all the rules that involve applying promotions to a shopping cart and it will still be the rule engine's job to determine the rule that should be fired next, if any.

The agenda group will be manually activated through an API call to the KieSession object (before calling fireAllRules), as follows:

```
KieSession ksession = …;
    ksession.getAgenda().getAgendaGroup("promotions").
        setFocus();
    ksession.fireAllRules();
```

It's worth mentioning here that, by default, all the rules have an implicit MAIN agenda group. The `KieSession` has the group active by default and all rules that don't define an agenda-group attribute fall into this group.

Also, every rule, whether it is in the active agenda group or not, will be evaluated when rule evaluations get triggered. The active agenda group will determine the group of rule matches that should be executed at rule-execution time.

It's also worth mentioning that, when a rule is fired, it can also define the agenda group that is going to be activated through the implicit global variable called kcontext, as follows:

```
rule "Done with promotions. Onward with printing invoice"
    salience -100 //last rule of group to run
    agenda-group "promotions"
    when
        OrderLine()
    then
        kcontext.getKnowledgeRuntime().getAgenda().
                getAgendaGroup("MAIN").setFocus();
end
```

Take a good look at the previous rule. There are many tricks placed together in there. First of all, you have a negative value in the salience attribute. This means that this rule will take a very low priority so that even if it is activated, as long as there is another rule match, it will take precedence to this one. This makes this rule the last rule of the group likely to run. The condition asks for an OrderLine object, therefore, as long as we have an order line and the rules have done everything they need with it, we'll execute this rule's action.

As the consequence of this rule, the kcontext default variable is used to access the KieSession, using the getKnowledgeRuntime method. Through this, it can activate the next agenda group just like it did on the plain Java code. You can see that the agenda group activated is the MAIN agenda group, which is the default agenda group so that the next set of rules to be matched and possibly fired is the group that didn't define an agenda group.

Other types of rule groups

Agenda groups are very useful to not only define a specific sequence in our rules, but also let the rules determine the next group of rules that is to be activated. Very complex situations where rules have to control, the next set of actions to follow can be represented using these types of rules. However, there are times when rules are exposed through user-friendly editors to business users and they usually want a more graphical way of defining rule group sequences.

There is a tool for **Business Process Management (BPM)** called jBPM, which uses Drools as its base API and rule engine. It allows the end users to define diagrams to show the sequence of steps in a process. Some of these steps can be rule executions and to determine the rules that should fire at that particular point, they use a common attribute between the rule step in the process and the rules that are going to be invoked: the ruleflow-group rule attribute.

Ruleflow groups are used for exclusive interaction with business processes and there isn't an exposed API to invoke the ruleflow group that should be activated. Instead, this is done directly by the runtime of jBPM.

Groupings are used to split rules in groups; however, sometimes, we need these groups to have an even more specific behavior. For example, we might define that a specific group of rules should be mutually exclusive. To define such behavior, Drools defines a rule attribute called activation-group, which defines that only one rule should fire in that group. If the data that we feed the KieSession matches five rules in the same activation group, the first one to fire will cancel the other four rules.

 Note that rule attributes can only be defined once per rule, however, you can have multiple rule attributes defined in a single rule. The combinations of rule attributes is a very powerful tool once we understand the purpose of all the attribute types.

Rule dates management

There are times when we want our rules to be considered only in specific moments in time. Some rules, specially company policies, such as special discounts for retail, tax calculations, and holiday specials, make sense only on specific dates or days of the week. There are rule attributes with this very purpose and they allow you to control whether or not a rule is enabled at a specific point in time.

Two of these attributes, date-effective and date-expires, determine the start and end date for a specific rule to be enabled. If we assume the government establishes a specific tax to be added to every purchase from 2015 to 2020, this would be a good way to define this rule, as follows:

```
rule "Add special tax of 3%"
    date-effective "01-Jan-2015"
    date-expires "31-Dec-2020"
    when $i: Item()
    then $i.setSalePrice($i.getSalePrice() * 1.03);
end
```

The dd-mmm-yyyy date format is supported by default. You can customize this by providing an alternative date format mask as a drools.dateformat system property.

There is another type of common case, where we might need to switch the rule from enabled to disabled periodically or based on a specific date configuration. In our eShop example, this could be related to promotions such as 2 x 1 on the purchase of beers on Saturdays. This rule should not apply to any other day, therefore, we use a special attribute called calendars to specify the days when a rule is enabled.

Also, we might need to retrigger a specific rule on a specific schedule as long as the condition of the rule continues to match the specific data. For this kind of situation, there is a timer rule attribute that allows you to set either cron or interval-based timers to your rules.

Here's an example of these two types of attributes working together on some rules:

```
rule "Weekday notifications of pending orders"
    calendars "weekdays"
    timer (int:0 1h)
    when Order($id: orderId)
    then emailService.sendEmail("Pending order: "+$id);
end
rule "Weekend notifications of pending orders"
    calendars "weekends"
    timer (cron:0 0 0/8 * * ?)
```

```
    when Order($id: orderId)
    then emailService.sendEmail("Pending order: "+$id);
end
```

As you can see, these two rules do pretty much the same. If there is an order on the working memory, they send an e-mail through a helper class set as a global variable called `emailService`. The main difference between the two rules is provided by the rule attributes. The first rule will only be active on the days the `weekdays` calendar tells it to be, while the second rule will only be active on the `weekends` calendar. Also, each rule will fire at different rates as long as the condition is still fulfilled, the first rule will fire at one hour intervals (with zero time of delay for the first time) and the second rule will fire exactly at 00:00, 08:00, and 16:00 hours. They both require that the rule execution is invoked so that fireAllRules should be called continuously in order to get the firing rate going.

The calendars have to be configured through the `KIESession` using the `getCalendars` method, as follows:

```
ksession.getCalendars().set("weekday", new Calendar() {
    //for simplicity, any date/time matches this calendar
    public void isTimeIncluded(long timestamp) {
        return true;
    }
});
```

You can find an example of its configuration in the chapter's code bundle, under the name `TimersAndCalendarsTest`. Any object that matches the `org.kie.api.time.Calendar` interface can define any form of calendar with any kind of business logic behind it.

Controlling loops in rules

So far, we've seen some ways in which we can manage our rules to trigger new rule invocations. This will help us enormously in order to be able to split our rules into simple components that interact in the background through the data in the working memory. Powerful as it is, however, it can bring us a few extra complications along the line of the rules getting fired more times than we desire. Fortunately, Drools provides us with a set of elements to control rule execution from the very syntax where we define them.

The first and the most simple case where we can get into an infinite rule execution loop happens when a rule modifies the working memory in a way that it retriggers itself. Let's see an example of this problem in the following:

```
rule "Apply 10% discount on notepads"
    when $i: Item(name == "notepad", $sp: salePrice)
    then modify($i) { setSalePrice($sp * 0.9); }
end
```

In this rule, our intention is to reduce the sale price of the notepads in our inventory. We just don't change the value of our items, however, we also want to notify the engine that it changed. This is done using the modify keyword, as discussed earlier in this chapter, and we do it as we might have other rules that need to re-evaluate the item now that the price is different.

The problem is that if the modified object still matches the condition of this rule (and it does as its name is still notepad), it will also re-evaluate itself. This will lead to an infinite amount of rule executions for the same element.

The method to avoid this unwanted loop is a very simple attribute called, by no surprise, no-loop. The no-loop rule attribute prevents a rule from reactivating itself, irrespective of the changes the rule makes to the working memory. Its syntax is very simple, as the following example depicts:

```
rule "Apply 10% discount on notepads BUT ONLY ONCE"
    no-loop true
    when $i: Item(name == "notepad", $sp: salePrice)
    then modify($i) { setSalePrice($sp * 0.9); }
end
```

The `true` condition is optional, and writing `no-loop` is enough. The boolean parameter is there because, as we previously mentioned, it can be a variable from the context that determines whether or not this rule is to be set as no loop or not.

It's worth mentioning that `no-loop` only prevents this rule from refiring for the same data if it was the last rule to fire. If another rule changes the working memory in a way that matches this rule again, the `no-loop` condition won't prevent it from executing a second time. Sometimes, this is a desired behavior, however, if this isn't the case, there are other types of loop-prevention strategies that we need to discuss.

Lock-on-active

Let's see an example of how this works:

```
rule "Give extra 2% discount for orders larger than 15 items"
    no-loop true
    when $o: Order(totalItems > 15)
    then modify ($o) { increaseDiscount(0.02); }
end
rule "Give extra 2% discount for orders larger than $100"
    no-loop true
    when $o: Order(total > 100.00)
    then modify ($o) { increaseDiscount(0.02); }
end
```

These rules have the no-loop attribute so that even if they modify the order object, they won't retrigger themselves. However, nothing is stopping them from activating each other. Therefore, the first rule will trigger the second one, which will trigger the first one again, and so on and so forth. This type of infinite loop requires something a bit stronger than the no-loop attribute.

One quick way of making sure that a rule doesn't get retriggered for the same objects is to add an attribute called lock-on-active to the troublesome rules. Whenever a ruleflow-group becomes active or an agenda-group receives the focus, any rule within this group that has lock-on-active set to true will not be activated any more for the same objects. Irrespective of the origin of the update, the activation of a matching rule is discarded. The following is an example of one of the rules rewritten to use lock-on-active:

```
rule "Give extra 2% discount for orders larger than $100"
    lock-on-active true
    when $o: Order(total > 100.00)
    then modify ($o) { increaseDiscount(0.02); }
end
```

In this second case, the rules will trigger only once for the same objects. You can see a running example of these rules in the `LoopingExamplesTest` class of the chapter's code bundle.

This is a stronger version of no-loop as the change can now be caused not only by the rule itself. It's ideal for calculation rules, where you have a number of rules that modify a fact and you don't want any rule re-matching and firing again. Only when the ruleflow-group is no longer active or the agenda group loses the focus; these rules, with lock-on-active set to true, become eligible again for matching on the same objects to be possible again.

Model properties execution control

The no-loop and lock-on-active attributes give us a great amount of power when it comes to controlling undesired execution loops. The problem with these attributes, however, arises from the fact that the whole objects used in the condition will not retrigger the rule, no matter how much they are modified by the same or other rules. This might not be the desired behavior for a lot of cases where the model is complex or hard to change and we might still need to re-evaluate some of the changes if they occur to specific properties.

This sort of fine-grained control is possible, in its most simple form, by adding flag attributes to the objects that store the conditions that we want to check. Some rules will alter these flags and some other rules will check against them to see whether they should or should not evaluate again. Here's an example:

```
rule "Add 2% discount for orders larger than $100"
  when $o:
    Order(total > 100.00, has100DollarsDiscount == false)
  then
    modify($o){
      increaseDiscount(0.02);
      setHas100DollarsDiscount(true);
    }
end

rule "Add 2% discount for orders larger than 15 items"
  when $o:
    Order(total > 100.00, has15ItemsDiscount == false)
  then
    modify($o){
      increaseDiscount(0.02);
      setHas15ItemsDiscount(true);
    }
end
```

In the previous rule, there was no need to add the rule attributes to the rules as the use of two flag attributes (has15ItemsDiscount and has100DollarsDiscount) had already flagged the object to not be evaluated again. If any other modification was done to the object in the working memory, it would retrigger the rule.

This solution has two main problems. One problem is that we will eventually saturate the model with extra properties with no direct relation to the actual content of the model, however, they are more related to the execution of rules. The second problem arises when we have so many rules that we need to check on too many flags in order to make the rule easy to understand. Remember our main goals when writing rules: keep them independent and as simple (atomic) as possible. If we have too many flags that relate to specific rules, the independence starts to break.

Let's not worry. There are more tricks within Drools that will help us with these situations.

Declared types

Drools rules conditions are build, based on Java types. This means that we need to have a defined set of Java classes to define our model and use it from our rules. All our previous examples have been based on the existence of Java classes to represent orders, discounts, clients, and so on.

This is not the only way that Drools has to define a data model. Within the DRL files, where we define our rules, we can also define new types that will be created, compiled, and made available in the runtime at the same moment as the rules and it can be changed just as easily. These are called **declared types** and they play a very useful part in defining data models that only make sense for specific groups of rules (such as inference objects that might not necessarily be a part of the rules output result). They are defined before the rules in the DRL structure, with the following syntax:

```
declare SpecialOrder extends Order
      whatsSoSpecialAboutIt: String
      order: Order
      applicableDiscount: Discount
   end
```

The previous example contains a few things all together that are worth mentioning, as follows:

- They are defined between the **declare** and **end** keywords
- They can define object attributes (such as String) and primitive attributes (such as long)
- They can extend other types, including Java classes and other declared types
- They can even declare attributes that are a part of your own model (such as the `applicableDiscount` attribute in the previous example, of type Discount) and they can also have other declared types as attributes

These types can be used from the conditions and consequences of the rules in the same way as any other Java class. You can access the getters/setters of all the attributes that will be automatically generated by the rule engine at the compilation time. The only difference arises from trying to access these objects from outside the rules in the plain Java code. It is possible to do so, however, it requires using a reflection API accessible through the KieBase, as follows:

```
KieSession ksession = ...; //previously initialized
FactType type = ksession.getKieBase().getFactType(
        "chapter04.declaredTypes", "SpecialOrder");
Object instance = type.newInstance();
type.set(instance, "relevance", 2L);
Object attr = type.get(instance, "relevance");
```

Due to this complex syntax for use in Java code, it is best to use declared types only if they're going to be used exclusively from the rules code. The use of declared types can be seen in the DeclaredTypesTest class in the `chapter-04/chapter-04-tests project` of the code bundle.

Property-reactive beans

Whenever we use the modify or update keywords in the consequence of a rule, we're notify the engine that rules that filter similar object types should re-evaluate the object again. This re-evaluation, by default, occurs on the whole object; As long as one property of the object changes, the rules will consider it as a new object to match.

This could lead to some issues when we don't wish to have a rule re-evaluated for some changes. The loop-control mechanisms, such as no-loop and lock-on-active, could be helpful in these situations. However, if we want the rule to control changes on some properties only, we need to write very complex conditions. Also, if the model changes in the future for a large rule base, you may have to modify a lot of rules to avoid undesired rule re-executions.

Fortunately, Drools provides a feature that allows the engine to work around this problem. It allows the rule writers to define the attributes of a bean that should be monitored if they're updated in the working memory. This feature is defined in the data model (Java classes or declared types) that are used in the rules and it is called property-reactive beans.

To use this feature, we first need to mark the types that we will use in the rules with the Property Reactive annotation. This annotation allows the engine know that whenever an object of this type is added to the working memory, special filtering on its changes needs to apply. This annotation can be added to a Java class (at class level) or declared type (right after the first line, defining the type name), as follows:

```
declare PropertyReactiveOrder
    @propertyReactive
    discount: Discount
    totalItems: Integer
    total: Double
end
```

After we have our types "marked" as property-reactive beans, we can make our rules define the properties of these beans that should be monitored for changes, and the properties that should not. To do so, we use the @Watch annotation after each specific condition of the rule that should have this type of filtering applied, as shown in the following:

```
rule "Larger than 20 items orders are special orders"
    when
        $o: PropertyReactiveOrder(
            totalItems > 20
        ) @Watch (!discount)
    then
        modify ($o) {
            setDiscount(new Discount(0.05));
        }
end
```

In the previous rule, the @Watch annotation makes the rule behave similar to adding a no-loop or a lock-on-active rule attribute. It will avoid this and the other rules to be re-fired for the same element. However, if any rule modifies the object in a way other than changing its discount, it will not avoid the retriggering of this rule. This is the main power of the property-reactive beans; you can determine which attribute changes could retrigger the rule and which could not.

The @Watch annotation can be used in the rule to monitor different situations regarding the attributes of a property-reactive bean. If not present, the watched fields can be inferred by default, depending on the condition structure. Here, we can see a few examples:

- **@Watch(discount, total)**: This only monitors changes in the discount and total attributes

- **@Watch(!discount)**: This means that we should disregard changes to the `discount` attribute of the bean

- **@Watch(!*, total)**: This means that we should disregard all the attributes of the bean, except for the `total` attribute

- **@Watch(!*, total, totalItems)**: This means that we should only pay attention to changes of the `total` and `totalItems` attributes, other changes are disregarded

Property reactive beans changes should be notified to the rule engine only using the `modify` keyword. The update keyword won't be able to tell the difference between the attributes of the bean that are being changed. This is another reason to discourage the use of the update keyword.

We've seen, so far, how malleable and extensible the data model that we use in our rules is. Based on its modifications and the conditions that our rules define, we can create very complex environments in very simple ways. The next thing we need to learn is how to define the conditions in our rules in a simple yet powerful way. To do so, let's take a look at some of the most used operations that we can use to compare our data in our rule definitions.

Special Drools operations

We've seen, so far, the simplest cases to check attribute values against the boolean expressions in our rules. We've also discussed all the different ways in which rules can manage data updates, which might retrigger checking our rules. However, the power of rules doesn't stop there as there are many different ways in which the rule conditions can be written, which will allow us to create rules that are both powerful and simple to understand.

Drools already provides a set of operations that you can use to compare different objects against each other. These objects might be living directly on the working memory, global variables, literal values, or any combination of these types. We're going to enumerate the most used ones in the following sections, splitting them into the following:

- Boolean and numeric operations

- Collection-based operations

- Regex operations

- Custom operations

Boolean and numeric operations

We've seen some examples of these operations in our previous rules as they are the simplest to understand for anyone with programming experience. Boolean operations are the ones that use AND, OR, XOR, and so on. Numeric operations are the ones that compare two numeric values. Here's an example of some of these operations against an attribute of the Item type:

```
Item(
        salePrice > 100.00 && salePrice <= 500.00
        && salePrice != 101.00
    )
```

In the previous example of a condition, we checked whether the salePrice attribute of our Item object has a value greater than 100, lesser or equal to 500, and different from 101, in that order.

Some of these operations are intrinsic to Drools, such as the use of the AND operation. Using the && method is not necessary in the conditions of the previous example as any comparison that is separated by a comma is considered a new condition that must be checked as well. However, boolean conditions are required to express the situations where either one of the two conditions needs to be true (that is, an OR boolean expression).

Using boolean expressions is possible, but if required, they will usually mark places where the design of our rules needs revision. This is because the AND expressions are intrinsic to the language and rules that use OR expressions should be considered as more than one condition in the same rule (and therefore, non-atomic). Whenever an OR expression is required to express a rule, consider splitting the rule into two different rules, as shown in the following example:

```
rule "Add 5% discount for minors or seniors"
    when $o: Order(customer.age < 18 || customer.age > 60)
    then $o.increaseDiscount(0.05);
end
```

This could be broken into this two rules:

```
rule "Add 5% discount for minors"
    when $o: Order(customer.age < 18)
    then $o.increaseDiscount(0.05);
end
rule "Add 5% discount for seniors"
    when $o: Order(customer.age > 60)
    then $o.increaseDiscount(0.05);
end
```

It might seem that boolean expressions are something to avoid as much as possible, however, we will see some other uses that they have when combining other operations later in this chapter. For the moment, let's just remember that they exist and try to use them only if really needed.

Regex operations – matches

Matches is an operator that we can use against string-based objects and attributes. It allows us to check whether they follow a specific regular expression. Most common uses of them are to check whether a string represents a valid number, e-mail, or any special character order that we need to validate. Regular expressions are a very complex topic to cover here and you can learn more about them online. We will see a small example of how matches are used in a rule condition by creating a rule to check whether customers in our KieSession have a valid e-mail address, as follows:

```
rule "validate customer emails"
    when $c: Customer(email not matches
        "[A-Za-z0-9-.]+@[A-Za-z0-9-.]+$")
    then $c.setEmail(null); //invalidate email
end
```

The previous rule has a simplified regular expression to validate e-mails. Any Java regular expression could be used with the **matches** and **not matches** operators and they can both work with variables and literal values. This means that the regular expression could be a global variable defined somewhere else.

Collection operations – contains and memberOf

The collection operations are the ones prepared to work with one or more collections, whether they are variables, attributes, or literal values. They are used to determine whether a collection has an element in them. An example of using these operations would be something similar to the following:

```
rule "print orders with pencils in them"
    when
        $i: Item(name == "pencil")
        $ol: OrderLine(item == $i)
        $o: Order($ol memberOf orderLines,
            orderLines contains $ol)
    then
        System.out.println("order with pencils: " + $o);
end
```

In the previous rule, we're using both operations one after the other. They are both checking for the same condition, whether the found order line is in the orderLines collection of the order object.

Operations in Drools have an open syntax. This means that you can write your own operation if you need to. This is a useful tool when a comparison of two objects has too many complexities to be easily written as a simple boolean operation. Some common uses for custom operations are comparing GPS location data to determine facts near to each other in space or comparing time data to determine time relationships between events. We will see more about custom operations in the next chapter.

Working memory breakdown: the from clause

We've seen how rule conditions are written. So far, all these conditions have filtered data that was inserted in our KieSession (that is, inserted in the working memory). However, in some situations, we might need to check special conditions on collections that are different from the working memory, such as attributes of some objects, global variables, or subsets of the working memory itself that we can create dynamically. To be able to do so, Drools provides the from clause, which we can be used to define a specific search space outside of the working memory.

The following rule is a simple example of how we can use the from clause to look for specific attributes:

```
rule "For every notebook order apply points coupon"
    when
        $o: Order($c: customer, $lines: orderLines)
        OrderLine($item: item) from $lines
        Item(name == "notebook") from $item
    then
        insert(new Coupon($c, $o, CouponType.POINTS));
    end
```

The previous rule looks for orders in our working memory first. It will store both the order lines collection as a $lines variable and the customer in a $c variable (this last variable is stored to use it from the consequence of the rule). After finding an order, it looks in the $lines variable (which holds all the order lines) and stores the item in another variable. After that, the third line of the rule condition directly searches a single object (the item), and checks whether the item is a notebook.

As you can see, if we only have the Order object in our working memory (and not all of its subcomponents), we can still go deep into its structure in a way that the following conditions are satisfied:

- It is easy to read and break down into multiple conditions
- It can take into account the situations where we might have collections of objects to dig into (such as the `orderLines` attribute in the second part of our rule condition)
- It can make a rule easier to read

The `from` clause is a very versatile tool. It can be used to get data from multiple sources and not only from attributes. You can invoke methods from global variables that return specific values or lists and use it from the `from` clause. You can basically use it with anything that returns a value.

Drools 6.3, and higher, comes with a feature called OOPath expressions, which allows to define the previous rule in a more compact way, as follows:

```
rule "For every notebook order apply points coupon"
    when
        $o: Order($c: customer,
            /orderLines/item{name == "notebook"}
        )
    then
        insert(new Coupon($c, $o, CouponType.POINTS));
    end
```

One common use of global variables is to retrieve data that doesn't need to be in the working memory all the time. Thanks to the `from` clause, we can directly filter this data from our rules as soon as we execute a global variable method, as follows:

```
global QueryService qServ

rule "get stored coupons for new order"
    when
        Order(totalItems > 10, $c:customer)
        Coupon(customer == $c) from qServ.queryCoupons()
    then
        System.out.println("We have a stored coupon");
    end
```

This can be useful to compare the data between the working memory and outside storages, such as databases and web services. We need to be careful when using these external queries by realizing when the engine will invoke the global variable method, though. In the previous example, every time we add a new Order object to the working memory, the first line will be evaluated once again. If the first line fills the required conditions, it will call the second line, invoking the global variable method. If we add 50 orders that fill the first condition, the global variable method will be called 50 times by this rule.

Another thing to be careful about when using from clauses like these is how deep you nest them; if you have to execute five global variable methods one after the other in the same rule and they are all process-intensive, you will have a very slow rule. If you need to do something of this type, it is best to work with caches for your slow methods whenever possible.

Note that if the return value of a global variable method changes, it will not retrigger a rule that invokes it, even if it is the first condition of the rule. This is because global variables are outside the working memory, and therefore, they are not re-evaluated when they change. If you need to re-evaluate things used in the `from` clause, the best way to go is to use a subset of the working memory, which you can create using collect or accumulate keywords along with the `from` clause. These keywords and their uses are described in the following two sections.

Collect from objects

So far, we've seen ways to write conditions in our rules that will get triggered for every single match against the working memory. Let's analyze a simple rule to fully understand this mechanism:

```
rule "Simple order condition"
    when $o: Order()
    then System.out.println("order found: " + $o);
end
```

The previous rule is defined in such a way that if we insert 50 orders in the KieSession, we will trigger this rule 50 times when we fire the rules. This is useful when we want to do something on each element that matches a condition. However, if we want to act against all the elements that match a condition at once, we need an extra syntax to help us. This is where the `collect` keyword comes into play.

The "collect" keyword is used to find all the elements that match a specific condition and group them into a collection. Later on, this collection can be assigned to a variable or submitted to further conditions, as follows:

```
rule "Grouping orders"
    when $list: List() from collect(Order())
    then
        System.out.println("we've found " +
            $list.size() + " orders");
    end
```

In the previous case, if we insert 50 orders to KieSession and then fire the rules, the rule will fire only once, producing a list of 50 orders. However, if we fire all the rules without inserting any orders first, this rule would still fire returning an empty list in the $list variable. To avoid so, we should add conditions in the List object by writing it as follows:

```
$list: List(size > 0) from collect(Order())
```

The `collect` keyword can be combined with the `from` clause to create new collections from different sources. It is very useful whenever we can find objects through the rule conditions and add them directly to a collection.

Accumulate keyword

In the previous section, we saw that the `collect` keyword allows us to gather information directly from a source into a collection. This is a very useful component when we already have the elements as we need them to be somewhere accessible in the working memory. However, sometimes we need to apply transformations to the data that matches a condition. For these cases, the `accumulate` keyword is used to transform every match of a condition to a specific type of data.

You can think of the `accumulate` keyword as a `collect` on steroids. You not only get to group every item that matches a condition, but also extrapolate the data from these elements in a specific programmatic way. Some common examples where the accumulate keyword is used are counting elements that match a specific condition, get average values of an attribute of certain type of objects, and to find the average, minimum, or maximum values of a specific attribute in a condition.

Perhaps an example could help clarify the use of accumulate. In the previous rules, we've used a method of the Order object, called `getTotalItems`, to return the count of items that we were purchasing in this order. So far, this has been the only way we would have to get this information from the Order object. However, using accumulate, we can obtain this information while filtering specific items using the full power of rules. Let's see this in an example:

```
rule "10+ items with sale price over 20 get discount"
     when
         $o: Order($lines: orderLines)
         Number(intValue >= 10) from accumulate(
             OrderLine(
                 item.salePrice > 20.00,
                 $q: quantity
             ) from $lines,
             init(int count = 0;),
             action(count += $q),
             reverse(count -= $q),
             result(count)
         )
     then
         $o.increaseDiscount(0.05);
 end
```

We've got a lot to explain from the previous rule. It's main objective is to get the total number of items in the order that follows a specific condition: having a sale price value higher than 20. The getTotalItems method would be able to give us a count of all the items, however, it wouldn't be able to filter through them. The accumulate here, however, would allow us to apply a condition to the elements and apply a predicate to transform the elements that match the accumulate condition in the information that we need. Let's analyze the parts of the accumulate to fully understand its structure, as follows:

- **$o: Order($lines: orderLines)**: This part is simple. We're checking every Order object that we have in our working memory and storing the order lines attribute in a variable for later use.

- **Number(intValue >= 10)**: Our rule is trying to check whether we have at least, 10 items with price higher than 20. This first part of the accumulate line is checking the return value from the accumulate. It can be anything that you want, but for this first example, it is going to be a number. If that number is 10 or more, we consider the return value of the accumulate to be fulfilling our rule. This means that the accumulate should count all the items that match the specific condition.

- **Condition inside accumulate**: In the accumulate, we have a first part that matches a specific condition. In this case, it goes all over the OrderLine objects of the order (which were stored in the `$lines` variable), checks whether the sale price is over 20 and stores the quantity attribute value in a $q variable to be used later. Notice how you have a second `from` clause in the accumulate as you can nest them when needed.

The following four parts of the accumulate (init, action, reverse, and result) contain information about what to do whenever we find an object that matches the condition:

- **init**: This is done at the beginning of the accumulate. It initializes the variables to be used every time we find a match in the accumulate condition. In our case, we're initializing a count variable.

- **action**: Whenever we find an element in the working memory that matches the accumulate condition, the rule engine will trigger the action section of code in the accumulate. In our example, we're increasing the count of the elements by the value of the $q variable, which holds the quantity of the OrderLine object.

- **reverse**: This is an optional code block. As every object inserted, modified, or deleted from the working memory might trigger the condition (and activate the action code block), it can also make an element that had already matched the accumulate condition to stop doing so. In order to increase the performance, the reverse code block can be provided to avoid having to recalculate all the accumulate again if it is too processor-intensive. In our example, whenever OrderLine stops matching the condition, the reverse code will just decrease the count variable by the amount of the $q variable that is previously stored.

- **result**: This code block holds the return variable name or formula for the finished accumulate section. Once every object that matches a condition has been processed and all the `action` code blocks have been called accordingly, the `result` code block will return the specific data that we collected, which will dictate the type that we'll write on the right-hand side of the `from` `accumulate` expression. In our example, we return the count value (an integer value), which is matched against the first part of the accumulate function: `Number(intValue > 10)`.

Although this is the full syntax for using `accumulate`, it doesn't necessarily have to be this complex every single time. Drools provides a set of predefined accumulate functions that you can directly use in your rules. Here's the previous rule that is rewritten to show how to use one of these built-in functions:

```
rule "10+ items with sale price over 20 get discount"
    when
        $o: Order($lines: orderLines)
        Number(intValue >= 10) from accumulate(
            OrderLine(
                item.salePrice > 20.00,
                $q: quantity
            ) from $lines,
            sum($q)
        )
    then
        $o.increaseDiscount(0.05);
end
```

The already provided accumulate functions are as follows:

- **count**: This keeps a count of a variable that matches a condition
- **sum**: This sums up a variable, as shown in the previous example
- **avg**: This gets the average value of a variable for all the matches in the accumulate
- **min**: From all the variable values obtained in the accumulate condition, this returns the minimal one
- **max**: From all the variable values obtained in the accumulate condition, this returns the maximum one
- **collectList**: This stores all the values of a specified variable in the condition in an ordered list and returns them at the end of the accumulate
- **collectSet**: This stores all the values of a specified variable in the condition in a unique elements' set and returns them at the end of the accumulate

Using a predefined function is preferred as it makes the rule more readable and is less prone to errors. You can even use many of them at once, one after the other, separated by a comma, as shown in the following example:

```
rule "multi-function accumulate example"
    when accumulate(Order($total: total),
      $maximum: max($total),
      $minimum: min($total),
      $average: avg($total)
    )
    then //...
  end
```

The previous rule stores the maximum, minimum, and average of the totals of all the orders in the working memory. As you can see, the `from` clause is not mandatory for the `accumulate` keyword. It is even discouraged with multifunction accumulates as it might return completely different types of objects (such as `Lists` and `Numbers`).

If you want to do an accumulate in a way that is not provided by these functions, Drools provides an API to create our own accumulate functions, similar to that used to create our own custom operators. We will see more about the API in the next chapter.

Advanced conditional elements

The previous sections have been about how to extract data, however, we've been very straightforward with the order of our conditions. Always every condition has been separated by a comma and the execution of the rule was basically each condition followed by an implicit AND. It is time to see how to apply more complex boolean operations to our rules.

We've seen how to use boolean operations in a single object, checking whether its internal attributes matched the specific combinations of conditions. We'll see now how to do the same with different objects and how it would get translated to the rule language.

NOT keyword

Whenever we've written a condition so far, it's been translated to a search for any object (or group of objects) that matches the condition in the working memory. If we precede the condition of an object (or group) with the not keyword, we can check whether no incidence of the condition is found in the working memory and trigger a rule for these cases. Let's see the following example of this keyword:

```
rule "warn about empty working memory"
    when
            not(Order() or Item())
        then
            System.out.println("we don't have elements");
    end
```

The previous rule uses the not keyword to make sure that at the moment of firing the rules, we have at least an Order or Item object. If we don't, it will print a warning.

Notice how we use the **OR** keyword to share a condition in not. This is because the **NOT** keyword will contain a boolean expression. In this case, since we want to search for both Orders or Items to exist in the working memory, we can group them together in a single expression inside **NOT**. Another way of writing this rule would be as follows:

```
rule "warn about empty working memory"
    when
            not(Order())
            not(Item())
        then
            System.out.println("we don't have elements");
    end
```

It would act in the same way.

EXISTS and FORALL keywords

In a similar fashion to the not keyword, we have a few other keywords that we can use to check the existence of elements in the working memory. The exists keyword is used for the purpose of checking whether any object is present in the working memory that fulfills the condition in it.

Let's take a look at the following two rules, one with exists and one without it:

``
rule "with exists"
    when
        exists(Order())
    then
        System.out.prinltn(
            "We have orders");
end
``
	``
	rule "without exists"
	    when
	        $o: Order()
	    then
	        System.out.println($o);
	end
	``

The main difference between them is how many times these rules will fire for one or many Order objects. For the case on the right-hand side, if you have multiple orders, the rule will fire once for every order. On the left-hand side, whether you have one element, five, or five million Orders, you will fire the rule once.

The other difference that you can see in the declaration is that the rule on the right-hand side has a variable declaration. This can be done only in the case of the right-hand side components as it will execute for every Order in the working memory and you can have a reference to each one of them. In the case of the left-hand side component, it is only checking for a boolean expression (whether or not the Order objects exist in the working memory), so it is not storing any reference we could use in the consequence of the rule.

A similar pattern is used in the forall keyword. When using forall, we check two conditions against the working memory. Any object that matches the first condition must match the second condition to make forall true.

Let's see the following example of forall and exists working together:

```
rule "make sure all orders have at least one line"
    when
        exists(Order())
        forall(
            Order()
            Order(orderLines.size() > 0)
        )
    then
        System.out.println("all orders have lines");
end
```

In the previous rule, you can see the first condition uses exists to check whether there's any Order object in the working memory. If there is one order or a thousand, this will evaluate once.

The second part of the rule is using two conditions. For every item that fills the first condition (being an Order object), it will also need to fill the second one (having at least one order line). This means that every order in the working memory must have at least one order line for this rule to fire.

There's a reason for using both `exists` and `forall` in the same rule, beyond just providing a short example of both. The `forall` structure checks whether the collection of objects that fills both conditions are the same. This means if nothing fills the first and second conditions of the `forall`, it will evaluate to true. To avoid this, before every `forall`, we usually use `exists` with the first condition that we will use in the `forall`.

You can find examples of running rules about these advanced conditional elements in `ConditionalElementsTest` of the code base.

Drools syntactic sugar

Drools provides all sorts of special syntactic features. As much as we'd like, all of them won't fit in this book and more features are added constantly. Some of them, however, come in very handy when having to define our rules in a simple and comprehensive manner. We'll discuss the top three of these extra features, as follows:

- Nested accessors for the attributes of our types
- Inline casts for attributes of our types
- Null-safe operators

Nested accessors

Nested accessors allow us to simplify our conditions when we have to define conditions on nested beans. Using parentheses, it allows us access the nested properties without having to redeclare the path to get to them. Let's see the following example to fully understand it:

```
OrderLine( item.cost < 30.0, item.salePrice < 25.0 )
```

In the previous condition, we're filtering order lines that have an item with a cost under 30 and a sale price under 25. We could simplify the expression using nested accessors, as follows:

```
OrderLine( item.( cost < 30.0,salePrice < 25.0) )
```

This allows us to access multiple properties of the item attribute, without having to rewrite the path to reach these properties.

Inline casts

Inline casts allow us to quickly filter properties in a type without having to abuse from clauses. It allows us to cast an attribute of a type to a specific subclass and add a condition that would only make sense after casting. Let's see the following example to clarify it:

```
Order(customer#SpecialCustomer.specialDiscount > 0.0)
```

Here, we used the # symbol to mark our inline cast. We have a customer associated with our order. For some cases, the customer will not be of the Customer type, but a subclass of it called `SpecialCustomer`. This type of specialized customer has a special discount attribute. In the previous condition, we're trying to filter the orders that have a `SpecialCustomer` type of object and for these cases, the ones where the special customer has a discount greater than zero. Using inline casts, we can check all of these conditions in a single line.

Null-safe operators

Null-safe operators are very useful when dealing with possibly incomplete models, where we might not have to write the null-checking conditions over and over again. Using a special character, we can make sure that the conditions we write on attributes are only checked if the attribute is not null. Here's a case where we're using the null-safe operators to access the category of the customer of an order:

```
Order(customer!.category != Category.NA)
```

The previous condition, without null-safe operators, would be similar to the following:

```
Order(
    customer != null,
    customer.category != Category.NA
)
```

For deeply nested attributes, the null-safe operator allows us to save a lot of writing.

Decorating our objects in memory

We've seen examples where we modify the working memory whenever we detect that a specific condition is happening. We might remove objects, modify existing ones, and even delete them to trigger other rule executions. We've also seen that, sometimes, these elements make sense mostly within the rule executions and used declared types for these cases.

Whether we use declared types of external classes, most of the cases imply one of the following two strategies:

- We add new objects (declared types or Java classes) to the working memory, representing some inference about our domain model
- We modify attributes of existing objects in the working memory, adding the inferred data to these properties

These strategies have a few disadvantages when it comes to decorating an existing model. The first case (adding new objects) might imply having to keep a reference between the domain model object and the new inferred object in some form. The second case (modifying attributes) might imply modifying the domain model when we might not wish to do so.

There is a third alternative to these strategies, which implies adding a new nature to already existing objects without having to create extra attributes in the original beans. This dynamic decoration of existing objects in the working memory is known as traits.

Traits are like adjectives from an object-oriented perspective. We can say a house is pretty or a car is pretty. Adjectives can apply to many different types. However, these types don't need to share a common structure. This means that traits act like a flag that we can apply to multiple types and have specific attributes that apply to the adjective itself, and therefore, to the beans that apply the trait.

To explain this in a simpler way, think of traits as extra characteristics that we can dynamically add to certain objects in the working memory. We can filter these objects using these characteristics later in other rules. To do so, we need to do the following two things:

- **Define a trait**: We can do this using Java classes, marking them with the `@Trait` annotation at class level, or with declared types such as the following:

    ```
    declare trait KidFriendly
        kidsAppeal: String
    end
    ```

- Mark the classes and declared types that will have the trait applied with the `@Traitable` annotation.

Once we follow these steps, we can define the rules that apply the trait to the traitable objects. Let's consider an example based on our eShop case. Consider that we want to start classifying specific elements as `kid-friendly` in order to add advertising to them based on an age tier.

We can have items that are kid friendly, such as colored paper, toys, or special clothes. We might also have kid-friendly providers (they provide us with a lot of school-related items) or kid-friendly sales channels (such as parent-based sites where our eShop placed offers). If it wasn't for this qualification as kid-friendly, these elements wouldn't have any common structure. This is a good situation to apply traits.

Before we start using these traits, we need to see how to apply traits to our objects. To do so, we'll see the syntax of the don keyword.

Adding traits with the don keyword

Whenever we have an object where we want to apply a trait, we can do so using the don keyword. It receives the traitable object first, the trait type second, and an optional third boolean parameter to decide whether it should be logically inserted in the working memory. It returns an object casted to the type of the trait. Let's see the following example of its use:

```
rule "toy items are kid friendly"
      no-loop
      when $i: TraitableItem(name contains "toy")
      then
            KidFriendly kf = don($i, KidFriendly.class);
            kf.setKidAppeal("can play with it");
      end
```

The previous rule defines the conditions where we would consider a `TraitableItem` object (an object similar to `Item`, except it is annotated with `@Traitable`) as being kid-friendly. The reason for the no loop attribute on the rule is that `don` is not creating a new element, it is only decorating an existing one in the working memory. As this decoration doesn't make the object stop fulfilling the rule condition, the no loop avoids re-evaluations.

After using the don keyword, we will be able to treat this object as a kid-friendly object in any other rule. This means that rules that filter objects by the **KidFriendly** type can treat the traited object as a `KidFriendly` element.

Removing traits with the shed keyword

If, at some point, after applying a trait to an object, we decide that this trait needs to be removed, we can do so with the `shed` keyword. Shed will cause the deletion of the trait corresponding to the given argument type, as follows:

```
Object o = shed( $traitedObject, KidFriendly.class)
```

This syntax, and the use you can give to the traits, is also exemplified in `TraitTest` of the code base.

Logical insertion of elements

As we've discussed earlier, we should strive to keep our rules simple. To do so, sometimes, we break down a rule into multiple rules, making insertions of new data in the engine to trigger other simple rules. This helps in keeping the rules manageable as simpler rules will be easily understood. Here's a small example of how we can do such a thing:

```
rule "determine large orders"
    when $o: Order(total > 150)
    then insert(new IsLargeOrder($o));
end
```

In this way, we won't have to define what we consider a large order more than once. If we want to change this consideration in the future to, let's say, a total larger than 200, we will only have to change it once.

The one consideration that we need to have with this approach is that if the condition that triggered the insertion of `IsLargeOrder` might stop being true in the future. If some rule or a piece of code changes the order to have a smaller total, the `IsLargeOrder` object would still be in the working memory. We can avoid this by creating a rule to sanitize the working memory when the condition is not true anymore, but rules helps in avoiding this unnecessary rule duplication using **logical insertion**.

Logical insertion of objects binds the inserted objects with the condition that triggered their insertion. This means that if we rewrite the previous rule as follows:

```
rule "determine large orders"
    when $o: Order(total > 150)
    then insertLogical(new IsLargeOrder($o));
end
```

Then, if at some point in the future, the order changes its total to less than `150`, the `IsLargeOrder` object will be automatically removed from the working memory.

Handling deviations of our rules

Logical insertion not only avoid needing extra rules to sanitize our working memory, but also open the possibility of locking objects to specific conditions. This is very powerful because if we bind some form of `negation` of object to a condition, we can define the deviations or exceptions to our inferences.

Binding a negation of an object is simple. Just use the `insertLogical` keyword with a second parameter with the `neg` string on it. Let's see the following example, where we will add an exception for what we consider a large order, the total items being less than five, regardless of the price:

```
rule "large orders exception"
        when $o: Order(total > 150, totalItems < 5)
        then insertLogical(new IsLargeOrder($o), "neg");
    end
```

If we take the previous two rules, we will have one `IsLargeOrder` object in the working memory for every order that has a total greater than `150` and more than five items. If, at some point, the total of an order decreases below `150`, the corresponding `IsLargeOrder` object will automatically be deleted. If an order with a total above 150 and only four items gets another item, a corresponding `IsLargeOrder` object will automatically be inserted.

This deviation management has the advantage of keeping the rules independent of each other. The deviation rules don't need to understand how many rules are adding an `IsLargeOrder` object to the working memory, but only the situation where the object should not be added.

Note that the logical insertion can be done also for creation of traits. The `don` keyword has a third optional boolean parameter and if you set it to true, the trait gets logically inserted in the working memory and only exists in it while the rule is evaluated to true, as follows:

```
don($traitObj, SomeTrait.class, true);
```

Deviations to our deviations

The previous approach allows us to have independent rules, but it doesn't let us add more than one level of deviations. If, at some point, we want to nest deviations (which means to add a deviation to an existing deviation), the previous syntax won't be enough. Let's first discuss an example of this double deviation situation:

- If you have an order over 150 dollars, you consider it a large order

- In these orders, if they have less than five items, you consider them a large order

- If it's less than five items, but over 300 dollars (well over 150 dollars), you also consider them a large order

For these cases, Drools provides a set of annotations that allows us to implement deviation trees in our rules. This method of writing rules, however, comes with a disadvantage. Using these annotations will break the rule independence as we have to specify that to which rules we are providing a deviation or else you might find yourself having rules and deviations to deviations competing with each other and possibly lead to the rules getting executed more than designed.

Nevertheless, we might still require to do a case involving deviations to deviations and this strategy manages the situation quite nicely. The set of provided annotations mark the rules to identify which of them are deviations and which of them can or cannot have them. These annotations are as follows:

- **@Strict**: This marks a rule that cannot be defeated. In this type of scenario, it is useful to mark rules that should not be overridden by any other.

- **@Defeasible**: This marks a rule that can have deviations.

- **@Defeats**: This annotation receives a list of specific rules it can defeat. It is the point where the rule independence gets broken as it has to know the name of other rules.

- **@Defeater**: This marks a special case of defeats. It can defeat other rules, but the changes it makes won't be propagated in the working memory. This means that the rules marked with `@Defeater` won't trigger other rules. In very complex scenarios, this can be useful to stop deviation chains.

Each of the rules should use `insertLogical` to bind their inferences to the rule engine. Let's see the following example of the previous double deviation case implemented in Drools:

```
rule "large orders" @Defeasible
    when Order($id: orderId, total>150.00)
    then insertLogical(new IsLargeOrder($id));
end
rule "large orders exception" @Defeats("large orders")
    when Order($id:orderId, total>150.00, totalItems < 5)
    then insertLogical(new IsLargeOrder($id), "neg" );
end
rule "large orders double exception"
  @Defeats("large orders exception")
    when Order($id:orderId, total>300.00)
    then insertLogical(new IsLargeOrder($id));
end
```

In the previous set of rules, we first check for orders of more than 150 dollars and mark everything we find as a large order. The second rule establishes an exception, stating orders with less than five items are not large orders. The third rule, an exception to the second case, establishes that orders with less than five items are considered large as long as the total is over 300 dollars.

You will also need to specify in the kmodule.xml configuration that the KieSession will use defeasible logic. To do so, define your kbase and ksession tags as follows:

```
<kbase name="ruleExceptionsKbase"
        equalsBehavior="equality"
        packages="chapter04.ruleExceptions">
    <ksession name="ruleExceptionsKsession"
                beliefSystem="defeasible"/>
</kbase>
```

You can run this example in the `RuleExceptionsTest` class in the code base.

Rule inheritance

One last important aspect of rule creation is the possibility of having a rule hierarchy. Just like classes, rules allow inheritance between them. If rule B inherits rule A, it will be the same as having all the conditions in rule A at the beginning of the conditions of rule B. The following table shows two rules using inheritance and their equivalent without it:

```rule "A" when s: String(this == "A") then System.out.println(s); end```
 	
```rule "B" extends "A" when i: Integer(intValue > 2) then System.out.println(i); end```
	```rule "A" when s: String(this == "A") then System.out.println(s); end```
	
	```rule "B" when s: String(this == "A") i: Integer(intValue > 2) then System.out.println(i); end```

This can be a good strategy to manage rules that have repetitive conditions but still change structure. However, you need to be careful when deciding to use rule inheritance. Inheriting from another rule means that your sub-classed rule will not be independent; people reading your rule will need to refer to the parent rule to fully understand the behavior of your rule. Use this feature with caution.

Conditional named consequences

Rule inheritance allows us to avoid rewriting conditions as separate rules by extending an existing rule. Another interesting feature that allows us to avoid rewriting conditions is the possibility of using conditionally named consequences. They are basically extra then clauses marked by an identifier to make one rule behave as several. The same identifier has to be used in the rule condition with the go keyword to identify when you should go to that specific consequence. For example, if we wanted to write the two rules that we saw in the rule inheritance subsection as a single rule, we could do it in the following way:

```
rule "A and B combined"
    when
        s: String(this == "A")
        do[aCase]
```

```
        i: Integer(intValue > 2)
    then
        System.out.println(i);
    then[aCase]
        System.out.println(s);
  end
```

As you can see in the previous rule, we can use the do keyword to mark a point in the conditions where we can go to a specific consequence. If all the conditions in the rule are true, both consequences would execute, similar to the case that we would see if we defined two different rules.

Same as with rule inheritance, we must be very careful of using this feature. It can save us a lot of rewriting, but it can also provoke one rule to become very cumbersome to read in the long run. It is usually a good workaround when required to quickly update an existing rule, but not something you want to abuse so much that the rule becomes hard to read. Simplicity is key to making rules easy to understand and modify.

Summary

Throughout this chapter, we've acquired a large amount of tools to write very powerful rules. Working memory manipulation, communication with outside of the rule engine through global variables, and control of the flow through groupings will come in handy for different aspects of each specific rule.

The next step is to get everything that we've defined so far working together. Rule engines provide an enormous amount of flexibility by taking care of all the optimizations from a code perspective. In a way, we're here to write all the rules, and let the engine sort them out.

In the next chapter, we will start tuning our runtime environment to control how the rules should be executed, what information is to be logged in, and the rest of the details that exceed rule definition and are related to rule runtime configuration.

Understanding KIE Sessions

5

So far, we have covered what Kie Sessions are and how to create them and interact with them. In this chapter, we are going to dive deeper into some of the advanced configuration options and components available in Drools 6, when configuring and defining a Kie Session.

Before going deeper though, we are going to cover the two flavors of Kie Sessions that are present in Drools: stateless and stateful. The type of Kie Session that we choose for our applications has its advantages and disadvantages, which will eventually determine the way we interact with them—whether it's storing information between calls or satisfying a single use case for our business rules.

Once we have a better understanding of the different types of Kie Sessions provided by Drools, we will move on to some of their configuration aspects. In this section, topics such as globals, channels, and event listeners will be covered. All these elements will allow us to create better applications where dependencies with external services and monitoring over the Kie Sessions can be easily decoupled.

The last section of this chapter will focus on the options that we have to enhance the DRL language by creating functions, custom operators, and accumulate functions. These features are one of the most powerful tools we have in Drools to create customized rules without affecting their readability or maintainability.

The following topics will be covered in this chapter:

- Stateless and stateful Kie Sessions
- Globals, channels, and event listeners
- Queries both on-demand and live
- Functions
- Custom operators and accumulate functions

This chapter has a corresponding module in the chapter-05 code bundle. Most of the examples described in this chapter, and more, can be found in this module in the form of unit tests.

Stateless and stateful Kie Sessions

As we already know, Kie Sessions come in two different flavors: stateless and stateful. Most of the examples we covered so far involved only stateful Kie Sessions; and there is a good reason why, stateful Kie Sessions are, by far, the most powerful type of sessions supported by Drools.

Before we can decide which kind of session we want to use for a particular situation, we need to understand the differences and similarities between these two type of sessions. In order to do so, we are going to start with the most simple type of session: the stateless Kie Session.

Stateless Kie Sessions

From a development perspective, the type of session we want to use for a particular scenario is not determined by the rules—or any other asset type—we want to use. The type of session is determined either when we define it in the kmodule.xml file or when we programmatically instantiate it in our code. In most of the cases, the same set of assets (.drl files, decision tables, and so on) can be executed inside either a stateless or a stateful session.

So, what is a stateless Kie Session? One of the best analogies to understand what a stateless Kie Session is would be to describe this kind of session as a function.

Typically, a function is something that receives a set of predefined parameters, processes them, and generates an output or result. In many programming languages, the result of a function can be the return value itself, or it can also be the modification of some of the input parameters. Ideally, a function shouldn't have any collateral effect, meaning that if it is invoked multiple times with the same set of parameters, the result should be the same.

A stateless Kie Session shares some of the concepts we described for functions: it has some loosely defined set of input parameters, it processes these parameters in a way, and generates a response. In the same way as a function does, different invocations on the same stateless Kie Session don't interfere with each other.

In order to get a stateless Kie Session, we first need to define the Kie Base we want to use to instantiate it. One way to do this is by creating a `kmodule.xml` file, as follows:

```
<kmodule xmlns:xsi="http://www.w3.org/2001/XMLSchema-instance"
 xmlns="http://jboss.org/kie/6.0.0/kmodule">
<kbase name="KBase1">
    <ksession name="KSession1" type="stateless" default="true/">
</kbase>
```

The important thing to notice in the previous code is that we are specifically defining `KSession1` as a stateless session.

 If not specified, the default type of a Kie Session is `stateful`.

The next step is to get an instance of the `Ksession1` session. For this, we may use the following code snippet:

```
KieServices kieServices = KieServices.Factory.get();
KieContainer kContainer = kieServices.getKieClasspathContainer();
StatelessKieSession statelessKsession = kContainer.newStatelessKieSession("KSession1");
```

The API exposed by the `StatelessKieSession` class is a subset of the one exposed by its stateful counterpart, `KieSession`. The way we usually interact with a stateful session is that we insert a set of facts into it, execute any activated rule, and then we extract the response we are looking for in some way. In a stateful session, the insertion and execution is separated into two different methods: `insert()` and `fireAllRules()`. In the case of a stateless session, these two operations are combined in a single method called `execute()`. The `execute()` method of `StatelessKieSession` comes in the following three versions:

```
execute(Object fact)
execute(Iterable facts)
execute(Command command)
```

These first two versions of `execute()` will insert the facts passed as arguments, fire all the activated rules, and dispose the created session. Successive invocations of these methods will execute all these three steps again. Remember that everything related to any previous invocation will be discarded after `execute()` ends.

The third version of `execute()` allows us to interact with the session using a command pattern (http://en.wikipedia.org/wiki/Command_pattern). Drools already comes with a predefined set of available commands such as `InsertObjectCommand`, `SetGlobalCommand`, `FireAllRulesCommand`, and so on. All the available commands can be instantiated using the `CommandFactory` class. Commands can be grouped together using an instance of the `BatchExecutionCommand` interface.

A typical use of a stateless Kie Session would be as shown in the following code:

```
List<Command> cmds = new ArrayList<>();
cmds.add( CommandFactory.newSetGlobal( "list1", new ArrayList(), true
) );
cmds.add( CommandFactory.newInsert( new CustomerBuilder().withId(1L).
build(), "customer1" ) );
cmds.add( CommandFactory.newQuery( "Get Customers" "getCustomers" );
ExecutionResults results = ksession.execute( CommandFactory.
newBatchExecution( cmds ) );
results.getValue( "list1" ); // returns the ArrayList
results.getValue( "customer1" ); // returns the inserted Customer fact
results.getValue( "Get Customers" );// returns the query as a
QueryResults instance
```

If stateless sessions provide a subset of the operations present in the stateful counterpart, why do we need them? Well, technically, we don't. Everything that could be done by `StatelessKIESession`, can be also done using a `stateful` one. Using a stateless session is more like an explicit statement saying that we just want to use a single-shot session that it is going to be used just for a one-time evaluation. Stateless sessions are ideal for stateless scenarios such as data validation, calculations (such as risk evaluation or mortgage rate), and data filtering.

Due to its stateless nature, a stateless Kie Session doesn't need to be disposed. After each invocation of any of the `execute()` methods, the resources used for the execution are freed. At this point, the same stateless Kie Session is ready for another execution round if required. Each `execute()` invocation will then be independent from the previous one.

Summing up, `stateless Kie Sessions` are ideal for stateless evaluations such as:

- Data validation
- Calculations
- Data filtering
- Message routing
- Any complex function or formula could be described as rules

Stateful Kie Sessions

We have already covered stateful Kie Sessions in great detail in the previous chapters. This kind of session is the most powerful type of session supported by Drools. Whenever we read or hear about a session in Drools, 99% chances are that it refers to a stateful one. In fact, the stateful Kie Session is so common that they changed its class name from StatefulKnowledgeSession in Drools 5 to simply KieSession in Drools 6.

The main advantage of a stateful session over a stateless one is that the former keeps its state between interactions. We already explained how different invocations to the execute() method on a StatelessKieSession object are isolated from each other. For stateful scenarios, this is not enough. These kinds of scenarios require a session to span across multiple invocations. A common example for these type of scenarios is a session that we are using to monitor a process. Ideally, we would like to insert any incoming event from the process that we are monitoring as soon as we can. We also want to detect a problem as soon as possible. In these situations, we can't wait until we have all the incoming events (maybe they never end) so that we can create our BatchExecutionCommand object to execute it against a stateless session. A better approach here would be to insert each event as soon as it arrives, execute an activated rule, get a generated result, and then wait for the next event to arrive. When the next event arrives, we don't want to treat it in a new session, we want to use the same session where any previous event already is.

When we don't want to use a KieSession anymore, we must explicitly state this by invoking its dispose() method. The dispose method will free any resource the session may have acquired and release any memory it may have allocated. After dispose() is invoked, the session stays in an invalid state, further interactions with this session will throw a exception as java.lang.IllegalStateException.

Just like StatelessKieSession, the KieSession interface also supports the command pattern-like interaction via its execute() method. This command pattern-like interaction is relevant when we are dealing with persistent sessions. In this situation, all the commands passed in a single execute() call are executed in a single transaction. More about the persistent session can be found in *Chapter 10, Integrating Rules and Processes*.

Now that we have a better understanding about the different type of sessions provided by Drools, let's take a look at some advanced configuration options we have for them.

Kie runtime components

Drools presents us with several configuration options for its sessions—whether they are stateless or stateful. In this section, we are going to cover some of the options that we have in order to configure our sessions in a way that allows us to make full use of Drools' potential.

The most common way we usually interact with a Drools session is by inserting/modifying/retracting facts from it and executing any rule activation that may have happened as a consequence of these operations. All these operations target different aspects of the rule engine—such as knowledge assertion and inference—but there are also some other ways to interact with a session that can be used to provide or extract information to or from it. These operations are more oriented to the application where Drools is running and not to the rule engine itself. The options that we are going to review in this section are globals, channels, queries, and event listeners.

 Even if the four options are available in both stateless and stateful sessions, we are going to focus on the examples of stateful ones.

Globals

Global variables were briefly mentioned in *Chapter 3, Drool Runtime* and explained in greater detail in *Chapter 4, Improving Our Rule Syntax*. In this section, we are going to cover the most common patterns of globals usage inside a session.

Even when globals can be used internally in a session and never be exposed to the outside world, they are typically used as a way to introduce/extract information to/from a session. A global is, in many cases, a contact point between a session and the external word.

When working with stateful sessions, there are three methods in the `KieSession` class that are related to globals. These methods are shown in the following table:

Method	Description
`void setGlobal(String identifier, Object value)`	This method is used to set the value of a global. Invoking this method more than once in the same session will update any previously set value of the global.
	The identifier used in the invocation of this method must match the identifier (name) of the global in the knowledge base.

Method	Description
`Globals getGlobals()`	This method is used to retrieve all the globals in a session. The resulting object can be used to retrieve individual globals by their identifiers.
`Object getGlobal(String identifier)`	This method is used to retrieve a global using its identifier.

As you can see, there is not too much to learn about how to interact with global variables inside a session. The three methods described in the preceding table are almost self-explanatory.

There are four common ways to use a global in Drools, as shown in the following:

- In the LHS of a rule, as a way to parameterize the condition of a pattern
- In the LHS of a rule, as a way to introduce new information in a session
- In the RHS of a rule, as a way to collect information from a session
- In the RHS of a rule, as a way to interact with external systems

No matter how a global is used in a session, it is important to notice that a global is not a fact. Drools will treat globals and facts in a completely different way; changes in a global are never detected by Drools, and thus, Drools will never react upon them.

 Globals in Drools are not facts! Drools will never be notified nor react when a global is set or modified.

Let's analyze each of the four common scenarios for a global that we have previously listed.

Globals as a way to parameterize the condition of a pattern

One way globals are normally used in Drools is as a way to externally parameterize the condition of a rule. The idea is to use globals instead of hardcoded values in the conditions of our rules.

As an example, let's go back to our eShop example. Let's say that we want a Drools session to detect suspicious operations for customers in our eShop application. We will define a suspicious operation as a customer with pending operations summing more than 10,000 dollars.

The input of our session will be the customers of our application and their orders. For each customer with pending orders for more than 10,000 dollars, we are going to insert a new object of the SuspiciousOperation type. The SuspiciousOperation class has the following structure:

```
public class SuspiciousOperation {
    public static enum Type {
        SUSPICIOUS_AMOUNT,
        SUSPICIOUS_FREQUENCY;
    }
    private Customer customer;
    private Type type;
    private Date date;
    private String comment;

    public SuspiciousOperation(Customer customer, Type type) {
        this.customer = customer;
        this.type = type;
    }

    //setters and getters
}
```

The following rule is enough to accomplish our goal of detecting suspicious operations:

```
rule "Detect suspicious amount operations"
when
    $c: Customer()
    Number( doubleValue > 10000.0 ) from accumulate (
        Order ( customer == $c, state != OrderState.COMPLETED, $total:
total),
        sum($total)
    )
then
    insert(new SuspiciousOperation($c, SuspiciousOperation.Type.
SUSPICIOUS_AMOUNT));
end
```

The rule is straightforward: for each Customer, it collects any Order whose OrderState is not COMPLETED and calculates the sum of their totals. If the total is more than 10,000, then the rule is activated. When the RHS of the rule is executed, it will insert a new object of the SuspiciousOperation type in the session.

As we already know, if we want to execute this rule, we need to include it as part of a knowledge base, create a session from it, and provide some facts to it, as follows:

```
//Create a customer with PENDING orders for a value > 10000
Customer customer1 = new CustomerBuilder()
            .withId(1L).build();
Order customer1Order = ModelFactory.getPendingOrderWithTotalValueG
reaterThan10000(customer1);

//Create a customer with PENDING orders for a value < 10000
Customer customer2 = new CustomerBuilder()
            .withId(2L).build();
Order customer2Order = ModelFactory.getPendingOrderWithTotalValueL
essThan10000(customer1);

//insert the customers in a session and fire all the rules
ksession.insert(customer1);
ksession.insert(customer1Order);
ksession.insert(customer2);
ksession.insert(customer2Order);

ksession.fireAllRules();
```

A running example of the preceding code can be found in the code bundle under the `chapter-05` module.

The previous example works fine as long as the threshold for what we consider a suspicious operation remains unchanged. However, what if we want to make this threshold variable?

One way of the many different ways to achieve this is to replace the hardcoded value in our rule with a global variable that can be defined whenever we want to run our session, as follows:

```
global Double amountThreshold;

rule "Detect suspicious amount operations"
when
    $c: Customer()
    Number( doubleValue > amountThreshold ) from accumulate (
        Order ( customer == $c, state != OrderState.COMPLETED, $total:
total),
        sum($total)
    )
then
    insert(new SuspiciousOperation($c, SuspiciousOperation.Type.
SUSPICIOUS_AMOUNT));
end
```

In the preceding example, we can see how the hardcoded threshold is no longer present in the DRL. We are now using a global of the `Double` type in the condition of our rule. Using this approach, the threshold of what we consider a suspicious operation can now be modified among the different executions of the session.

 There is nothing that prevents us from modifying our global variables during the execution of our session from within a rule. Even if this is possible, modifying the value of a global that is being used in a constraint during runtime is not encouraged. Given the declarative nature of Drools, we can't predict what is the effect of modifying the value of a global variable in these situations.

One important thing to mention is that when global variables are used as part of a rule constraint, the global must be set before the pattern where it is being used is evaluated. To avoid race conditions, it is considered good practice to set the global variables of a session before any fact is inserted. A downside of using global variables in the constraints of our rules is that their values are not cached by Drools. Every time a global variable needs to be evaluated, its value is accessed. In large knowledge bases, this could create performance issues.

 Given all the drawbacks of using globals to parameterize our rules, this pattern is not recommended. A much better approach to parameterize the conditions of our rules would be to make the parameters as facts themselves in our session and treat them as any other type of fact. The inclusion of this pattern in this book was just for the sake of completeness.

Globals as a way to introduce new information into a session in the LHS

Another common pattern related to globals is their usage as data sources for a session. Usually, this type of globals encapsulate the invocation of a service (database, in-memory map, web service, and so on) that introduces new objects into the session. This usage pattern always involves the `from` conditional element.

In order to demonstrate this scenario, we are going to modify the example introduced in the previous section and introduce a service call to retrieve the orders of our customers. The service will be modeled as an `OrderService` interface, containing a single method—`getOrdersByCustomer`—as shown in the following code:

```
public interface OrderService {
    public Collection<Order> getOrdersByCustomer(String customerId);
}
```

The idea here is to use this interface as a global that our rule can use to retrieve all the orders related to a customer. The final version of the DRL for this example will look similar to the following code:

```
global Double amountThreshold;
global OrderService orderService;

rule "Detect suspicious amount operations"
when
    $c: Customer()
    Number( doubleValue > amountThreshold ) from accumulate (
    Order ( state != OrderState.COMPLETED, $total: total) from
        orderService.getOrdersByCustomer($c.customerId), sum($total))
then
    insert(new SuspiciousOperation($c,
    SuspiciousOperation.Type.SUSPICIOUS_AMOUNT));
end
```

In this version of our example, we are still using a global to hold the threshold of what we consider a suspicious operation, but we now also have a new global called orderService. Our rule is now invoking the global's getOrdersByCustomer method to get all the orders for a particular customer instead of getting the orders from the customer's orders property.

In this simple example, we may not realize the advantage of this approach—the orders of a customer are now being fetched only when/if required. In the previous version of the rule, we had to prefetch all the orders for all the customers before inserting them into the session. We didn't know, at the insertion time, whether the session will actually require all the orders for all the customers or not.

As mentioned earlier, we need to remember to set the value of the orderService global before we insert any Customer into the session, as follows:

```
OrderService orderServiceImpl = new OrderServiceImpl();
//a concrete implementation of OrderService.
ksession.setGlobal("orderService", orderServiceImpl);
ksession.insert(customer1);
ksession.insert(customer2);
ksession.fireAllRules();
```

One important thing to notice in the previous code is that we are no longer inserting the Orders as facts. The Orders will be retrieved on demand by the rules themselves. There is a catch though, a condition of a rule could be evaluated multiple times while rules are being executed. Every time the rule is re-evaluated, the data source will be invoked. When using this kind of pattern, the latency of the data source has to be taken into account.

We saw how to use a global as an interface to an external system in order to retrieve and introduce (but not insert) new information into the session. The question now is how to extract the generated SuspiciousOperation objects out of the session?

Globals as a way to collect information from a session

The rule from the previous example inserted a SuspiciousOperation object for each suspicious operation found. The problem is that these facts are not accessible from outside the session. A common pattern to extract information from a session is by using globals.

The idea behind this pattern is to use a global variable to collect the information we want to extract from the session. As the global is accessible from outside the session, any fact, object, or value that it references will also be accessible. The most common class of this type of globals is any instance of java.util.Collection or java.util.Map.

We are now going to modify the knowledge base we used in the previous section by adding a new rule that will collect any SuspiciousOperation fact into a global set:

```
global Double amountThreshold;
global OrderService orderService;
global Set results;

rule "Detect suspicious amount operations"
when
    $c: Customer()
    Number( doubleValue > amountThreshold ) from accumulate (
        Order ( state != OrderState.COMPLETED, $total: total) from
            orderService.getOrdersByCustomer($c.customerId),
                sum($total))
then
    insert(new SuspiciousOperation($c, SuspiciousOperation.Type.
SUSPICIOUS_AMOUNT));
end

rule "Collect results"
when
    $so: SuspiciousOperation()
then
    results.add($so);
end
```

The code shows that we now have a new global called `results` and a new rule that will collect any instance of the `SuspiciousOperation` class into it.

The relevant Java code to execute this new version of the example is shown in the following:

```
Set<SuspiciousOperation> results = new HashSet<>();
ksession.setGlobal("results", results);

ksession.insert(customer1);
ksession.insert(customer2);
ksession.fireAllRules();

//variable 'results' now holds all the generated SuspiciousOperation
objects.
```

After the rules are executed, the global set will contain the references of any `SuspiciousOperation` object generated during the session's execution. We can then use these objects outside the session where they were created.

Globals as a way to interact with external systems in the RHS

The last common usage pattern regarding globals that we are going to cover is the usage of globals on the right-hand side of a rule as a way to interact with an external system. The idea behind this pattern is simple, we saw that we can use a global to introduce new information into a pattern (using the `from` conditional element). We can also use a global to interact with external systems on the right-hand side of a rule. The interaction with this external system could be unidirectional (getting information from the system or sending information to the system) or bidirectional (sending and receiving information from the system).

Continuing the previous example, let's say that now we want to notify each `SuspiciousOperation` found to an external audit system. We have two options here, we now know that we can access these generated facts using the global set introduced in the previous section. We could, from within the Java code, iterate over this list and send each of its elements to the audit system. Another option is to leverage this in the session itself.

This new interface will be represented in our code by an interface called `AuditService`. This interface will define a single method — `notifySuspiciousOperation` — as shown in the following code:

```
public interface AuditService {
    public void notifySuspiciousOperation(SuspiciousOperation
        operation);
}
```

We need to add an instance of this interface as a global and create either a new rule that invokes its `notifySuspiciousOperation` method or modify the `Collect results` rule so that it now invokes this method too. Let's take the first approach and add a new rule to notify the audit system:

```
...
global AuditService auditService;
...
rule "Send Suspicious Operation to Audit Service"
when
    $so: SuspiciousOperation()
then
    auditService.notifySuspiciousOperation($so);
end
```

In the preceding code snippet, we are only showing the new code that we have introduced in the previous example. The new rule we have created is using the new global that we defined to notify the audit system about each generated `SuspiciousOperation` objects. It is important to remember that Drools will always execute the rules in a single thread. Ideally, the RHS of our rules should not involve blocking operations. In the case where blocking operations are required, the introduction of an asynchronous mechanism to execute the blocking operation in a separate thread is considered as a good option most of the time.

We have covered the four common usage patterns of globals in Drools. We are now going to introduce a similar concept: channels.

Channels

A channel is a standardized way to transmit data from within a session to the external world. A channel can be used exactly for what we discussed in the previous section: globals as a way to interact with external systems in the RHS. Instead of using a global, we can accomplish the same task by using a channel.

Technically, Channel is a Java interface with a single method—void send(Object object)—as shown in the following:

```
public interface Channel {
    void send(Object object);
}
```

Channels can only be used in the RHS of our rules as a way to send data to outside the session. Before we can use a channel, we need to register it in our session. The KieSession class provides the following three methods to deal with channels:

Method	Description
void registerChannel(String name, Channel channel)	This method is used to register a channel in the session. When a channel is registered, a name must be provided. This name is then used by the session to identify the channel.
void unregisterChannel(String name)	This is the counterpart of registerChannel and it is used to unregister a previously registered channel. The name parameter passed to this method is the same name used during the registration.
Map< String, Channel> getChannels()	This method can be used to retrieve any previously registered channel. The key of the returned Map corresponds to the name that was used during the channel registration.

In the RHS of a rule, whenever we want to interact with a channel, we can obtain a reference to it through the predefined channels RHS variable. This variable provides an interface similar to a map that allows us to reference a specific channel by its name. For example, if we have registered a channel with the notifications name, we can interact with it using the following code snippet in the RHS of our rules:

```
channels["notifications"].send(new Object());
```

Concrete implementations of the Channel interface can be used to route data to external systems, notify about events, and so no. Just remember that a channel represents a unidirectional way to transmit data: the send() method in the Channel interface returns void.

Let's refactor the example from the previous section to make use of a channel instead of a global to notify an audit system about suspicious operations.

The first thing we need to do is to get rid of the `auditService` that we had in our knowledge base. The whole point of this example is to replace this global with a channel. Then, we need to replace the RHS from the `"Send Suspicious Operation to Audit Service"` rule so that it makes use of a channel instead of the old global:

```
rule "Send Suspicious Operation to Audit Channel"
when
    $so: SuspiciousOperation()
then
    channels["audit-channel"].send($so);
end
```

Now, before we can execute a session based on this knowledge base, we need to register a new channel in the session with the `audit-channel` name. In order to do so, we can use the `registerChannel` method we have already covered, as follows:

```
ksession.registerChannel("audit-channel", auditChannel);
```

In this case, the `auditChannel` object is an implementation of the `Channel` interface.

As we can see, a channel provides a more rigid, but well-defined, contract than a global. Just like with globals, we can use different implementations of a channel to provide different runtime behaviors in our rules.

One of the advantages of channels is the versatility they provide due to the fact that they are indexed using a `String` key. The key of a channel could be determined in runtime either in the LHS as a binding or in the RHS of a rule. This gives us more flexibility than plain variables, where the name of the variable we want to use is fixed in the DRL.

Let's move to a much more flexible way to extract information from within a session: queries.

Queries

A query, in Drools, can be seen as a regular rule without its right-hand side section. A major difference between a query and a rule is that the former may take arguments. With queries, we can use all the power of Drools' pattern-matching syntax to extract information from within a session. During runtime, we can execute a query and do whatever we want with its results. In some way, a query is a rule with a dynamic right-hand side.

A query can also be used as a regular pattern inside a rule. This is the foundation of Drools' backward chaining reasoning capability. This section is only focused on queries as a way to extract information from a session. Queries used as patterns are covered in *Chapter 9, Introduction to PHREAK*.

Continuing with the example we were using before, let's now create a query to extract all the generated SuspiciousOperation facts from the session. The query required to do this looks similar to the following one:

```
query "Get All Suspicious Operations"
    $so: SuspiciousOperation()
end
```

As we can see, the query we have created looks exactly like a rule without its right-hand side. If we are interested in a particular customer, we can define another query that takes the customer ID as a parameter and filters all their related SuspiciousOperation objects, as follows:

```
query "Get Customer Suspicious Operations" (String $customerId)
    $so: SuspiciousOperation(customer.customerId == $customerId)
end
```

The arguments of a query are defined like the parameters of a method in a Java class: each argument has a type and a name.

There are two ways to execute a query from outside a session: on-demand queries and live queries. Let's analyze them in more detail.

On-demand queries

A query is evaluated on-demand by invoking KieSession's getQueryResults method:

```
public QueryResults getQueryResults(String query, Object...
arguments);
```

This method takes the name of the query and the list of its arguments (if any). The order of the arguments corresponds to the order of the parameters in the query definition. The result of this method is a QueryResults object:

```
public interface QueryResults extends Iterable<QueryResultsRow> {
    String[] getIdentifiers();
    Iterator<QueryResultsRow> iterator();
    int size();
}
```

The `QueryResults` interface extends `Iterable` and represents a collection of `QueryResultsRow` objects. The `getIdentifiers()` method returns an array of the query's identifiers. Any bound variable defined in the query will became an identifier in its result. For example, our `Get All Suspicious Operations` query only defined one identifier, `$so`. Identifiers are used to retrieve the concrete value of a bound variable when a query is executed.

The following code can be used to execute the `Get All Suspicious Operations` query:

```
QueryResults queryResults = ksession.getQueryResults("Get All
Suspicious Operations");
for (QueryResultsRow queryResult : queryResults) {
    SuspiciousOperation so = (SuspiciousOperation)
                                    queryResult.get("$so");
    //do whatever we want with so
    //...
}
```

The preceding code executes the `Get All Suspicious Operations` query and then iterates over the results extracting the value of the `$so` identifier, in this case, instances of the `SuspiciousOperation` class.

Live queries

On-demand queries are used when we want to execute a particular query at a particular point in time. Drools also provides another way to execute queries, it allows us to attach a listener to a query so that we can be notified about the results as soon as they become available.

Live queries are executed using the following Kie Session's method:

```
public LiveQuery openLiveQuery(String query,Object[] arguments,
    ViewChangedEventListener listener);
```

Just like with on-demand queries, the first argument we need to pass to this method is the name of the query we want to attach a listener to. The second parameter is the array of arguments that the query is expecting to receive. The third parameter is the actual listener that we want to attach to the query. The result of this method is a `LiveQuery` class instance.

Let's take a closer look at the `ViewChangedEventListener` interface:

```
public interface ViewChangedEventListener {
    public void rowInserted(Row row);
    public void rowDeleted(Row row);
    public void rowUpdated(Row row);
}
```

As we can see, the `ViewChangedEventListener` interface is used not only for receiving new facts matching the specified query, but we can also detect modifications or retractions of these facts. Drools engine will notify this listener as soon as a fact matches the specified query, when a previously matching fact gets modified or the modifications of a previously matching fact excludes it from the query's filter.

In the previous section, we saw how to use global variables to communicate the results, actions, and general rule execution information to the outside world. However, what if we wanted to do so in a generic way — for every rule — without modifying existing rules? To do so, we have other mechanisms such as Event Listeners.

Event Listeners

Drools framework provides the users a mechanism to attach event listeners into two of its main components: **Kie Bases** and **Kie Sessions**.

Events from a Kie Base are related to the structure of the packages it contains. Using `org.kie.api.event.kiebase.KieBaseEventListener`, for example, we can be notified after or before a package is added or removed from a `KieBase`. Using this same event listener, we can go deeper into detail about what is actually being modified inside a KieBase, such as individual rules, functions, and processes being added/removed.

A `KieBaseEventListener` can be attached to a `KieBase` using `KieBase public void addEventListener(KieBaseEventListener listener)` method. A `KieBase` could have none, one, or more event listeners attached to it. When a particular event has to be fired, the `KieBase` will sequentially execute the corresponding method in each of the previously registered event listeners. The order of execution of the listener doesn't necessarily corresponds to the order they were registered.

Kie Session's events are related to the Drools' runtime execution. The events that a Kie Session could fire are separated into three different categories: rules execution runtime (`org.kie.api.event.rule.RuleRuntimeEventListener`), agenda-related events (`org.kie.api.event.rule.AgendaEventListener`), and processes execution runtime (`org.kie.api.event.process.ProcessEventListener`).

All these three types of event listeners can be attached into a Kie Session using one of `KieSession addEventListener` methods:

```
public void addEventListener(RuleRuntimeEventListener listener)
public void addEventListener(AgendaEventListener listener)
public void addEventListener(ProcessEventListener listener)
```

A `RuleRuntimeEventListener` can be used to notify about the events that are related to the state of the facts inside a Kie Session. The state of the facts inside a Kie Session is modified when they are inserted, modified, or retracted from the session. This kind of listener is usually used for reporting or statistical analysis of the execution of the session.

The `AgendaEventListener` is the interface we could use to be notified about the events happening inside Drools' agenda. Agenda events are related to rules match being created, canceled, or fired; agenda groups being pushed or popped from the active agenda stack and about rule-flow groups being activated and deactivated. The `AgendaEventListeners` are a fundamental aid for auditing tools. Being able to know when a rule gets activated, for example, is a valuable piece of information when analyzing the execution of a Kie Session.

The `ProcessEventListeners` are related to **jBPM** events and allow us to be notified when a process instance is started or completed or before/after the individual nodes inside a process instance are triggered.

A more declarative way to configure the event listeners that we want to use in a session is to define them inside the `kmodule.xml` file as part of a `<ksession>` component:

```
<kmodule xmlns:xsi="http://www.w3.org/2001/XMLSchema-instance"
xmlns="http://jboss.org/kie/6.0.0/kmodule">
  <kbase name="KBase1" default="true" packages="org.domain">
    <ksession name="ksession1" type="stateful">
      <ruleRuntimeEventListener type="org.domain.
RuleRuntimeListener"/>
      <agendaEventListener type="org.domain.FirstAgendaListener"/>
      <processEventListener type="org.domain.ProcessListener"/>
    </ksession>
  </kbase>
</kmodule>
```

All the event listeners in Drools are executed in the same thread where the Drools framework is running. This behavior has two implications: the event listeners should be lightweight and fast and they should never throw an exception. Event listeners that perform heavy processing tasks—or even worst, blocking tasks—should be avoided, if possible. When an event is fired, the Drools execution will not continue until all the registered listeners for such events are completed. The execution time of an action in Drools that may fire events is the sum of the execution time of the task itself, plus the execution time of each individual event listener that is fired. Drools current implementation not only executes the event listeners in the same thread where it is running, but it doesn't take any precaution when an event listener is fired either. An event listener throwing an exception will break the execution of the underlying action that was being executed. Catching any possible exception in an event listener is then mandatory if we don't want to interfere with the Drools execution when something goes wrong in our listener.

In the code bundle of this chapter, there are some unit tests showing how listeners are registered and used in Drools. We strongly recommend the reader to take a look at these tests and run, debug, and even enhance them in order to get a better understanding of Drools' event listeners capabilities.

Kie Base components

We have covered some of the most used components in a knowledge base, such as rules, globals, queries, and channels. It is time to move on to more advanced topics that will allow us to create more concise and reusable knowledge.

In this section, we are going to cover topics such as functions, custom operators, and custom accumulate functions. All these components can be used to model our knowledge in a simpler yet powerful way.

Functions

So far, we have covered three of the most common knowledge declarations that we have in Drools: rules, queries, and declared types. There is another kind of knowledge declaration that can be used to express stateless logic in a knowledge base: functions. **Functions** in Drools are basically isolated pieces of code that will optionally take arguments and may or may not return a value. Functions are useful for situations where we want to define some logic in a knowledge base instead of having it, for example, in an external Java class.

The syntax to define a function is similar to the one used in Java to declare a method with the addition of the keyword function at the beginning. A function has a return type (it could be any Java class including declared types or void), name, and optional set of typed parameters, as follows:

```
function String formatCustomer(Customer c){
    return String.format(
        "[%s] %s", c.getCategory(), c.getName());
}
```

In the preceding example, a function called formatCustomer is defined. This function takes a Customer instance as a parameter and returns a String parameter. The body of the function uses a regular Java syntax; in this case, it is using String. format() to concatenate the category and name of the provided customer.

Just as with declared types, functions defined in the knowledge base are a good way to keep logic together in just one place. Functions in Drools also give us the flexibility to modify them without having to recompile any code.

 The *without having to recompile any code* part of the last paragraph is not 100% accurate. Behind the scenes, when the knowledge base gets compiled, Drools will create a helper class containing the functions defined in it.

Even if the use of functions in Drools gives us a certain degree of flexibility, they do have some limitations, which are as follows:

- A function can't be used outside the package where it is defined. This means that a function defined inside a DRL file can't be used in any other DRL file, unless both have the same package declaration.

- Functions can't make use of any global variable, fact, or predefined variables such as kcontext. The context of a function is only the set of arguments that are passed when it is invoked.

- As a corollary of the previous limitation, functions can't insert, modify, or retract facts from the session.

When thinking about reusability and maintainability, the functions declared inside a knowledge base may not be the best approach. Drools, fortunately, also allows us to import a static method from the Java classes as a function and use it in our rules. In order to import a static method, we need to make use of the function keyword combined with the import keyword.

```
import function org.drools.devguide.chapter05.utils.CustomerUtils.
formatCustomer;
```

As you can see, importing a static method of a class as a function resembles, in a way, how static methods can be imported in Java.

It does not matter if our function is being imported from a Java class or declared inside the knowledge base, the way we invoke them in our rules or from another function is by simply using its name, as shown in the following code:

```
rule "Prepare Customers List"
when
    $c: Customer()
then
    globalList.add(formatCustomer($c));
end
```

The preceding example shows the use of the formatCustomer function within the right-hand side of a rule, but functions can be also used in the conditional part of a rule, as follows:

```
rule "Prepare Customers List"
when
    $c: Customer($formatted: formatCustomer($c))
then
    ...
end
```

Let's now move to another powerful feature in Drools that allows us to enhance the DRL language with tailored operators that can be used to create more concise, readable, and maintainable rules: custom operators.

Custom operators

In *Chapter 4, Improving Our Rule Syntax*, we saw most of the comparison operators that can be used when specifying the left-hand side of our rules. Operators such as ==, !=, <, > ,and so on are already supported by Drools, out of the box. There are some situations though, when the available operators are not enough. Comparisons involving complex logic, external services, or semantic reasoning are good examples of situations where the power of Drools falls short. However, there's nothing to be worried about; Drools provides a mechanism for the creation of custom operators that can then be used when authoring our rules.

In Drools, custom operators are defined as Java classes implementing the org. drools.core.base.evaluators.EvaluatorDefinition interface. This interface represents only the definition of the operator. The concrete implementation is delegated to an implementation of the org.drools.core.spi.Evaluator interface.

Before a custom operator can be used as part of a rule, it must be first registered in the knowledge base being used. The registration of a custom operator is performed using a configuration file in the classpath or by specifying it inside the kmodule.xml file. However, before we move on to see how a custom operator is registered, let's see an example first.

In order to clarify what a custom operator is and how it is defined, let's use an example from our eShop use case. For this example, we are going to implement a trivial operator that will tell us whether an Order function contains a specific Item given its ID. This example may not be the most interesting example for custom operators as it can be resolved in many different ways. Nevertheless, it represents a good and concise example to show how custom operators are built.

The idea of our new custom operator is to be able to write rules as the following:

```
rule "Apply discount to Orders with item 123"
when
    $o: Order(this containsItem 123) @Watch(!*)
Then
    modify ($o){ setDiscount(new Discount(0.1))};
end
```

The important thing to notice in the previous rule is the use of a custom operator called containsItem. All custom operators—and by extension, any operator in Drools—take two arguments. In this particular case, the first argument is of the Order type and the second is of the Long type. An operator will always evaluate to a boolean value. In this case, the boolean result will indicate whether the specified item is present in the provided Order or not.

The first thing we need to do in order to implement our custom operator is to implement org.drools.core.base.evaluators. EvaluatorDefinition. In our example, the implementation class will be called ContainsItemEvaluatorDefinition:

```
package org.drools.devguide.chapter05.evaluator;
public class ContainsItemEvaluatorDefinition implements
    EvaluatorDefinition {

    protected static final String containsItemOp = "containsItem";

    public static Operator CONTAINS_ITEM;
    public static Operator NOT_CONTAINS_ITEM;

    private static String[] SUPPORTED_IDS;

    private ContainsItemEvaluator evaluator;
```

```
    private ContainsItemEvaluator negatedEvaluator;


    static {
        if (SUPPORTED_IDS == null) {
            CONTAINS_ITEM = Operator.addOperatorToRegistry
                (containsItemOp, false);
            NOT_CONTAINS_ITEM = Operator.
                addOperatorToRegistry(containsItemOp, true);
            SUPPORTED_IDS = new String[]{containsItemOp};
        }
    }

    @Override
    public String[] getEvaluatorIds() {
        return new String[]{containsItemOp};
    }

    @Override
    public boolean isNegatable() {
        return true;
    }

    @Override
    public Evaluator getEvaluator(ValueType type, Operator
        operator) {
        return this.getEvaluator(type, operator.
            getOperatorString(),
                operator.isNegated(), null);
    }

    @Override
    public Evaluator getEvaluator(ValueType type, Operator
        operator,
            String parameterText) {
        return this.getEvaluator(type, operator.getOperator
            String(),
                operator.isNegated(), parameterText);
    }

    @Override
    public Evaluator getEvaluator(ValueType type, String
        operatorId,
            boolean isNegated, String parameterText) {
        return getEvaluator(type, operatorId, isNegated,
parameterText,
                Target.BOTH, Target.BOTH);
```

```
        }

        @Override
        public Evaluator getEvaluator(ValueType type, String
            operatorId,
                boolean isNegated, String parameterText,
                    Target leftTarget,
                        Target rightTarget) {
            return isNegated ?
                    negatedEvaluator == null ?
                        new ContainsItemEvaluator(type, isNegated) :
                            negatedEvaluator
                    : evaluator == null ?
                        new ContainsItemEvaluator(type, isNegated) :
                            evaluator;
        }

        @Override
        public boolean supportsType(ValueType type) {
            return true;
        }

        @Override
        public Target getTarget() {
            return Target.BOTH;
        }
        ...
    }
```

There is a lot of information to process in the previous class, so let's go by parts. The static block at the beginning registers two new operators into Drools' operators registry. The two new operators are indeed our new containsItem operator and its counterpart not containsItem. The next important method is getEvaluatorsIds(), which tells Drools all the possible IDs for the operator that we are defining. Following this method, comes isNegatable(), which indicates whether the operator that we are creating can be negated or not. Then, four different versions of the getEvaluator() method are defined. These methods will return, at compile time, the concrete instance of org.drools.core.base.evaluators. EvaluatorDefinition, which should be used for each specific scenario. The arguments that are passed to these methods are as follows:

- type: This is the type of operator's operands.
- operatorId: This is the identifier of the operator being parsed. A single operator definition can handle multiple IDs.

- isNegated: This indicates whether the operator being parsed is using the not prefix (is negated) or not.

- parameterText: An operand in Drools could have fixed the parameters that are defined in the angle brackets. Examples of operators with parameters are the CEP operators from Drools Fusion. Refer to *Chapter 6, Complex Event Processing* for more information about Drools Fusion.

- leftTarget/rightTarget: These two arguments specify whether this operator operates on facts, fact handles, or both.

The four versions of getEvaluator() return an instance of ContainsItemEvaluator. The ContainsItemEvaluator is the concrete implementation of Drools' org.drools. core.spi.Evaluator and is the class in charge of the runtime behavior of our operator. This class is where the real logic of our operator—check whether a specific Item is contained by an Order—is implemented:

```
public class ContainsItemEvaluator extends BaseEvaluator {

    private final boolean isNegated;

    public ContainsItemEvaluator(ValueType type, boolean
        isNegated) {
        super(type ,isNegated?
            ContainsItemEvaluatorDefinition.NOT_CONTAINS_ITEM :
                ContainsItemEvaluatorDefinition.CONTAINS_ITEM);
        this.isNegated = isNegated;
    }

    @Override
    public boolean evaluate(InternalWorkingMemory workingMemory,
        InternalReadAccessor extractor, InternalFactHandle
            factHandle,FieldValue value) {
        Object order = extractor.getValue(workingMemory, factHandle.
getObject());
        return this.isNegated ^ this.evaluateUnsafe(order,
            value.getValue());
    }
    @Override
    public boolean evaluate(InternalWorkingMemory workingMemory,
            InternalReadAccessor leftExtractor,
                InternalFactHandle left,
                    InternalReadAccessor rightExtractor,
                        InternalFactHandle right) {
        Object order = leftExtractor.getValue(workingMemory,
            left.getObject());
```

```
        Object itemId = rightExtractor.getValue(workingMemory, right.
getObject());
        return this.isNegated ^ this.evaluateUnsafe(order,
            itemId);
    }


    @Override
    public boolean evaluateCachedLeft(InternalWorkingMemory
workingMemory,
            VariableRestriction.VariableContextEntry context,
            InternalFactHandle right) {
        Object order = context.getFieldExtractor().
getValue(workingMemory,
                right.getObject());
        Object itemId = ((ObjectVariableContextEntry)context).left;

        return this.isNegated ^ this.evaluateUnsafe(order, itemId);
    }


    @Override
    public boolean evaluateCachedRight(InternalWorkingMemory
workingMemory,
            VariableRestriction.VariableContextEntry context,
            InternalFactHandle left) {
        Object order = ((ObjectVariableContextEntry)context).right;
        Object itemId = context.getFieldExtractor().
getValue(workingMemory,
                left.getObject());

        return this.isNegated ^ this.evaluateUnsafe(order, itemId);
    }

    private boolean evaluateUnsafe(Object order, Object itemId){
        //if the object is not an Order return false.
        if (!(order instanceof Order)){
            throw new IllegalArgumentException(
                    order.getClass()+" can't be casted to type
Order");
        }

        //if the value we are comparing against is not a Long, return
false.
        Long itemIdAsLong;
        try{
```

```
        itemIdAsLong = Long.parseLong(itemId.toString());
    } catch (NumberFormatException e) {
        throw new IllegalArgumentException(
                itemId.getClass()+" can't be converted to Long");
    }

    return this.evaluate((Order)order, itemIdAsLong);
}

private boolean evaluate(Order order, long itemId) {
    //no order lines -> no item
    if (order.getOrderLines() == null) {
        return false;
    }

    return order.getOrderLines().stream()
        .map(ol -> ol.getItem().getId())
        .anyMatch(id -> id.equals(itemId));
    }
}
```

Instead of implementing `org.drools.core.spi.Evaluator`,
`ContainsItemEvaluator` extends from `org.drools.core.base.BaseEvaluator`,
which is a class that implements the boilerplate code of the interface, leaving the
implementation of the concrete methods where the operator evaluation actually
happens to us. There are four methods that we have to implement, as follows:

- `evaluate`: There are two versions of this method that need to be
  implemented. These methods are used by Drools when the operator appears
  as part of a condition involving a single fact (in Phreak algorithm, these type
  of conditions are part of the so called alpha network. Phreak will be covered
  in more detail in *Chapter 9, Introduction to Phreak*). The first version is used
  when literal constraints are involved and the second when variable bindings
  are involved.

- `evaluateCachedLeft`/`evaluateCachedRight`: These two methods are used
  by Drools when the operator is used in conditions involving multiple facts
  (in Phreak algorithm, these conditions are part of it's beta network).

Before we can actually use this new operator in our rules, we need to register it in the
knowledge base where we want to use it. There are two ways of doing this: using the
`drools.packagebuilder.conf` file or via the `kmodule.xml` file.

The first way to register a custom operator is by using a special file in Drools called `drools.packagebuilder.conf`. This file, which must be located under the `META-INF` directory, is automatically used by the Drools' package builder to read configuration parameters of the knowledge base being created. In order to register a custom operator, we need to add the following line to this file:

```
drools.evaluator.containsItem= org.drools.devguide.chapter05.
    evaluator.ContainsItemEvaluatorDefinition
```

The line must start with `drools.evaluator` and the ID of the custom operator must follow. After that, the fully qualified name of the class, where the custom operator is defined, must be specified.

The second way to register a custom operator in Drools is to use the `kmodule.xml` file. A specific section for configurations can be defined in this file, where properties can be specified as key/value pairs. In order to register our created custom operator in a `kmodule.xml` file, the following configuration section must be added to it:

```
<kmodule xmlns:xsi="http://www.w3.org/2001/XMLSchema-instance"
        xmlns="http://jboss.org/kie/6.0.0/kmodule">
    <configuration>
        <property key="drools.evaluator.containsItem" value="org.
drools.devguide.chapter05.evaluator.ContainsItemEvaluatorDefinition"/>
    </configuration>
</kmodule>
```

A complete example of a custom operator can be found in the code bundle under the `chapter-05` module. This module defines the custom operator covered by this section and it also includes a couple of unit tests showing its behavior. The tests can be found in `chapter-05/chapter-05-tests/src/test/java/org/drools/devguide/chapter05/CustomOperatorTest.java`.

So far, we have covered how to define our own custom operators to create tailored solutions for our domain and enhance Drools pattern-matching capabilities. Let's move to another way, we have to create a customized logic in order to be used in our rules: the custom accumulate functions.

Custom accumulate functions

In *Chapter 4, Improving Our Rule Syntax*, we covered the accumulate conditional element and the different ways we can use it. The structure of an accumulate conditional element is composed of a pattern section and one or more accumulate functions. In the previous chapter, we saw two different types of accumulate functions: inline accumulate functions and built-in accumulate functions.

Inline accumulate functions are explicitly defined in the rule being created. These functions have the four sections that are already explained in the previous chapter: init, action, reverse, and result. On the other hand, the built-in functions are supported by Drools, out of the box. These functions include count, sum, avg, collectList, and so on.

Even if the inline accumulate functions are a powerful and flexible way to enhance Drools' capabilities, their definition and maintainability is fairly complex. Inline accumulate functions are cumbersome to write, debug, and maintain. Inline accumulate functions are basically chunks of the Java/MVEL code embedded in DRL. Writing the code in each section can be very confusing if we are not implementing a trivial function. Even worst, debugging what's going on inside an inline accumulate function is almost impossible. However, maybe the worst thing about inline accumulate functions is that they can't be reused. If the same function is required in multiple rules, it has to be redefined in each of them. Due to all of these inconveniences, the use of inline accumulate functions is kind of discouraged. Instead of defining our accumulate functions embedded in DRL, Drools allows us to define them in Java and then import them into our knowledge base. Decoupling the definition of the accumulate function from its usage in the rules solves all the problems that we have mentioned before.

A custom accumulate function is a Java class that implements Drools' org.kie.api. runtime.rule.AccumulateFunction interface. As an example, let's implement a custom accumulate function to retrieve the one item with the biggest total (including discounts) from a group of Orders, as follows:

```java
public class BiggestOrderFunction implements AccumulateFunction{

    public static class Context implements Externalizable{
        public Order maxOrder = null;
        public double maxTotal = -Double.MAX_VALUE;

        public Context() {}
        ...
    }

    @Override
    public Serializable createContext() {
        return new Context();
    }

    @Override
```

```java
    public void init(Serializable context) throws Exception {
    }

    @Override
    public void accumulate(Serializable context, Object value) {
        Context c = (Context)context;

        Order order = (Order) value;
        double discount =
                order.getDiscount() == null ? 0 : order.
                    getDiscount()
                        .getPercentage();
        double orderTotal = order.getTotal() - (order.getTotal()
            * discount);

        if (orderTotal > c.maxTotal){
            c.maxOrder = order;
            c.maxTotal = orderTotal;
        }

    }

    @Override
    public boolean supportsReverse() {
        return false;
    }

    @Override
    public void reverse(Serializable context, Object value) throws
Exception {
    }

    @Override
    public Object getResult(Serializable context) throws Exception {
        return ((Context)context).maxOrder;
    }

    @Override
    public Class<?> getResultType() {
        return Order.class;
    }
    ...
}
```

The `BiggestOrderFunction` class can be found in the source bundles of this chapter. Let's analyze the different sections of this class now. The first thing to notice is that this class is implementing Drools' `org.kie.api.runtime.rule.AccumulateFunction` interface. This interface defines all the methods required to implement a custom accumulate function. However, before we can even start implementing these methods, we need to define a context class. Every time an accumulate function is used in Drools, an individual context will be created for it. The context will contain all the necessary information for the accumulate function to work. In this case, a `Context` static class is defined, containing an `Order` instance and a double `maxTotal` attribute. This context will keep track of the biggest `Order` class found so far.

Once we have defined our context, we can implement the methods from the `AccumulateFunction` interface. The name of these methods, except for `createContext()`, and their semantics are closely related to the name of the different sections of the inline accumulate functions, as shown in the following:

- `createContext`: This method is created the first time the accumulate function is being used. The purpose of this method is to create the context that is going to be used for this particular instance of the accumulate function. In our example, it is creating a new instance of our `Context` class.

- `init`: This method is also invoked the first time the accumulate function is used in a rule. The argument of this method is the context created in `createContext()`.

- `accumulate`: This is where the real accumulate logic happens. In our case, we are detecting whether current `Order` being processed is bigger than the one held by the context. If it is, the context is updated accordingly. This method corresponds to the action section of an inline accumulate function.

- `supportsReverse`: This method indicates whether this accumulate function supports the reverse operation. In our case, we don't support it (otherwise, we would need to keep the collection of all analyzed `Orders` in the context).

- `reverse`: This method contains the logic involved when a fact that had previously matched the pattern of the accumulate conditional element no longer does. In our case, given that we don't support the reverse operation, this method remains empty.

- `getResult`: This method returns the actual result of the accumulate function. In our case, the result is the `Order` instance contained in our context object.

- `getResultType`: This method tells Drools the result type of this accumulate function. In our case, the type is `Order.class`.

Before our custom `accumulate` function can be used in our rules, we need to import it in our knowledge package. A custom accumulate function can be imported into a DRL asset in the following way:

```
import accumulate org.drools.devguide.chapter05.acc.
BiggestOrderFunction biggestOrder
```

The import statement starts with the `import accumulate` keywords and what follows is the fully qualified name of the class, implementing the function. The last part of the import statement is the name that we want to give to this function in our DRL.

Once the function is imported, we can use it as any of the Drools built-in accumulate functions:

```
rule "Find Biggest Order"
when
    $bigO: Order() from accumulate (
        $o: Order(),
        biggestOrder($o)
    )
then
    biggestOrder.setObject($bigO);
end
```

Summary

In this chapter, we saw an overview of the different type of sessions that Drools supports and their advantages and disadvantages. Knowing the available type of sessions will allow us to take better decisions when implementing our solutions with Drools.

We also covered the common patterns of interactions between Drools and our applications. The way how global variables, channels, and queries can be used to extract or provide information to Drools was also explained in great detail. When and what is needed for getting information on what is going on inside Drools internals, we now know that we have a powerful mechanism in our hands by using event listeners.

The last part of this chapter focused on the different ways to enhance and customize the DRL language to create more readable and maintainable rules.

It is time now to move to another important topic in Drools that deals with temporal reasoning inside a Kie Session: Complex Event Processing.

6
Complex Event Processing

So far, we've seen how to use rules to make decisions based on a set of data (called facts). This information is pretty much any group of Java objects describing the state of the domain on which we're making the decisions, but it has always represented the state of the world at one particular point in time. In this chapter, we're going to see a set of concepts, configurations, and rule syntax components that will allow us to make decisions based on time relationships between facts. These concepts are often called **complex event processing** (CEP).

Drools provides support for this under the name of **Drools Fusion** or **Drools CEP**, a conceptual module fully integrated into the Drools core features. This is just a conceptual separation as all the CEP features are fully supported by the same modules that provide the rule engine functionality. To fully understand this, the chapter will cover the following topics:

- Discussing different concepts associated with complex event processing, including sliding windows, entry points, and time operations

- Fitting complex event processing into a special kind of architecture called event-driven architecture

- Writing rules and configuring the runtime to take full advantage of the Drools CEP features

What is complex event processing?

The main focus of CEP is to correlate small units of time-based data within an ever-changing, ever-growing data cloud in order to detect hard-to-find special situations and to do something for these cases. In order to fully understand how it works, we first need to define a few other concepts. Let's start by defining events.

What are events and complex events?

In order to understand events, let's first talk about a familiar concept. So far, we've dealt with facts that we insert into a Kie Session and how they can match a specific rule. Facts are very similar to events, except events have one extra feature: time of occurrence. Events are simply the data about any domain (represented as a Java object), along with the information about the time in which this information was true.

Pretty much anything that we record taking place at a specific time can be an event, as follows:

- A sale in our eShop has a time for the transaction
- A phone call has a starting time and ending time
- Any sort of sensor reading will tell you its specific reading (temperature, humidity, and movement) in relation to a specific moment in time

Events, by themselves, are the basic structure of event processing. Every input we have from the outside world can be perceived as an event. However, we're going to be mostly interested in detecting complex events.

A **complex event** is simply an aggregation, composition, or abstraction of other events. The real power of complex event processing comes from being able to correlate simple incoming events in such a way that we can detect complex situations, which cannot be detected by any device or individual directly, as shown in the following:

- All the transactions that we have at a specific moment can be correlated to detect any possible fraud attempts (and take preemptive measures against it)
- At a call center, all the incoming calls, grouped by specific areas, can determine a massive outage of service at these areas to automatically notify the users of the case

Even sensor readings, combined on a large scale, can detect complex situations by just combining simpler events. Let's consider a set of sensor readings all over the city as our input events. A group of seismic events can tell us where an earthquake is happening in the city and its intensity. A set of fire alarms can tell us where in the city there is a fire.

In case of a large earthquake, combined with the information of the city infrastructure, we can infer the possible structural collapses and send experts to evaluate the current situation. If we have fire alarms going off, we can send the fire brigade to put the fire out.

If we find a set of small earthquakes, one after another and at the interval of one second, in the same direction, we might infer that something very large is moving in that general direction. If we also detect fires, one after the other in the same direction, we might aggregate all the seismic and fire-alarm events into a complex event, maybe Godzilla is moving in this direction, as shown in the following image:

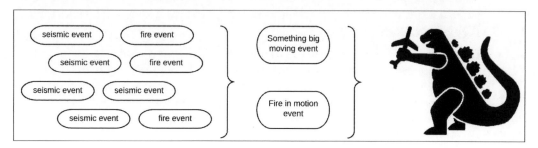

If that's the case, we might not want to send architects and fire brigades in that general direction (they will most likely be eaten). Instead, we might take a different action, such as sending the military. As you can see, very small simple events can correlate time wise for us to be able to infer a lot more information from them. This is the main power of complex event processing.

Declaring CEP-based Rules

Previously, we've discussed how rules should attempt to be atomic and work together to achieve management of complex scenarios. This is very well aligned with CEP as each different rule can deal with one aspect of the aggregation, composition, or abstraction of other events. They can work together to achieve real-time resolution of very complex event situations. We will still need a few added features of Drools to be able to do so, as follows:

- How to instruct Drools that an object is to be treated as an event
- How to compare two events in time

In the next subsections, we will see how to achieve this using the DRL syntax.

Semantics of events

Before we get into the detail about how to define an event, we need to understand a few characteristics of the events. The first characteristic marks a difference between two main types of events—punctual and interval events—as shown in the following:

- **Punctual events**: They are the events that occurred at a specific instance in time. They may represent the exact moment when a change in the reality of our domain model appeared, or they may have a lifespan that is too short to be considered. An example of punctual events is sensor readings, which will associate a specific value from the sensor with a specific time of the reading. Transactions can also be considered punctual events if they are so short lived that we can ignore their duration.

- **Interval events**: They are events that have two distinctive moments in time: the moment they started and the moment they ended. This makes the interval events a bit more complex to compare than the punctual events; if you have two punctual events, you can only compare whether they happened at the same time, before, or after each other. For interval events on the other hand, you might compare cases where one event started and ended during another one, just to name a scenario.

Also, regardless of being punctual or interval events, they share a set of conceptual characteristics worth mentioning before we look into the code:

- **They are usually immutable**: Events are supposed to be a record of the state of our domain model at a particular moment in time. You cannot change the past, therefore, you shouldn't have to change your event information. The engine doesn't force this feature, but it is something to keep in mind when designing our events. They might be decorated by adding extra information to them, but you shouldn't have to modify their internal data with which they were inserted in the Kie Session.

- **They have a managed lifecycle**: As the engine understands all the events as mere objects with a time relation, the Kie Session can determine, based on the rules defined in it, when an event will no longer trigger the rules (as it is too old for the relations considered in these rules) and can automatically delete it from a session.

Declaring time-based-events in Drools

The first thing we'll need to do in order to create the CEP rules is to specify the type of objects that need to be treated as events to the engine. That is, the objects that should have the time metadata. This will allow the Kie Session to apply temporal reasoning to these types. There are a few ways to define that a specific type should be treated as an event, but they all define the same set of metadata. The properties to be defined are as shown in the following:

- **Role of the type**: This is the only mandatory piece of metadata used to define a type as an event. It will have two specific types: fact and event.

- **Timestamp**: This is an optional property to define the attribute of the type that will define the moment when the event took place. If not present, the timestamp of each event instance will be the moment it was inserted in the Kie Session.

- **Duration**: This is an optional property to define the attribute of the type that will specify the duration of the event. If not present, the event will be treated as a punctual event. This property is required for interval events.

- **Expires**: This is an optional character string to determine how long this type of event should be present in the Kie Session before automatic deletion.

Now that we understand the properties, let's see the different ways to apply them to our types. This metadata can be directly defined as class-level annotations in our Java beans, as follows:

```
@org.kie.api.definition.type.Role(Role.Type.EVENT)
@org.kie.api.definition.type.Duration("durationAttr")
@org.kie.api.definition.type.Timestamp("executionTime")
@org.kie.api.definition.type.Expires("2h30m")
public class TransactionEvent implements Serializable {
    private Date executionTime;
    private Long durationAttr;
    /* class content skipped */
}
```

As you can see in the previous code section, we can define the annotations for the role, duration, timestamp, and expiration properties of an event type. Duration should identify an attribute of the `Long` type and Timestamp should identify an attribute of the `Date` type. This way, the Kie Session will be able to understand the inserted objects of said type as events.

Another way to define these properties is in the declared types. Similar annotations can be used to define a declared type as an event, as follows:

```
declare PhoneCallEvent
    @role(event)
```

```
        @timestamp(whenDidWeReceiveTheCall)
        @duration(howLongWasTheCall)
        @expires(2h30m)
        whenDidWeReceiveTheCall: Date
        howLongWasTheCall: Long
        callInfo: String
    end
```

The previous code section shows that we can create our own declared type and annotate it accordingly in order to make it an event.

Another way to declare the events is to grab an existing class and declare it as an event inside the DRL. This is very common when events are created to be shared between different applications and we cannot directly modify them in order to have the annotations on the Java bean. We can do something as shown in the following code section to declare the existing Java beans as events:

```
    import path.to.my.shared.ExternalEvent;
    ...
    declare ExternalEvent
        @role(event)
    end
```

Just as the previous code section shows, we can redeclare this non-annotated Java bean inside the DRL to be treated as an event. As previously stated, all the annotations are optional. The only necessary annotation to treat the declared type as an event type is to have the `@role(event)` annotation. You can see the examples of events like these in the `chapter-06/chapter-06-events` project of the code bundle.

Now that we've seen how to declare our event types, we need to start seeing how to compare them. To do so, we will review the existing temporal operators.

Temporal operators

Once we define our event types, we need a way to compare the events based on their timestamp. To do so, there are 13 temporal operators that we can use in Drools. Some of these operators only make sense for comparing interval events, but given two events, they can compare them as the following code snippet shows:

```
    declare MyEvent
        @role(event)
        @timestamp(executionTime)
    End
    rule "my first time operators example"
    when
        $e1: MyEvent()
```

```
    $e2: MyEvent(this after[5m] $e1)
Then
    System.out.println("We have two events" +
        " 5 minutes apart");
end
```

In the previous example, we make use of the `after` operator to determine whether an event is at least five minutes newer than another event. As you can see, the comparison is done on the specific event instances. Internally, the time comparison will happen against the timestamp attribute called `executionTime`, but we can disregard that fact when dealing with events. This provides an advantage if we need to modify the timestamp nature of an event type in the future as we don't have to change the CEP rules where it is used.

Also, we can notice the use of a parameter in the operator, passed inside the square brackets. Each temporal operator will be prepared to receive between zero and four parameters to make use of the operator in a more specific way. In the previous scenario, we pass a `5m` parameter to specify that an event should be at least five minutes after the other.

There are many temporal operators with which we can work. Here's a list of them and what they mean:

The previous diagram shows the different temporal operators and how they will compare between different events. They all share certain qualities, as shown in the following:

- They operate against two events. They are prepared to compare two events against each other.

- They can also be used to compare the Date objects as dates are, by definition, the most minimalistic representation of an event (only the temporal information without any extra data).

- They can receive parameters to specify their internal work. The operation of these parameters is thoroughly explained at the product documentation at https://docs.jboss.org/drools/release/latest/drools-docs/html/ under the Temporal Operators title.

One more thing worth mentioning about events is that they are still facts too. The engine will add the temporal features to the event types, but we can still compare any of their internal attributes and methods to create conditions and constraints on the rules, like we have done in the previous chapters.

In order to get familiar with a CEP rule, let's analyze one of the rules that we can find in the chapter-06/chapter-06-rules project of the code bundle and aim to detect fraud attempts, as follows:

```
rule "More than 10 transactions in an hour from one client"
    when
        $t1: TransactionEvent($cId: customerId)
        Number(intValue >= 10) from accumulate(
            $t2: TransactionEvent(this != $t1,
                        customerId == $cId, this meets[1h] $t1),
            count($t2) )
        not (SuspiciousCustomerEvent(customerId == $cId,
                reason == "Many transactions"))
    then
        insert(new SuspiciousCustomerEvent($cId,
                "Many transactions"));
    end
```

This example DRL file can be found at chapter-06-rules/src/main/resources/chapter06/cep/cep-rules.drl. In order to run this example, we start with our previously defined TransactionEvent event type. We will check two main things in our rule: whether we have 10 transactions from the same customer within an hour, and that we still don't have a complex event to reflect this situation.

The first condition is written inside an accumulate. We count the number of TransactionEvent objects we have that contain the same customer ID and we also check whether they happened within an hour of the original reference transaction using this meets [1h] $t1.

The consequence of this rule is not a particular action against the outside. Instead, we just detect a complex event called SuspiciousCustomerEvent (a declared type in our example). This will represent an aggregation of our transaction events.

The second condition is a simple not clause, where we just check whether we haven't already fired this rule for the specific customer by checking the SuspiciousCustomerEvent object, which we need to add in the consequence if in case it hasn't been already added.

This rule will only detect the situation as that's the smallest responsibility we can break it down to. We could do a lot with suspicious customers, but this rule only has the responsibility of understanding a specific situation where a customer acts suspiciously. We need to remember to always keep our rules as atomic as possible. Other rules might detect a suspicious activity from a customer by other means.

Once the suspicious customer is detected, another rule can take care of deciding what to do when we detect a few suspicious customer events. For that case, we will create a different rule:

```
rule "More than 3 suspicious cases: warn the owner"
  when
    SuspiciousCustomerEvent($cId: customerId)
    not (AlarmTriggered(customerId == $cId))
    Number(intValue >= 2) from accumulate(
      $s: SuspiciousCustomerEvent(customerId==$cId),
      count($s)
    )
  then //warn the owner
    System.out.println("WARNING: Suspicious fraud" +
            " case. Client " + $cId);
    insert(new AlarmTriggered($cId));
end
```

As we previously stated, we can have multiple rules detecting suspicious customer activities. This rule will trigger when two or more of these rules get triggered for the same customer. Once this happens, we send a warning to the owner. In this example, it is represented as a system output for simplicity, but it could just as easily be a helper method or global variable method programmed to send an e-mail or SMS.

As we can see from the previous examples, we can break down our complex event processing cases into multiple rules, each one connected to the rest of the CEP scenario by the events it consumes or produces. These aggregations of events lead to a special kind of architecture for our systems, where events and their relation with isolated application components allow us to create very decoupled, highly extensible components. This architecture is known as event driven architecture, and we'll describe it in the next subsection.

Event-driven architecture

Event-driven architecture is a concept that is very easy to bond to the CEP as it defines a simple architecture to promote the production, detection, consumption, and reaction to the events. The concept of this architecture is to focus on application components as one of the four possible elements, related as shown in the following diagram:

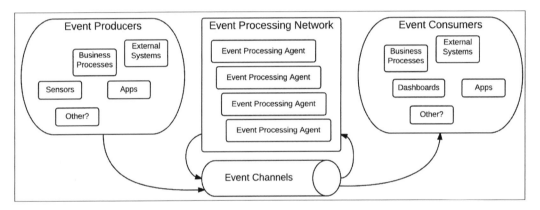

The idea of **event-driven architecture (EDA)** is to classify the components in the following four different categories:

- **Event Producer**: Their role in EDA is solely to be creators of events. Everything that can produce an event is considered a producer, whether it is a hardware-based sensor, application-gathering requests, business processes, or any other form of application that can introduce a new event into our architecture.

- **Event Consumer**: Their role in EDA is to listen to the events produced by other components. They can also range from a wide variety of components, from simple listeners in apps to complex dashboards. They usually represent the final output of this architecture and point the produced value to the outside world.

- **Event Channels**: They are communication protocols between all the other components. Event channels encapsulate any component used to transmit events from one component to another, from a physical wire transmitting a sensor reading to a logical component, such as a **Java Message Service (JMS)** queue.

- **Event Processing Agents**: These are the core components that group the events to detect and process complex events. In Drools, every rule that deals with CEP would be considered an event processing agent. The grouping for them to detect and react to more complex situations is called the **event processing network**.

This architecture is a very useful concept when designing a system around complex event processing. It can easily be integrated into any other type of architecture as it is only concerned about how events interconnect the components, leaving room for all sorts of other features.

Most applications that start using CEP need to consider, at some point in their design, a concept similar to the one proposed by EDA, where multiple event producers are connected to a network of event processing agents (our CEP rules) and produce data to multiple event consumers. Drools provides this concept of source pluralism through a component called entry points, which we'll discuss in the next subsection.

Split event sources with entry points

Entry points are provided in Drools as a way to partition the working memory. Each Kie Session can have multiple entry points that it can use to determine the source of incoming data. For complex event processing, entry points are a great way of defining multiple sources for events.

In order to insert objects of any kind into an entry point, all we need to do is use the following API:

```
KieSession ksession = …; //kie session initialization
    ksession.getEntryPoint("some entry point").
        insert(new Object());
```

The previous code section will only work if we have declared an entry point in our DRL file with the name **some entry point**; otherwise, it will throw an exception. Declaring and using an entry point is something that can occur directly in any rule. They can be used within the condition or consequence of a rule, as shown in the following example:

```
rule "Routing transactions from small resellers"
    when
        t: TransactionEvent() from
            entry-point "small resellers"
```

```
    then
        entryPoints["Stream Y"].insert(t);
end
```

In the previous rule, we're filtering the `TransactionEvent` objects that came from the `small resellers` entry point. Then, in the consequence, we will insert each one of these matching events into another entry point, called `Stream Y`. As you can see, we can create as many entry points as needed to split the sources of our information.

Events inserted in one entry point will never lose a reference to it. This means that the Kie session will treat different entry points as a completely different group of events. You will need to specify, in your rules, from which entry point you want to filter the data and to which entry point you want to modify the data. However, you can cross reference information from multiple entry points in a single rule and also between entry points and the regular working memory.

You can see an example of rules working on different entry points in the `CEPEntryPointsTest` class, in the `chapter-06-tests` project of the code bundle. In the example, we use two entry points to separate the incoming transactions from big and small clients. Each one will have a different amount of transactions that they would consider suspicious, therefore, each one handles the case with a different rule.

Sliding windows

Another very useful concept among Drools CEP features is the use of sliding windows. As events have a timestamp associated, they also have an intrinsic order. We can filter the events coming directly from the working memory or any entry point by this particular order. We have two types of sliding windows, as follows:

- Length-based sliding windows
- Time-based sliding windows

Length-based sliding windows

The simplest type of sliding window is the length-based sliding window. You use it to specify the last N elements inserted into a stream. Every time a new event is added into the stream, the last element of the window is replaced by a new one. Using a length-based sliding window is easy. The following rule shows a simple way to declare a sliding window to get the last six events of the `TransactionEvent` type from the working memory:

```
rule "last 6 transactions are more than 100 dollars"
    when
```

```
Number(doubleValue > 100.00) from accumulate(
    TransactionEvent($amount: totalAmount)
    over window:length(6),
    sum($amount)
)
then
    //... TBD
end
```

In the previous rule, we will sum up all the amounts of the last six transactions and trigger the rule if this amount is over 100 dollars. To get the last six transactions, we are using a sliding window.

If there are six or less elements in the working memory of the TransactionEvent type, the window will have all the elements. The moment we add the seventh TransactionEvent object, we will only have the last six returned by this sliding window. This is why it is called sliding window. You will see only a specific group of events and every time you add a new one, the window will move to see the last elements that fit the condition.

Time-based sliding windows

A similar window can be created that will return any elements that happened within a specific time lapse from now. This is done through a time-based sliding window. Let's take a look at the following example of this case:

```
rule "obtain last five hours of operations"
    when
        $n: Number() from accumulate(
            TransactionEvent($a: totalAmount)
            over window:time(5h),sum($a)
        )
    Then
        System.out.println("total = " + $n);
end
```

In the previous example, we will have a transaction added between now and five hours ago. If a transaction took place five hours and one second ago, it will no longer be active here. It doesn't matter if we had one transaction or five hundred transactions during this time, the time window will contain all of them.

 Note that this window will slide following an internal clock of the Kie Session, which we will see how to configure in the *Testing with the session clock* section later in this chapter.

Declared sliding windows

Sliding windows are usually defined within the rule that uses them. This is a very common practice as it was originally the only way to use sliding windows. Nevertheless, this caused the rules that needed to filter elements from the same window to have to redefine it in every rule. If we define our sliding windows like this and later need to change the nature of the window that we use, for example, to transform a length-based sliding window to a time-based sliding window, we would have to edit every rule that uses it. To avoid doing this, there is a feature in Drools called window declaration.

Window declaration allows you to define a window as a pre-established component and invoke it through any number of rules by name. This allows the changes in the declared window that should be shared among multiple rules to be done in a single place. The syntax is as follows:

```
declare window Beats
    @doc("last 10 seconds heart beats")
    HeartBeat() over window:time( 10s )
    from entry-point "heart beat monitor"
end
```

Rules can then use the declared window by referencing the name, as shown in the following example:

```
rule "beats in the window"
    when
    accumulate(
      HeartBeat() from window Beats,
      $cnt : count(1)
    )
  then
    // there has been $cnt beats over the last 10s
end
```

As you can see, the window declaration allows simple reuse of windows and even declares initial common filters for a particular entry point. This can be used to avoid rewriting many rules that might share a logically identical sliding window.

Running CEP-based Scenarios

Now that we've seen the main components of CEP rules, we need to start paying attention to some configuration steps required to run the CEP scenarios successfully in Drools. Both the Kie Base and Session that run the CEP cases need special management and we will see in the next subsections, as follows:

- How to configure the Kie Base to support complex event processing
- The difference between continuous and discrete rule execution
- How the Kie Session internal clock works to evaluate temporal events

Stream processing configuration

In order to create a CEP Drools runtime, we need to provide a few extra configurations from the default initialization. The first one we need to add is the event processing mode of the Kie Base that we'll use.

The event processing mode will determine the manner in which the new data inserted into the runtime will be processed. The default event processing mode is called the CLOUD mode and basically treats any incoming data the same way, regardless of being events or simple facts. This means that the runtime will not understand the concept of events, so that we cannot use it for CEP.

We will need to configure our Kie Base to use the STREAM event processing mode. This configuration will inform the runtime that it should manage events and keep them internally ordered by their timestamp. Due to this ordering, we are able to run time operations against events and use sliding windows on them.

There are many ways to configure the STREAM event processing mode in a Kie Base. The simplest one is to do it directly in the `kmodule.xml` as an attribute of the `kbase` tag:

```
<kbase name="cepKbase" eventProcessingMode="stream"
    packages="chapter06.cep">
    <ksession name="cepKsession"/>
</kbase>
```

In this way, we can later on use the Kie Base or Kie Session directly from the corresponding Kie Container and the configuration for its runtime will be using the STREAM event processing mode. We can see an example of this configuration in the `chapter-06/chapter-06-rules/src/main/resources/META-INF/kmodule.xml` file.

Another way to configure this event processing mode is programmatically. To do so, we will make use of a `KieBaseConfiguration` bean and its `setOption` method, as follows:

```
KieServices ks = KieServices.Factory.get();
    KieContainer kc = ks.getKieClasspathContainer();
    KieBaseConfiguration kbconf = ks.
        newKieBaseConfiguration();
    kbconf.setOption(EventProcessingOption.STREAM);
    KieBase kbase = kc.newKieBase(kbconf, null);
```

In the previous example, we used the Kie classpath container for simplicity, but we could be using any Kie Container to create the Kie Base. It is very useful when defining dynamic knowledge modules.

Once we define a Kie Base with the STREAM processing mode, we will need to understand the different options that we will have to run a KIE Session and manage our CEP scenarios.

Continuous versus Discrete rule firing

The first thing we'll need to understand when running our CEP rules is whether or not we need to run them in a continuous or discrete fashion. The main difference between the two is as follows:

- Discrete rule firing will fire rules at specific points in time. Our application will add events and facts to the Kie Session, and at a specific point, it will use the `fireAllRules` method to fire any rules that matched with the working memory at that specific moment.

- Continuous rule firing will have a specific thread dedicated to firing the rules the very moment some data matches a rule. It will use the `fireUntilHalt` method of the Kie Session to do so, while one or more other threads will be inserting events and facts into the Kie Session.

These two ways of firing rules will depend entirely on our case and the situations that might trigger a rule. If we have a scenario where the absence of events will trigger a rule, or to put it in other words, the absence of events could be abstracted into another event, then you should use continuous rule firing. If, on the other hand, the only thing that could trigger new rules is the insertion of new events into the Kie Session, then discrete rule firing will be enough for our case.

Let's discuss a couple of examples to understand these two scenarios.

First, let's discuss a common case for discrete rule firing: fraud detection. Most fraud detection systems will work based on the cumulative information from transactions. Basically, if we have a specific number of transactions with specific parameters, we might consider the possibility of fraud. In this type of scenario, the only way we would trigger a rule is if we insert a new transaction to match the conditions of our rules. For this case, we can just call `fireAllRules` after every transaction or transaction batch is inserted in our Kie Session. No rules will need to fire if they don't do it immediately after adding the latest data.

In a different scenario, let's imagine that a heart monitor is sending events to our CEP engine. About once every second, we get a heart beat event from an oscilloscope. If we get events too close in time or at an irregular pace, we might detect a stroke or arrhythmia complex events. What would happen if we wanted to detect whether the heart stops beating? This case would be a cardiac arrest event. If we want to detect it, our system will need the ability to fire rules when no events are being inserted. This type of scenario is typical of a continuous rule firing case.

Testing with the session clock

One more useful configuration when creating Kie Sessions to run CEP-based scenarios is the possibility to configure its internal clock. By default, Kie Sessions will understand the passing of time using the clock of the machine on which it is running. However, this is just one of the two available configurations, called runtime clock. The other configuration allows us to define a clock controlled by the application, called pseudo clock.

Both runtime and pseudo session clocks only move in one direction (forward in time). However, the pseudo clock will only do so if you call a specific method on it, called `advanceTime`. Here's a small example of how you can use the pseudo clock from inside the Kie Session:

```
SessionPseudoClock clock = ksession.
    getSessionClock();
clock.advanceTime(2, TimeUnit.HOURS);
clock.advanceTime(5, TimeUnit.MINUTES);
```

In the previous example, we told the clock to advance two hours and five minutes. These two calls will take only milliseconds, which make this clock an excellent option for testing CEP scenarios. If you had to check the case where two events with default timestamps (the moment they are inserted in the Kie Session) happen apart from each other by two hours, the pseudo clock would let you run this case almost immediately, while the runtime clock would need at least two hours to run.

In order to use the pseudo clock in our Kie Session, we need to provide a specific configuration for it through the `kmodule.xml` file:

```
<kbase name="cepKbase" eventProcessingMode="stream"
    packages="chapter06.cep">
    <ksession name="cepKsession" clockType="pseudo"/>
</kbase>
```

We can even use it through a `KieSessionConfiguration` bean:

```
KieServices ks = KieServices.Factory.get();
KieContainer kc = ks.getKieClasspathContainer();
KieSessionConfiguration ksconf = ks.
    newKieSessionConfiguration();
ksconf.setOption(ClockTypeOption.get(
    ClockType.PSEUDO_CLOCK.getId()));
KieSession ksession = kc.newKieSession(ksconf);
```

You can see an example of this code running in the `chapter-06-tests` project of the code bundle.

Even if the most common use for the pseudo clock is to test, another case where it is commonly used is, oddly, distributed production environments. The reason for this is that, for large environments where CEP scenarios might be executed in multiple servers, the pseudo clock is usually used to easily synchronize the clocks of all the sessions in different servers. An extra thread or server can have the responsibility of invoking a ticking mechanism in each server at almost the same time and each server with a Kie Session can advance the time to make sure that they all are operating at almost the same clock values. This is usually simpler than having all the internal clocks of multiple servers synchronized, which is a requirement when rules are in charge of real-time decisions.

Drools CEP limitations

Drools CEP features are really powerful and are as quick to resolve decisions as any other type of Drools-based rules. However, it has a few architectural elements that we need to be aware of in order to make the most of it.

First of all, all Kie Sessions operate in memory. This means that all events living inside a Kie Session have to be in memory while they are still relevant to at least one rule in its Kie Base. This can be overcome by the `@expires` annotation of an event type, but it will still require to plan ahead for the amount of memory required to define a Drools CEP service. One quick way of determining how much memory a server will need to run a Drools CEP scenario is as follows:

- Determine how long each event instance should be present in the Kie Session (because it might still be used in triggering a rule). Let's call this value A.

- Determine how many events can be received in a specific period of time. Let's call this value B.

- Determine how big an event instance is (using any Java profiler tool such as JProfiler available at `https://www.ej-technologies.com/download/jprofiler/files`). Let's call this value C.

A times B times C equals X, a very rough estimate of the minimal amount of memory required by the Kie Session only to keep the reference of all live events. We'll need to be careful though as we're still not considering the memory consumption of storing interrelations between events provoked by rule conditions and the Beta network. We'll discuss these topics in more detail in *Chapter 9, Introduction to PHREAK*.

Another limitation to take into account involves the possibility of storing the Kie Session in any persistence mechanism (something that we will discuss in *Chapter 10, Integrating Rules and Processes*). The KIE Session is usually persisted when something changes in its internal representation, whether it is the working memory or its matching agenda. For the case of a regular CEP scenario, this might mean storing all the working memory data every time a rule fires or a new event is inserted. Doing so with a CEP-based KIE Session could mean as much as gigabytes of data being stored multiple times per second. Therefore, other mechanisms for replicating a Kie Session in another system are required.

Currently, the only methods available for replicating a CEP-based Kie Session involve replicating small deltas between Kie sessions (as to not have to replicate the whole working memory) and coordination strategies for firing the rules (so that only one of the replicated Kie Sessions actually fires the rules for the replicated matching data). These are custom mechanisms and each user should implement their own at their own risk, therefore, the suggested alternative is to break down the CEP scenarios by domain and have different servers handle only a subgroup of cases.

To do so, usually the first step is to filter the events by type or specific components in its data and forward it to the specific Kie Sessions that take care of managing a specific scenario at a time.

To name an example, all the fraud detection cases from small providers are handled in a server and fraud detection for two large providers could be done in two dedicated servers. Even the filtering could be a Kie Stateless session, created to redirect each event to its corresponding Kie Stateful session, as shown in the following diagram:

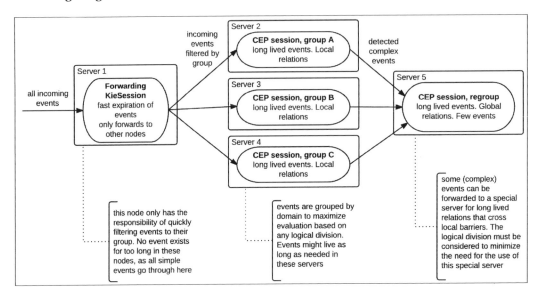

In this way, an increase in the event throughput can be achieved within a Drools CEP Session and handled (at least to some extent) by adding additional servers.

Summary

In this chapter, we've learned about complex event processing and its relation to Drools. CEP can provide a lot of value to make complex decisions on a large number of events for the same reasons Drools is a great tool for making fast reliable decisions. We've seen the use of time and length-based sliding windows, temporal operators, and entry points.

We've also seen how to declare our events from new classes, declared types, and existing types. We've covered a few examples of rules for fraud detection cases and how they align with CEP principles. Among these principles, we've also briefly discussed event-driven architecture, a very useful design for applications that need to focus on CEP solutions.

In the next chapter, we will start looking into defining our rules in more user-friendly ways by studying how to define rules in natural language and decision tables.

7
Human-Readable Rules

The title of this chapter could be offensive to some developers. Aren't all the rules we have covered so far human-readable? Aren't we humans? The idea behind this chapter is to introduce other ways to define rules in Drools that are more user-friendly. In this chapter, "human" means a non-technical person.

So far, we have covered a single way to define rules and knowledge: the DRL language. This language—even if powerful—is inappropriate, most of the time, for users without a technical background. And even then, DRL requires a certain amount of time to become familiar with it. Drools provides other means of knowledge creation by supporting different abstractions over DRL that make the language simpler.

Having a simpler and more concrete language provides us with a great advantage: we can include **Subject Matter Experts (SME)** in the development cycle. Business requirements no longer have to be translated into technical artifacts (such as classes, rules, and so on) by the developers. The people writing these artifacts can be the people who have business expertise. This is one step towards to the holy grail of business rule engines: business rules written by business people.

This chapter will cover some of the abstractions that Drools provides over DRL, and some other ways in which we can generate DRL from various resource types. The topics included in this chapter are:

- How to define and use a Domain-Specific Language (DSL) in Drools
- How to define rules using spreadsheets
- How to use templates to generate DRL from structured data
- An introduction on how to use PMML (Predictive Model Markup Language) in Drools

Domain Specific Languages

The first abstraction over DRL that we are going to cover is Domain Specific Languages, or simply DSL. DSL is a great way to tailor DRL for a specific context. In the previous six chapters, we covered all the concepts required to create rules and execute rules in Drools. These concepts require a certain amount of knowledge. For the left-hand side of a rule, we need to understand the DRL syntax and to have an idea of things such as pattern matching, the internal structure of our model, invocation to external systems, and so on. For the right-hand side, we need to know Java and some of the automatic variables present in this context, such as **kcontext** and **drools**. Having to master all this knowledge in order to write a business rule seems like overkill, and indeed it is. One of the ways to fill the gap between the technical requirements from DRL and the SMEs is by using a DSL.

The concept behind a Drools DSL is simple: to create a dictionary file containing business-oriented concepts and their translations to DRL. The SME then only has to know about the business-oriented concepts when writing rules without worrying about the technical aspects of DRL.

The dictionary file that defines the translation between business concepts and DRL is simply called DSL in Drools. A file containing rules defined using business concepts is called DSLR. While the technical team is in charge of the creation and maintenance of the dictionary file (DSL), the SME is in charge of the creation and maintenance of the business rules (DSLR).

DSL is supported out of the box by Drools; there are no special dependencies, and no configuration is required before we can start using it.

The Dictionary file

The Dictionary file (or DSL) is a text file (with a `.dsl` extension) that contains DSL entries. Each line of this file starting with an opening bracket "[" is considered a DSL entry. Lines starting with hash character # are considered comments. Lines starting with something other than an opening bracket or a hash symbol are considered to be part of the previous DSL entry. The format of a DSL entry is as follows:

```
[<scope>][<type definition>]<dsl expression>=<replacement text>
```

The `<scope>` section currently supports four different types:

- `[when]` or `[condition]`: This DSL entry can only be used in the left-hand side of a rule

- `[then]` or `[consequence]`: This DSL entry is only valid for the action part of a rule

- [*]: This DSL entry is valid in both the condition and action part of a rule
- [keyword]: This DSL entry is valid in any part of a DSLR file, even outside a rule definition

The <type definition> section is not mandatory (we can either omit it or use empty brackets []) and it is used as a hint for editors such as KIE-Workbench.

After the <type definition> comes the <dsl expression>. This is the text that will be matched and replaced in the DSLR file. A <dsl expression> consists of a Java regular expression (https://docs.oracle.com/javase/8/docs/api/java/util/regex/Pattern.html) and any number of embedded variable definitions. A variable definition is enclosed in braces ("{" and "}") and it consists in a variable name and two optional sections separated by a colon ":". If only one optional section is present, it is used as a regular expression to match text that will be assigned to the variable; if the two optional sections are present, the first one is used as a hint for an editor (such as the KIE-Workbench) and the second one is the regular expression. A <dsl expression> always ends with an equal sign (=).

What follows after the equals sign is the <replacement text> that will be used to replace any part of the DSLR file matching the <dsl expression>. Variables defined in the <dsl expression> section can be used in this section, just like named regular expression matching groups, by using the name of the variable enclosed in braces. Optionally, the variable name may be followed by an exclamation point "!" and a transformation function. The supported transformation functions are detailed in the following table.

Name	Description
uc	Converts all letters to upper case.
lc	Converts all letters to lower case.
ucfirst	Converts the first letter to upper case, and all other letters to lower case.
num	Extracts all digits and - from the string. If the last two digits in the original string are preceded by (.) or (,) a decimal period is inserted in the corresponding position.
a?b/c	Compares the string with string a, and if they are equal, replaces it with b, otherwise with c. But c can be another triplet a, b, c, so that the entire structure is, in fact, a translation table.

A typical (and very simplistic) DSL entry might look like the following:

```
[when]There is a Customer=Customer()
```

The previous entry is defining a DSL entry that will replace any occurrence of the text There is a Customer inside a DSLR file with the corresponding DRL Customer().

Adding constraints to patterns

A common requirement when creating a domain-specific language is to have the ability to add an arbitrary number of constraints to a pattern. For example, we may want to be able to express filters, such as `a customer with age greater than 40`, `a customer with GOLD category`, and even combined expressions such as `a customer in the GOLD category and older than 40 years`. Having an individual DSL entry for each possible combination of constraints in our model makes no sense at all. Drools allows us to specify individual constraints for a pattern in DSL and to combine them in any way we want in the DSLR file. This magic is done by appending a hyphen sign "-" to the `<dsl expression>` section of a DSL entry:

```
[when]There is a Customer=Customer()
[when]- age greater than {years:\d*} years=age > {years}
[when]- category is {category:\w*}=category == Customer.Category.
{category}
```

The previous DSL definition allows us to create a rule such as the following in DSLR:

```
rule "A GOLD Customer older than 31 years"
when
    There is a Customer
        - age greater than 31 years
        - category is GOLD
then
    ...
end
```

When a hyphen-prefixed `<dsl expression>` is processed, its result is not added as a new line in the generated DRL, but instead it is added to the last pattern line preceding it as a constraint. The previous DSLR code will then be translated into the following DRL:

```
rule "A GOLD Customer older than 31 years"
when
    Customer(age > 31, category == Customer.Category.GOLD)
then
    ...
end
```

When multiple constraints are present for a single pattern, they are always appended using a comma (,). This means that constraints are always ANDed in DSL.

Hyphens can also be used for DSL entries, which are defined inside the [then] context. In this case, the entry is assumed to be part of a modify statement and its content is added to the previous line (this must be a valid modify statement):

```
[when]There is a Customer=$c: Customer()
[when]- age greater than {years:\d*} years=age > {years}
[then]Update Customer=modify($c)\{\}
[then]- set Category to {category:\w*}= setCategory(Customer.Category.
{category})
```

Using the previous DSL, we can write the following rule in DSLR:

```
rule "Mark Customers older than 31 years as BRONZE"
when
    There is a Customer
        - age greater than 31 years
then
    Update Customer
        - set Category to BRONZE
end
```

The resulting DRL from the following example will be:

```
rule "Mark Customers older than 31 years as BRONZE"
when
    $c: Customer(age > 31)
then
    modify ($c) { setCategory(Customer.Category.BRONZE) }
end
```

Rules files

A rules file, also referred to as a DSLR file, is a text file with a .dslr extension. DSLR files define Drools rules using a domain-specific language. Previous versions of Drools required the DSLR file to specify which DSL had to be used to process it. This is no longer the case in the current version of Drools; all DSL files included in a KIE Base are going to be used to process any DSLR file also found in that same KIE Base.

The translation of a DSLR file into DRL follows these steps:

1. Each of the [keyword] entries is applied to the entire DSLR. If the [keyword] contains variables, these variables are captured and replaced by the corresponding value.

2. The left-hand side and right-hand side of all the rules present in the DSLR are processed. Each of the lines in the DSLR text is matched against each individual DSL entry in the order in which they are defined in the DSL file. This means that the order of the entries in a DSL file matters. When a match is found, the DSLR text is replaced by the corresponding DRL. If the DSL entry defines any variable, its value is taken from the DSLR and copied into the generated text.

3. If a DSLR line is written with a leading hyphen, the expanded result is added to the previously expanded pattern—if the context is [when]—or to the previously expanded **modify** statement, if the context is [then].

A detailed explanation of the translation process can be found in Drools' documentation: `http://docs.jboss.org/drools/release/6.3.0.Final/drools-docs/html/ch08.html#d0e11300`.

By default, plain DRL or Java syntax is not allowed in a DSLR file. However, there is a mechanism to mix DRL and Java sentences along with DSL inside a DSLR file for experienced users. Any line in a DSLR resource starting with a greater than sign > will be skipped by the translator and will remain unmodified in the final DRL resource. This facility provides the means to overcome some limitations of DSL.

DSL troubleshooting

One of the most difficult aspects of working with DSL/DSLR is understanding and fixing errors. The fundamental issue is that errors are reported based on the generated DRL, and will not refer to the high-level DSLR statements used to create the DRL.

There are some methods we can use though to make the detection and correction of errors easier.

The first handy feature we have resides in the DSL itself. Using a special type of comment starting with # we can make Drools log certain information regarding the DSL translation process. This special comment could contain the following keywords that will enable specific features of the DSL debug capabilities:

Keyword	Description
result	Prints the resulting DRL text, with line numbers.
steps	Prints each expansion step of condition and consequence lines.
keyword	Dumps the internal representation of all DSL entries with scope "keyword".
when	Dumps the internal representation of all DSL entries with scope "when" or "*".
then	Dumps the internal representation of all DSL entries with scope "then" or "*".
usage	Displays a usage statistic of all DSL entries.

As an example, we could add the following line to one of the DSL examples in the source bundle:

```
#/ debug display result, steps and  usage
```

By adding this line, Drools will log some statistics regarding the usage of each DSL sentence (`usage`), the conversion steps involved in each DSLR sentence (`steps`), and the final DRL (`result`).

 Drools will use SLF4j to log the output of the debugging options in DSL. Make sure you have a proper logger configured for the `org.drools` package.

There is another way we can use to generate DRL from DSL/DSLR for debugging purposes, and it involves the internal classes that Drools' compiler uses for this task: `org.drools.compiler.compiler.DrlParser`, and `org.drools.compiler.lang. dsl.DefaultExpanderResolver`. Using a combination of these two classes we can convert DSL and DSLR resources into DRL to analyze what the final result looks like. The following lines will convert some DSL and DSLR resources into plain DRL:

```
String dslContent = //Get the DSL content from somewhere
String dslrContent = //Get the DSLR content from somewhere
DrlParser parser = new DrlParser();
DefaultExpanderResolver resolver = new DefaultExpanderResolver(new
StringReader(dslContent));
String drl = parser.getExpandedDRL( dslrContent, resolver);
```

After this code gets executed, the `drl` String will contain the expanded DRL code.

Let's now move to a concrete scenario showing all the topics introduced so far.

A simple scenario

Let's now put it all together in a simple example. Going back to our e-shop, let's assume we want to create some classification rules for our Customers. In this simple example, the classification logic will be based on the age of the Customer. Because we want SMEs to write the rules, we have to provide them with a simple, domain-specific language containing only those expressions that apply to this scenario. The SME will then use this tailored language to express the necessary business logic. Let's assume that the business logic we want to implement is the following:

Age	Category
Between 18 and 21 (inclusive)	N/A
Between 22 and 30 (inclusive)	BRONZE

Age	Category
Between 31 and 40 (inclusive)	SILVER
More than 40	GOLD

The categorization rules must only be applied if the customer doesn't have a category already assigned (meaning that the current category is N/A).

A proposed DSL for the described scenario is shown next:

```
# Simple DSL example file
[keyword]avoid looping=no-loop true
[when]There is a Customer=$c:Customer()
[when]- with age between {low:\d*} and {high:\d*}=age >= {low}, age <=
{high}
[when]- who is older than {low:\d*}=age > {low}
[when]- without a Category set=category == Customer.Category.NA
[then]Set Customer Category to {category:\w*}=modify($c)\{
setCategory(Customer.Category.{category}) \};
```

The first sentence after the initial comment is a `[keyword]` that will allow us to use a more user-friendly alternative for the `no-loop` attribute in our rules. Following the `[keyword]` we find four `[when]` sentences. These sentences will allow us to write the necessary rules for the scenario we are dealing with. The last sentence is a `[then]`. This sentence can be used to set a category to the customer. The braces belonging to the `modify` statement have to be escaped (`\{` and `\}`) so they don't conflict with a variable reference.

The following DSLR rule is only one of the four required rules the SME needs to write. A complete implementation and unit test of this scenario can be found in the source bundle associated with this chapter:

```
rule "Categorize Customers between 22 and 30"
avoid looping
when
    There is a Customer
        - with age between 22 and 30
        - without a Category set
then
    Set Customer Category to BRONZE
end
```

After the previous rule gets translated into DRL, the result will look like the following:

```
rule "Categorize Customers between 22 and 30"
no-loop true
when
    $c: Customer( age >= 22, age <= 30, category == Customer.Category.
NA)
then
    modify($c){ setCategory(Customer.Category.BRONZE) }
end
```

We can clearly identify which of the previous 2 rules is more business-oriented.

One of the limitations of DSL is that SMEs still need to know what the available sentences are and how they can interact with each other. They still need to manually write the rules in a text editor. But one of the advantages of DSL is that, by having a limited set of sentences, it is easy to build a tailored UI for the SMEs to use. Both the Drools Eclipse plugin and KIE-Workbench have support for DSL and DSLR creation and usage. These two applications are, unfortunately, beyond the scope of this book.

As mentioned before, the source bundle included with this chapter contains a complete implementation of the previously described scenario as well as a more elaborated scenario, where the categorization of the Customers is based on the number of Orders they have.

Categorization rules allow us to introduce the next topic in this chapter.

Decision tables

If there is a tool every business person—from a CEO to a secretary—knows how to use, it is a spreadsheet. In fact, most of the time, they know more about spreadsheets than most people in the IT department. If one of the goals of Drools is to be a business-oriented rule engine, then what could be better than to provide first-class integration with spreadsheets?

DSLs are very powerful, but, without a proper UI, the users still need to write their rules by themselves. Even if, by using a DSL, the available options to write rules are narrowed down to very specific sentences, the probability of syntax errors, misplaced statements, invalid code, and so on is still high.

Decision tables, on the other hand, provide a much more constrained environment than DSL, thus mitigating most of the risks DSL has.

What is a decision table?

A decision table in Drools is a document stored in an XLS (Microsoft Excel) or CSV (Comma Separated Value) formatted file, which defines a set of rules using a very compact syntax.

The advantage of using XLS and not any other spreadsheet format is that many of the office suite products already support it. An XLS file can be edited nowadays with any of the most popular office suites such as MS Office, LibreOffice, OpenOffice, and so on.

A decision table in Drools requires a specific structure in order to be executed. This structure aids the compiler in the identification of different sections of the spreadsheet that play different roles in the rules that get ultimately generated when the decision table is compiled. That's right, just like with DSL/DSLR, a decision table is first converted into DRL before it is compiled as part of a KIE Container.

Following our simple categorization scenario, where customer categories were assigned according to age, they could easily be rewritten using a very simple decision table, such as the one shown next:

	A	B	C	D	E
1					
2		RuleSet	chapter07.dtable.simple		
3		import	org.drools.devguide.eshop.model.Customer		
4		NO-LOOP	TRUE		
5					
6		RuleTable Simple Customer Categorization			
7		CONDITION	CONDITION	CONDITION	ACTION
8				$c: Customer	
9		age > $param	age <= $param	category == Customer.Category.$param	modify($c) { setCategory(Customer.Category.$param)}
10		More than	Less or equal to	Without previous Category	Set Category
11	18 – 21	18	21	NA	NA
12	22 – 30	21	30	NA	BRONZE
13	31 – 40	30	40	NA	SILVER
14	> 40	40		NA	GOLD

Even if we haven't talked about the structure of a decision table yet, it's quite simple to understand what's going on by simply looking at it. The tabular nature of a decision table makes it easy to read and modify.

Let's now analyze what the different sections of a decision table are and what they mean.

Decision tables structure

There are 2 main keywords when defining a decision table: **RuleSet** and **RuleTable**. The **RuleSet (B2)** keyword identifies where the decision table actually begins. The column where this keyword is used is also important; it determines the column that has to be used for any of the other keywords in the sheet. The **RuleTable (B6)** keyword identifies the beginning of a group of rules.

Only the first worksheet of an XLS file will be scanned for rule definitions.

RuleSet section

The cell after **RuleSet (C2)** is optional and defines the package name for all the rules contained in this sheet. If empty, the default package name is `rule_table`.

The following section the RuleSet can be used to define DRL construct (except for rules) and rule attributes for all the rules contained in the document.

In our example, two key-value pair entries (**B3-C3** and **B4-C4**) are used to specify the Java imports required by the rules and a global attribute of NO-LOOP. The available keywords in this section are:

Keyword	Value	Usage
RuleSet	The package name for the generated DRL file. Optional, the default is rule_table.	Must be the first entry.
Sequential	`true` or `false`. If `true`, then salience is used to ensure that rules fire from the top down.	Optional, at most once. If omitted, no firing order is imposed.
EscapeQuotes	`true` or `false`. If `true`, then quotation marks are escaped so that they appear literally in the DRL.	Optional, at most once. If omitted, quotation marks are escaped.
Import	A comma-separated list of Java classes to import.	Optional, may be used repeatedly.
Variables	Declarations of DRL globals — that is, a type followed by a variable name. Multiple global definitions must be separated with a comma.	Optional, may be used repeatedly.
Functions	One or more function definitions, according to DRL syntax.	Optional, may be used repeatedly.
Queries	One or more query definitions, according to DRL syntax.	Optional, may be used repeatedly.
Declare	One or more declarative types, according to DRL syntax.	Optional, may be used repeatedly.

Keywords inside a Drools decision table are case-insensitive.

Along with the previous keywords, a set of attributes could also be specified in the `RuleSet` section. These attributes will affect the behavior of all the rules present in the current document. A list of all available attributes is:

Keyword	Attribute
PRIORITY	An integer defining the "salience" value for the rule. Overridden by the "Sequential" flag.
DURATION	A long integer value defining the "duration" value for the rule.
TIMER	A timer definition. See "Timers and Calendars".
ENABLED	A Boolean value. `true` enables the rule; `false` disables the rule.
CALENDARS	A calendars definition. See "Timers and Calendars".
NO-LOOP	A Boolean value. `true` inhibits looping of rules due to changes made by its consequence.
LOCK-ON-ACTIVE	A Boolean value. `true` inhibits additional activations of all rules with this flag set within the same `ruleflow` or agenda group.
AUTO-FOCUS	A Boolean value. `true` for a rule within an agenda group causes activations of the rule to automatically give the focus to the group.
ACTIVATION-GROUP	A string identifying an activation (or XOR) group.
AGENDA-GROUP	A string identifying an agenda group, which has to be activated by giving it the "focus".
RULEFLOW-GROUP	A string identifying a `ruleflow` group.

All these attributes can only be used once per decision table.

> Attributes in the **RuleSet** section will affect the entire package where the rules are defined. This may include rules defined in other assets outside the decision table where they are defined. In order to get a more fine-grained control, the attributes can be used in the **RuleTable** section and its particular value for a particular rule can then independently be configured.

Let's now move on to the section where the rules themselves are defined: the **RuleTable** section.

RuleTable section

The second most important keyword after **RuleSet** is **RuleTable**. This keyword, which must be in the same column as **RuleSet,** identifies a section where rule templates are present. A single sheet in a decision table document could contain multiple **RuleTable** entries.

A String could be appended to the content of the **RuleSet** cell (C5) to specify a common prefix that will be shared among the names of all the generated rules. The name of the generated rules will be composed of this value and the row number where each rule is defined.

The row after **RuleTable** specifies the column type. There are five supported types of columns:

Keyword	Value	Usage
NAME	Provides the name for the rule generated from the row overriding the default name.	Optional, at most one column
DESCRIPTION	A text, resulting in a comment within the generated rule.	Optional, at most one column
CONDITION	Code snippet and interpolated values for constructing a constraint within a pattern in a condition.	At least one per rule table
ACTION	Code snippet and interpolated values for constructing an action for the consequence of the rule.	At least one per rule table
METADATA	Code snippet and interpolated values for constructing a metadata entry for the rule.	Optional, any number of columns

In addition, all the attributes introduced in the previous section can also be used in this row.

In our example, we have three conditions (**B7, C7,** and **D7**) and only one action (**E7**). Each condition corresponds to a pattern or a constraint inside a pattern. Each action represents the code to be executed in the right-hand side of the generated rules.

The cells in the row after the column type have a different meaning according to the type of the column.

For columns of type CONDITION, the values in these cells represent a pattern in the left-hand side of the generated rules. If multiple constraints inside a single pattern are intended, the cells can be merged into one (just like **B8** in our example). The second row below a CONDITION column is used to specify one or more constraints in a pattern. A special variable called **$param** can be used to specify parts of the cell that will be interpolated with the values further down in the column. If the columns below specify a comma-separated list of values—as opposed to a single value, as in our example—the variables **$1**, **$2**, and so on, can be used to access each individual value. A text value matching the pattern `forall(delimiter){snippet}` could also be used to expand the list of values by repeating the snippet once for each of the values, inserting the value in place of the symbol **$**, and by joining these expansions by the given delimiter.

For columns of type ACTION, the value of the cell in the next row is optional and, if present, it represents an object reference, a global variable, or a bound variable from the left-hand side.

The second row after an ACTION column is the action's code. This code, which also accepts interpolation variables, will be appended to the right-hand side of the corresponding rule. If the preceding cell contained an object reference (that is, it was not empty), the code in this cell is appended to the reference by adding a leading period and an ending semicolon. If the object reference cell was empty, the value in this cell—with its variables interpolated—is used as is. The **forall** construct is also allowed in this cell.

For columns of type METADATA, the first row below is ignored and the second row is used as the value of the generated rule metadata. Interpolation variables are also allowed in this cell. To the value of this cell after interpolation, a @ character will be prepended and the result will be added in the metadata section (between the name of the rule and the **when** keyword) of the generated rule.

For columns of type NAME and DESCRIPTION, the preceding two rows are not used. The third row after the column type row is used to provide a friendly name for the column. Drools will not use the values in this row at all, but having this row makes decision tables easier to read.

From the fourth row on, non-blank entries provide data for interpolation as described earlier. A blank cell results in the omission of the corresponding condition/action/metadata statement for this rule.

Coming back to our scenario

In the previous section, we introduced how a decision table could be used for our simple scenario of customer classification by age. Let's now analyze how the example decision table, shown next, gets converted into DRL:

	A	B	C	D	E
1					
2		RuleSet	chapter07.dtable.simple		
5					
6		RuleTable Simple Customer Categorization			
7		CONDITION	CONDITION	CONDITION	ACTION
10		More than	Less or equal to	Without previous Category	Set Category
11	18 – 21	18	21		NA
12	22 – 30	21	30	NA	BRONZE
13	31 – 40	29	40		SILVER
14	> 40	40			GOLD

The preceding spreadsheet can be found as part of the sources bundle associated with this chapter, along with the corresponding unit tests.

 As opposed to DSL, decision tables in Drools require a specific dependency that allows the translation to DRL. This dependency is `org.drools:drools-decisiontables`.

As we already know, the two keywords used in the **RuleSet** section of our decision table specify the package name and the **no-loop** attribute of the rules defined in it.

The rules, according to the spreadsheet, are composed of three conditions applied to a single pattern. In this case, the pattern is of type `Customer`. Notice that we have bound a variable to our pattern: `$c`. The first two conditions make reference to the `age` attribute of our `Customer` class. When a condition is only composed of a binary operator (such as ==, >, <, and so on), the use of `$param` is optional. The condition in cell **B9** could have been written as `age >`. In these cases, Drools will understand that the interpolation value has to be placed at the end of the condition. When the operator is ==, things are even simpler: it's enough to just name the attribute we want to use for the comparison—that is, `age`.

When a data cell is left empty (like **C14** in our example), the associated condition will not be included in the generated rule. In our scenario, the rule in row 14 doesn't impose a maximum value for the age of a customer; condition **C9** is then not required.

The spreadsheet also shows that the generated rules will contain a single action composed of a **modify** statement. This statement is used to set the category of the matching customer `$c`.

Starting from row 11, we find the definition of four rules. Column **A** for those rows is just a descriptive name of the rule and it is ignored by Drools. The values in columns **B**, **C**, **D**, and **E** provide the interpolation data used for the conditions and actions.

If we look closer, the values for the third condition (**D11-D14**) look suspicious. They all have the same "NA" value. For these types of fixed values, we have three options: we can repeat the value for each of the rules, we can merge all the cells together to avoid repeating the same value over and over, or we can set the value in the constraint itself. The latter option presents some challenges though. If we change the value of the condition (in **D9**) to "`category == Customer.Category.NA`" we still need to come up with a value for the cells **D11:D14**; otherwise, the entire condition will be omitted in the generated rules. The problem is that, if we do set a value in these cells, Drools will recognize that the condition doesn't contain any interpolation variable and will assume that we are trying to use an implicit " `== $param`" operator. The generated code will then become invalid. A possible solution to deal with conditions without interpolation variables is to append them to some other condition by using a comma. In our example, we could modify the **B9** condition to look like "`age > $param, category == Customer.Category.NA`" or "`category == Customer.Category.NA, age > $param`". The condition on cell **C9** is not a good candidate in this case because there is a blank cell in this column. As we can see, a condition is not restricted to a singular DRL condition.

Taking the rules in rows 11 and 14 as an example, let's see what the generated DRL for these rules looks like:

```
package chapter07.dtable.simple;
import org.drools.devguide.eshop.model.Customer;
no-loop true

rule "Simple Customer Categorization_11"
when
    $c: Customer(age > 18, age <= 21, category == Customer.Category.
NA)
then
    modify($c) { setCategory(Customer.Category.NA) }
end
rule "Simple Customer Categorization_14"
when
    $c: Customer(age > 40, category == Customer.Category.NA)
then
    modify($c) { setCategory(Customer.Category.GOLD) }
end
```

In the preceding DRL we can see the result of rows 11 and 14 being converted to DRL. There are some important things to be noted in that DRL:

- The package name is the one specified by the **RuleSet** keyword.

- The import sentence and global no-loop attribute also match with the attributes used in the **RuleSet** section.

- Because we didn't use a NAME column for our rules, the default name was used. The default name is composed of the **RuleTable** value and the row number that originated the rule.

- Given that row 14 contained a blank cell, the corresponding condition is not present in the generated rule.

Decision table troubleshooting

Because decision tables introduce a level of indirection between what the user writes and the DRL that actually gets generated, dealing with errors can be challenging.

As an example, let's assume that there is a typo in the condition present in C9. Instead of the correct value "age <= $param", let's assume that we inadvertently wrote "age =< $param". When the decision table containing this typo is compiled, it will generate the following error message:

```
Error while creating KieBase[

Message [id=1, level=ERROR, path=chapter07/dtable-simple/customer-
classification-simple.xls, line=8, column=0 text=[ERR 102] Line  8:29
mismatched input '=' in rule "Simple Customer Categorization_11"],

Message [id=2, level=ERROR, path=chapter07/dtable-simple/customer-
classification-simple.xls, line=16, column=0 text=[ERR 102] Line 16:29
mismatched input '=' in rule "Simple Customer Categorization_12"],

Message [id=3, level=ERROR, path=chapter07/dtable-simple/customer-
classification-simple.xls, line=24, column=0 text=[ERR 102] Line 24:29
mismatched input '=' in rule "Simple Customer Categorization_13"],

Message [id=4, level=ERROR, path=chapter07/dtable-simple/customer-
classification-simple.xls, line=0, column=0 text=Parser returned a null
Package]]
```

The messages make reference to errors in three different rules: Simple Customer Categorization_11, Simple Customer Categorization_12, and Simple Customer Categorization_13. In all the cases, the error is the same: "mismatched input '='". The problem here is that each error makes reference to the line and column inside the generated DRL, but we don't actually know what that DRL looks like.

One of the ways, and probably the best way, to deal with errors in a decision table's generated DRL is to dump it into a place where it can be analyzed.

A decision table can easily be converted into DRL by using the class `org.drools.decisiontable.DecisionTableProviderImpl` from the `drools-decisiontables` project:

```
InputStream dtableIS = //get the input stream to the decision table
file
DecisionTableProviderImpl dtp = new DecisionTableProviderImpl();
String drl = dtp.loadFromInputStream(dtableIS, null);
```

`DecisionTableProviderImpl` defines a `loadFromInputStream` method that takes two arguments:

- The `InputStream` to the decision table file
- An optional `org.kie.internal.builder.DecisionTableConfiguration` instance that allow us to configure some of the aspects of the DRL conversion

The sources bundle associated with this chapter has a working example of the preceding code.

Being able to reproduce the DRL generated from a decision table is a valuable help when we deal with errors. The line and column numbers in the error messages can be traced to the DRL generated by the `DecisionTableProviderImpl` class.

Enhanced decision tables

The example we just covered shows the basics of decision tables in Drools. There are many more interesting things we can do to make the life of the users of these spreadsheets easier. Most of the nice features spreadsheets support are also supported by Drools' decision tables. The features we are talking about are: collapsed/fixed/merged rows and columns, functions, colors, links between cells, and so on. By combining these features, we can create much more customized spreadsheets that enhance the overall experience of the user.

As an example, we can take the original decision table introduced in this chapter and apply some changes to leave it like the one bellow:

	A	B	C	D	E	F
1						
2		More than	Less or equal to	Without previous Category	Set Category	
3		18	21	NA	NA	
4		22	30	NA	BRONZE	
5		31	40	NA	SILVER	
6		41	150	NA	GOLD	
7						

This enhanced version of the original decision table can be found in the source bundle with the name `customer-classification-enhanced.xls`.

Some of the enhancements present in this new version of the decision table are:

- Rows 3, 4, 8, and 9 are hidden to avoid showing cells with technical content.

- **D11:D14** are merged to avoid duplicated "NA" values.

- **E11:E14** are now using a drop-down to select a value between **NA, BRONZE, SILVER,** or **GOLD**. This drop-down is not visible in the image but we can check this in the spreadsheet associated with this example in the source bundle.

- Cells in column **B** are using a conditional format that will mark them in red (that is, **B13**) when its value overlaps with the upper bound of the previous rule.

This example shows only a few of all the possibilities decision tables bring to the table to create a more elegant and concise way to define rules. The source bundle includes the decision table version of our advanced classification rules that uses the number of orders of a customer in order to set its category. The name of this decision table file is `customer-classification-advanced.xls`.

Decision tables provide an excellent way to easily create a considerable number of rules without too much work. Once the structure of the decision table is defined, the only job the rule author has is to add, update, or delete values in its cells. The possibility of making mistakes while authoring rules is still there, but, compared to DSLs/DSLRs, the risk is much lower.

Another advantage of decision tables over DSL is that we don't need any special UI for the former. Business users, most of the time, are already familiar with spreadsheets. There is no need to introduce a new UI to users before they can start writing their own rules.

But decision tables are not ideal for every situation: one of the biggest limitations is that rules we can model using decision tables must have the same structure. For cases like scoring, categorization, and classification, where the structure of the rules is almost the same and the only thing that changes is the values of their constraints, decision tables are a very efficient option. For situations where the structure of the rules doesn't necessarily remain the same, decision tables give us no benefits at all.

Another limitation decision tables have is that the structure of both the rules and the data is tightly coupled; they can't be reused separately from each other.

For situations where more flexibility is required, there is another option we may want to consider: rule templates.

Rule templates

Rule templates in Drools are a way to generate DRL rules on-the-fly using template files and tabular data sources. By tabular data sources, we mean data that can be expressed in a table. Typical examples of this kind of data source are spreadsheets and tables in databases.

Probably one of the most common questions in Drools mailing lists and forums is how to generate rules from data that is stored outside our application. The typical case is data inside a database. One of the ways to deal with this scenario is by using rule templates.

Another great advantage of rule templates is that the data and the structure of the rule are completely decoupled. The same template can be used for different data sets and the same data set can be used for different templates. This provides great flexibility in comparison with decision tables.

Rule template structure

A Drools rule template is a text file containing special keywords to demarcate the different sections of the template and to define what the variables inside a template are and where should they be used.

As an example, let's analyze the template file called `customer-classification-simple.drt` that can be found in the source bundle of this chapter:

```
template header
minAge
maxAge
previousCategory
newCategory

package chapter07.ruletemplate.simple;

import org.drools.devguide.eshop.model.Customer;

template "classification-rules"

rule "Categorize Customers_@{row.rowNumber}"
no-loop true
when
    $c: Customer(age >= @{minAge}, age <= @{maxAge}, category ==
Customer.Category.@{previousCategory})
then
    modify ($c){ setCategory(Customer.Category.@{newCategory}) };
end
end template
```

The first line of the template file contains the keyword that marks the beginning of a template: **template header**. The four lines below the template header are the names of the variables this template will use. In a template, the names of the variables are defined inline and are not part of the data set. Each of the columns in the data set used with this template will be named according to the corresponding variable name. The relation between a column and a variable is the position it has in the data set. In this case, the first column will be named minAge, the second maxAge, the third previousCategory, and the fourth newCategory. The white space that follows the variable definitions marks the end of that section.

After the template variable definitions section comes the standard rule header text containing the package definition and import statement. In the event we want to include globals, type declarations, or functions in our templates, this section is also the place to do it.

The keyword **template** indicates the beginning of a rule template. For each of the rows in the data set, an instance of this template will be generated. The name of the template must be unique in the entire template file.

What follows next is the rule template itself. Inside the rule template, variables previously defined can be accessed by using the syntax @{var_name}. For each row in the data set, the variables will be set and their placeholders substituted in the template. If any of the variables used in a rule template are empty, the entire template is omitted. A single **template** section can contain multiple rule definitions.

There is a special variable we can use in our templates called @{row.rowNumber}. This variable will contain the number of the row being processed and is useful, among other things, to avoid duplicated names in the generated rules.

> One of the advantages of rule templates over a decision table is that the variables in a rule template can be used anywhere in a rule: as the class name of a pattern, an operator, a property name, and so on.
>
> Another advantage of rule templates is that variables can be used in any order and can be used multiple times if needed.

To mark the end of a rule template, the keyword **end template** must be used.

Now that we understand the basics of the structure of a rule template, let's see how they are processed along with a data set in order to generate DRL rules.

Working with rule templates

Rule template-related classes are defined inside an individual project: drools-templates. This project contains the necessary classes to parse a template and create concrete DRL out of a data set. Four types of data source are already supported out of the box: spreadsheets, arrays, objects, and SQL result sets.

For spreadsheet-based templates, Drools supports their declarative definition in the kmodule.xml file using the special <ruleTemplate> configuration element of a KIE Base:

```
<kbase name="template-simple-KBase" packages="chapter07.template-
dtable">
        <ruleTemplate
            dtable="chapter07/template-dtable/template-data.xls"
            template="chapter07/template-dtable/customer-
classification-simple.drt"
            row="3" col="2"/>
        <ksession name="templateSimpleKsession"/>
</kbase>
```

The previous code snippet shows how a template named customer-classification-simple.drt with a data source file named template-data.xls is included in the template-simple-KBase KIE Base. This code snippet is part of the source bundle associated with this chapter.

The examples we will cover in the rest of this section will all use a programmatic way to process a template, create DRL out of it, and then, with the generated DRL, create a KIE Base.

All the tests associated with this section (look for the RuleTemplatesTest class) use a helper method to create a KIE Session from a String containing DRL code. To avoid repetition of this method in the following sections of this chapter, let's analyze this method here:

```
    private KieSession createKieSessionFromDRL(String drl){
        KieHelper kieHelper = new KieHelper();
        kieHelper.addContent(drl, ResourceType.DRL);

        Results results = kieHelper.verify();

        if (results.hasMessages(Message.Level.WARNING, Message.Level.
ERROR)){
            List<Message> messages = results.getMessages(Message.
Level.WARNING, Message.Level.ERROR);
            for (Message message : messages) {
```

```
        System.out.println("Error: "+message.getText());
    }

        throw new IllegalStateException("Compilation errors were
found. Check the logs.");
    }

    return kieHelper.build().newKieSession();
}
```

The implementation of the method is straightforward. It takes a String containing DRL syntax as a parameter and it uses the `KieHelper` utility class to compile it and create a KIE Base from it. This method also checks for errors or warnings during the DRL compilation. Once a KIE Base is built, a new KIE Session is returned.

 The `KieHelper` utility class is not part of Drools' public API. This class provides some convenient methods to avoid most of the boilerplate code required to get a Kie Base or KIE Session up and running. Given that this class is not part of the **kie-api** artifact, it may suffer from backwards-incompatible changes in the future.

Let's now take a detailed look at the four data source types supported by Drools rule templates.

Spreadsheet data source

The first type of data source we are going to cover resembles, in some ways, a decision table. When working with rule templates, the data we want to use to generate the concrete rules can be stored in a spreadsheet file. We have already discussed the benefits of using spreadsheets, especially for non-technical users.

As the input of our rule template, a spreadsheet like the following one could be used:

	A	B	C	D	E	F
1						
2		More than	Less or equal to	Without previous Category	Set Category	
3		18	21	NA	NA	
4		22	30	NA	BRONZE	
5		31	40	NA	SILVER	
6		41	150	NA	GOLD	
7						

The preceding spreadsheet contains only the necessary data for the template, plus some useful headers for the person who has to edit this table. The spreadsheet does not contain any information regarding the template that has to be used nor the structure of the rules that need to be generated.

In order to convert this spreadsheet into DRL, we are going to use the template file we have previously introduced (`customer-classification-simple.drt`) and the `createKieSessionFromDRL()` helper function:

```
InputStream template = RuleTemplatesTest.class.
getResourceAsStream("/chapter07/template-dtable/customer-
classification-simple.drt");
        InputStream data = RuleTemplatesTest.class.
getResourceAsStream("/chapter07/template-dtable/template-data.xls");
        ExternalSpreadsheetCompiler converter = new
ExternalSpreadsheetCompiler();
        String drl = converter.compile(data, template, 3, 2);
        KieSession ksession = this.createKieSessionFromDRL(drl);
```

The first two lines of the code are getting the template and data files as `InputStream` instances. The fourth line is using an instance of the helper class `ExternalSpreadsheetCompiler` to convert the template file and the data in the spreadsheet into DRL. The `compile()` method in `ExternalSpreadsheetCompiler` takes four arguments: the data, the template, and the row and column inside the spreadsheet where the data starts. In this case, the data starts in row **3** and column **2 (B)**.

Array data source

Another way to provide the data to a template is by using a two-dimensional array of Strings. In this case, the first dimension of the array is used as the row, and the second dimension as the column:

```
InputStream template = RuleTemplatesTest.class.
getResourceAsStream("/chapter07/template-dtable/customer-
classification-simple.drt");

        DataProvider dataProvider = new ArrayDataProvider(new String[]
[]{
            new String[]{"18", "21", "NA", "NA"},
            new String[]{"22", "30", "NA", "BRONZE"},
            new String[]{"31", "40", "NA", "SILVER"},
            new String[]{"41", "150", "NA", "GOLD"},
        });

        DataProviderCompiler converter = new DataProviderCompiler();
        String drl = converter.compile(dataProvider, template);

        KieSession ksession = this.createKieSessionFromDRL(drl);
```

The preceding code shows how an instance of the `DataProviderCompiler` class can be used to process a template using a two-dimensional array of Strings as the data source. The data is encapsulated inside an `ArrayDataProvider` instance. The `ArrayDataProvider` class implements the `DataProvider` interface. If you have a special, custom source of information that needs to be fed into your rule template, you could implement your own `DataProvider` and connect it with the template using a `DataProviderCompiler`.

Objects data source

A more object-oriented friendly way to present the data to a template is by using objects as the model. Instead of a two-dimensional array of Strings, we could use a collection of objects to hold the data required by our templates. When objects are used as the data source of a template, the name of the variables defined in the template must match the name of the attributes in our model class:

As an example, let's create a class to contain the data for our classification scenario:

```java
public class ClassificationTemplateModel {

    private int minAge;
    private int maxAge;
    private Customer.Category previousCategory;
    private Customer.Category newCategory;


  //constructors, getters and setters
  }
```

An instance of this class will correspond to a rule after the template is processed. Note that the names of the attributes of this class correspond to the name of the variables in the template header:

```java
        InputStream template = RuleTemplatesTest.class.
getResourceAsStream("/chapter07/template-dtable/customer-
classification-simple.drt");

        List<ClassificationTemplateModel> data = new ArrayList<>();

        data.add(new ClassificationTemplateModel(18, 21, Customer.
Category.NA, Customer.Category.NA));
        data.add(new ClassificationTemplateModel(22, 30, Customer.
Category.NA, Customer.Category.BRONZE));
        data.add(new ClassificationTemplateModel(31, 40, Customer.
Category.NA, Customer.Category.SILVER));
```

```
                data.add(new ClassificationTemplateModel(41, 150, Customer.
        Category.NA, Customer.Category.GOLD));

                ObjectDataCompiler converter = new ObjectDataCompiler();
                String drl = converter.compile(data, template);

                KieSession ksession = this.createKieSessionFromDRL(drl);
```

The preceding code shows how a `List` of `ClassificationTemplateModel` objects is used as the data source for the template. In this case, an instance of the `ObjectDataCompiler` class is used to process the template and the list of objects.

SQL result set data source

The last option we are going to be covering to process a template file is using SQL result sets as the data source. By SQL result sets we mean the `java.sql.ResultSet` class. A `ResultSet` class can be obtained in multiple ways using—for example, JDBC. Even if we could easily convert a `ResultSet` into a two-dimensional array, or a collection of objects, and use one of the previously introduced ways of processing a template, Drools already provides us with a way to deal directly with `ResultSet` instances.

Let's assume we have the following table, called `ClassificationRules`, inside a database:

id	minAge	maxAge	previousCategory	newCategory
1	18	21	NA	NA
2	22	30	NA	BRONZE
3	31	40	NA	SILVER
4	41	150	NA	GOLD

If we want to use the information in that table to generate DRL using a rule template, we can use the following code:

```
        Connection conn = //get a connection to our DB
        Statement sta = conn.createStatement();
        ResultSet rs = sta.executeQuery("SELECT minAge, maxAge,
previousCategory, newCategory " +
                                " FROM ClassificationRules");

        final ResultSetGenerator converter = new ResultSetGenerator();
        final String drl = converter.compile(rs, template);
```

The previous example uses standard JDBC classes, such as `Connection`, `Statement`, and `ResultSet`. This code executes a query against the `ClassificationRules` table and gets its result as a `ResultSet`. Then, using Drools' `ResultSetGenerator` class, the `ResultSet` and the template are converted into DRL.

It is important to notice that, even though Drools Templates comes with a handy set of functions, we can still use any other template engine, such as Velocity (https://velocity.apache.org/), or StringTemplate (http://www.stringtemplate.org/). Of course, we will not have any of the `DataProvider` classes, but remember that the ultimate goal of these classes is the generation of DRL code. And, after all, DRL is just plain text; so we can use whatever technique or framework we want.

Let's now move to the last topic of this chapter, which will teach us how to integrate Drools with PMML resources to allow non-rule based knowledge assets to be used inside the rule engine.

PMML

The **Predictive Model Markup Language (PMML)** is an XML-based language aimed at providing a way to exchange different predictive models, for classification or regression purposes, generated using a data mining or machine learning technique. PMML was originally developed by the Data Mining Group (http://www.dmg.org/) in 1997 and its latest version (4.2.1) dates from May 2014.

Even if PMML itself is not a business-oriented language, it is currently possible to generate PMML documents from a variety of well known applications, such as Knime (https://www.knime.org/), or R language (https://www.r-project.org/).

PMML support in Drools is relatively new. It originally started as an experimental module but, with effect from version 6.1, PMML is a first-class citizen of the Drools ecosystem. PMML standard can be used to encode and interchange classification and regression models, such as neural networks, decision trees, scorecards, and others. By adopting PMML, Drools has gained access to a broader set of options for knowledge representation.

Unfortunately, not all of the models supported in PMML are supported in Drools. The list of supported models is growing, and the currently supported set is this:

- Clustering
- Simple Regression
- Naïve Bayes
- Neural Networks

- Scorecards
- Decision Trees
- Support Vector Machines

An explanation of each of these model types is outside the scope of this section. More information about PMML and the models it supports can be found in the Data Mining Group website (http://www.dmg.org/v4-2-1/GeneralStructure.html).

PMML in Drools

A PMML document is an XML document composed of up to four main sections: Header, Data Dictionary, Data Transformation, and Model.

The Header section contains meta-information about the document itself. Elements such as information about the model being used, the application that was used to generate it, and a creation timestamp can be found in this section.

The Data Dictionary section defines all the possible data fields the document may use. For each data field, a name and its type are specified.

A Data Transformation section can be specified in the document to define any mapping between the incoming data and the data required by the model.

The concrete type of model is specified in the Model section of the document. The content of this section depends on the model being used (for example, neural network, scorecard, and so on.). The Model section may contain the following sub-sections:

- Mining Schema: this defines the subset of the fields in the Data Dictionary section used in the model, along with some metadata such as their usage type
- Output: this defines the model's output fields
- Targets: this allows post-processing of the output fields of the model.

Just like with any other resource type in Drools, a PMML asset can be compiled in two different ways: declaratively by using a `kmodule.xml` file or programmatically by using `KieHelper` or `KieBuilder` instances.

If we want to include PMML resources in our knowledge bases, our project must declare a dependency on the `org.drools:drools-pmml` Maven artifact (or include the `drools-pmml` JAR in the classpath).

The source bundle associated with this chapter contains a simple PMML example (`org.drools.devguide.chapter07.PMMLTest`) that programmatically creates a KIE Base from a PMML resource.

When a PMML document is compiled by Drools, its components are analyzed and the appropriate combination of rules, declared types, and entry points is created to emulate the calculations performed by the model being processed. The final result will be a set of Drools assets that will mimic the behavior of the original model.

The generated entry points are one possible way to evaluate a predictive model on some input data, facilitating the binding of external data streams (see later for alternative evaluation techniques). The declared types (implementing the base interface `org.drools.pmml.pmml_4_2.PMML4Field`) hold the current input, internal and output values, together with their metadata (for instance, probabilities and missing/invalid flags); the production rules generate the output values based on the model's evaluation semantics.

Evaluating a PMML model in Drools is slower than evaluating it in a native engine that compiles the model into a sequence of mathematical operations. Drools' goal is not performance at this point, but rather to provide a uniform abstraction of a hybrid KIE Base containing both rule-, and non-rule-based, reasoning elements.

> In a future version, Drools will support both compiled and "explicit" (rule-based) models and the ability to switch between the alternative implementations. An important feature of a rule-based model is that the model's parameters are always asserted as facts in working memory and can be modified by other rules implementing adaptive, online training strategies.

The way we have to specify the value of the input fields of a model in a KIE Session is by using the corresponding entry points that got generated by the PMML compiler. Each of the Mining Fields in the PMML model will create an entry point with the name `in_<FIELD_NAME>`, where `<FIELD_NAME>` is the name of the field.

There are three other ways to specify the inputs of a model:

Instantiating the input types directly, as declared types. We covered how to instantiate declared types in *Chapter 4, Improving Our Rule Syntax*. Now that we know that each input field in the model will generate a declared type, we can instantiate them and insert them into the corresponding session:

- Binding a Java bean to the model, which contains a field for each entry in the data dictionary.

- Enabling the declaration of a trait that mimics the data dictionary. Each input field in the model will generate a corresponding Trait class definition with the name `<FIELD_NAME>Trait`. We can then `don` an object containing a field for each entry in the data dictionary to feed the model.

After inserting the corresponding fields into a KIE Session, and calling `fireAllRules()`, the corresponding output fields will be generated inside the session. These output fields are also modeled as declared types. We can then use some of the techniques introduced in *Chapter 5, Understanding KIE Sessions* to extract these values from the session.

 PMML models are stateless. Any change in the input values will be reflected by a change in the outputs. Parallel or persistent evaluation is currently not supported.

In order to get a better understanding of how a PMML is compiled and used, let us implement a very simple model for our customer classification scenario.

Customer classification decision tree example

One of the supported PMML models in Drools is the Decision Tree. A decision tree allows the creation of a tree-like graph, where each node represents a condition that, when evaluated, determines whether the branches under it should also be evaluated. We can refer to Data Mining Group's website for more information about decision trees (`http://www.dmg.org/v4-2-1/TreeModel.html`).

For our simple classification scenario—where the category of a customer is dictated by his current category and age—the following decision tree would satisfy our requirements:

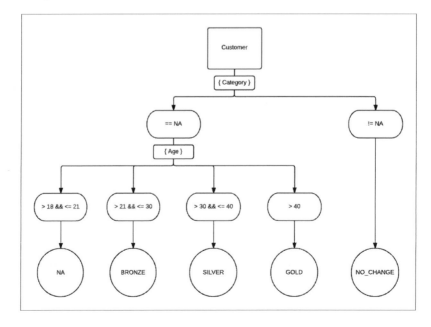

The preceding figure shows the decision tree for our example. We start with a Customer object and the first attribute we evaluate is its category. If the category is already set (that is, is not **NA**), then a special result is generated by the tree indicating that the current category should not be modified. If the category is **NA**, the next attribute to be evaluated is the age. For the age, we have our four well known segments. Each of them will generate a different category to be assigned to the customer. A PMML version of this decision tree can be found in the source bundle associated with this chapter (`customer-classification-simple.pmml.xml`). Let's now analyze the different sections of this PMML file.

Header

The first section is the `Header`:

```
<Header description="A simple decision tree model for customer
categorization."/>
```

In this case, this section only defines a description for the document.

DataDictionary

This section defines three fields: `previousCategory`, `age`, and `result`:

```
<DataDictionary numberOfFields="3">
        <DataField name="previousCategory" optype="categorical"
dataType="string">
            <Value value="NA"/>
            <Value value="BRONZE"/>
            <Value value="SILVER"/>
            <Value value="GOLD"/>
        </DataField>
        <DataField name="age" optype="continuous" dataType="integer"/>
        <DataField name="result" optype="categorical"
dataType="string">
            <Value value="NO_CHANGE"/>
            <Value value="NA"/>
            <Value value="BRONZE"/>
            <Value value="SILVER"/>
            <Value value="GOLD"/>
        </DataField>
    </DataDictionary>
```

PMML is not object-oriented; this is why we need to decompose the attributes of our customer into simple elements.

Each of these fields will create a declared type and an entry point when compiled.

Model

In this particular example, the model is defined by a `<TreeModel>` element. This section is composed of a series of `<Node>` elements defining the structure of the tree.

This section also defines two important sub-sections: mining schema and output.

The mining schema identifies the set of the fields from the data dictionary used in this model:

```
<MiningSchema>
<MiningField name="previousCategory"/>
<MiningField name="age"/>
<MiningField name="result" usageType="predicted"/>
</MiningSchema>
```

In this case, the field `result` is marked as `"predicted"`. This will tell the model that this field needs to be calculated when the model is executed.

The output section defines the output of the model:

```
<Output>
        <OutputField name="newCategory" targetField="result" />
</Output>
```

This output field, mapped to the `result` mining field, will also generate a declared type in Drools when the model is compiled. Instances of this declared type will contain the result of the execution.

The test included in the source bundle (`org.drools.devguide.chapter07.PMMLTest` class) uses a separate DRL resource that defines a query to extract the results generated by this model:

```
query getNewCategory()
    NewCategory($cat: value, valid == true)
end
```

The query basically filters all the objects of type `NewCategory` (this is the declared type generated by Drools) that are in a valid state and returns their value.

Once we have a session containing the compiled version of this PMML file, we can use the following code snippet to provide the value of the input fields of the model:

```
KieSession ksession = //obtain a KIE Session reference.
ksession.getEntryPoint("in_PreviousCategory").insert("NA");
ksession.getEntryPoint("in_Age").insert(34);
ksession.fireAllRules();
//execute 'getNewCategory' query to get the result.
```

As we have previously mentioned, each input field will generate a unique entry point that can be used to set its value. The preceding example sets the value "NA" to the `previousCategory` field and the value 34 to `age`. According to our decision tree, the expected result will be `SILVER`.

PMML troubleshooting

Just like with DSL, decision tables, and rule templates, PMML adds an abstraction level over the DRL that actually gets executed. When something goes wrong, the cause of the error is not always easy to identify.

The good news is that—unlike DSL, decision tables, and rule templates—PMML is an XML-based language that uses well defined schemas for it structure and values (`http://www.dmg.org/v4-2-1/pmml-4-2.xsd`). Having a schema to validate our documents against will eliminate premature errors caused by a malformed or invalid XML.

But if we still need to know what's going on under the hood when a PMML document is compiled, there is a way to dump the DRL that the compilation process generates. In the unit test associated with this section there is a method called `printGeneratedDRL()` that does exactly that. This method uses the `org.drools.pmml.pmml_4_2.PMML4Compiler` class to convert a PMML into DRL. This class is the same class used internally by the KIE Builder when compiling a PMML resource.

PMML limitations

We already mentioned that PMML support in Drools is relatively new, and there are some consequences to this. The first obvious consequence is that not all of the models supported by PMML are currently supported by Drools. This gap should shrink with every new version of the `drools-pmml` module. Another consequence is that this module has not yet been exposed to a considerable audience. While using this module, expect some rough edges, unsupported features, and even bugs.

When modeling our scenarios using PMML, we have to bear in mind that predictive models are quantitative and process primitive values—continuous or categorical. Coming from an Object Oriented environment such as Java could present some challenges when designing a solution involving PMML documents. As hinted in the model binding discussion, one or more objects can be used to deliver and collect the values of the features used by the model, but the predictive models themselves will not be aware of the domain-specific nature of those values. This is inherent to the nature of predictive models, and developers should not make additional assumptions.

Probably one of the biggest limitations of the current implementation of `drools-pmml` is the fact that a session can only be used to execute a single instance of a model. If we want to evaluate two customers in our sample tree, we will need to either create two independent KIE Sessions or sequentially evaluate each customer in a single KIE session. The problem with having simultaneous evaluations is that there is no way to identify which result instance corresponds to which set of input parameters.

Summary

In this chapter we have covered different ways to represent our knowledge in Drools.

For a tailored language for specific use cases, DSL/DSLR could be a solution that hides the complexity of the DRL syntax behind a language that is more familiar to an SME.

For situations where a big set of rules with a common structure is required, decision tables could be a perfect fit. The big advantage of decision tables is that they are very concise and user-friendly.

When more flexibility in the structure of the rules is required, rule templates could be a good help. The out of the box support for data sources such as spreadsheets, objects, or even a SQL store makes rule templates a very interesting option.

If we are dealing with non-rule based knowledge such as neural networks, decision trees, or scorecards, we must consider the use of the `drools-pmml` module. Maybe this is not the best performance solution but it allows us to easily integrate these models with our current rule-based solution.

Now that we have a better understanding about the DRL language and the more human-friendly alternatives that we can use to express our knowledge bases, it is time to understand the best practices regarding how rules can be tested in Drools and how to detect and troubleshoot our KIE Bases and KIE Sessions. The next chapter is all about this topic.

8
Rules' Testing and Troubleshooting

One of the most difficult aspects of working with Drools is probably dealing with errors or unexpected behavior of a rule. The problem is even harder if we are talking about a **knowledge base (KB)** composed of multiple rules. Add interaction with external systems to the equation and see how the complexity grows even further.

The declarative nature of Drools also presents some unique challenges when testing our code. Unlike classes and functions, rules can't be directly invoked. If we want to test a single rule, we need to recreate the necessary state of the session required by the left-hand side of this rule. The problem is that the same state could also trigger other rules in the same knowledge base. This is the reason why, usually, when testing a knowledge base, we test complete scenarios that may involve multiple rules.

In Drools, there is no magic bullet that allows us to easily test and debug our rules; instead, what we have is a set of good practices, techniques, and tips that will put us in a better position to identify, mitigate, and solve problematic situations in our Drools-based applications.

This chapter is a collection of these good practices, techniques, and tips, covering the following topics:

- KIE Base partition and testing
- Rules' left-hand side troubleshooting
- Rules' right-hand side troubleshooting

Let's start with some good practices regarding the partition of a knowledge base and how to facilitate its overall testing.

Create loosely coupled DRLs

The same principles that apply to a good system design apply to the resources in a KIE Base and even to the KIE Bases themselves: create tightly-integrated, loosely-coupled assets.

Regarding the **Drools Rule Language** (DRL) resources (and any other resource that will eventually be converted into DRL, such as Decision Tables, Rule Templates, DSL, and so on), it is always a good idea to keep them separated by some criteria. The criteria could be the input of the rules (that is, all the rules about Customers), the topic of the rules (that is, risk evaluation rules, customer scoring rules, and so on), or any other criteria that makes sense in our current implementation.

If the rules belong to independent modules of our system or even if these modules are not tightly related, it is also considered a good practice to create separate knowledge bases for them. Having separated knowledge bases not only makes our modules easier to test, but it will also render our system more flexible; the less rules we have in our Kie Base, the simpler it will be to test it as there will be lesser chance of triggering an unexpected rule from an unexpected resource in the classpath when we try to run our tests.

Depending on the structure of our rules, having separated knowledge bases could also lead to better execution times.

Prefer KieHelper over a KieContainer classpath

While testing, the use of a `KieContainer` classpath—the one you get from invoking `KieServices.Factory.get().getKieClasspathContainer()`—is not always the best approach. The thing with a `KieContainer` classpath is that it will scan the entire classpath looking for any `META-INF/kmodule.xml` file.

If we are only interested in testing a single rule or a subset of the rules present in the application's classpath, there is no need to scan the entire classpath looking for all the `kmodule.xml` files present.

There are different ways in Drools to create narrow containers with only the specific resources required for the specific scenario that we are testing. Probably, the easiest way is to make use of the `org.kie.internal.utils.KieHelper` class. The `KieHelper` class is a utility class that allows us to programmatically create a `KIEContainer` by specifying the resources that we want to include in it. We have already seen examples making use of this class in the previous chapters.

The `KieHelper` class provides different ways to add resources to the KIE Container that we want to build. It also contains methods to validate these resources and to, finally, create a `KieContainer` instance from them.

A typical use of the `KieHelper` class can be seen in the following code snippet:

```
KieHelper kieHelper = new KieHelper();
kieHelper.addResource(ResourceFactory.newClassPathResource("some/file.
drl"), ResourceType.DRL);
//add more resources if needed
Results results = kieHelper.verify();
if (results.hasMessages(Message.Level.WARNING, Message.Level.ERROR)){
    //fail
}
KieBase kieBase = kieHelper.build()
```

There is no factory for the `KieHelper` class, it can be simply instantiated in our code. Once we have an instance, we can use its `addResource()`, `addContent()`, and `addFromClassPath()` methods to add resources to it. Once we have added all the resources we want, we can verify them by invoking the `verify()` method. This method will return the verification results indicating whether or not the warnings or errors are present. If everything is OK, we can build a `KieBase` instances by invoking the `build()` method.

However, `KieHelper` is not only useful when dealing with unit/integration tests. Applications may also use this class when a fine-grained control over the resources that should be included in a KIE Container is required. Typical scenarios could be the creation of KIE Bases containing only a certain resources based on certain conditions or the creation of a dynamic KIE Base from a string containing DRL.

Benefits of using globals

In *Chapter 5*, *Understanding KIE Sessions*, global variables were introduced as a way of interacting with external services. Even if the chapter never explicitly stated this, its tests showed another important benefit of using `global`: different implementations of the same global may be provided, depending on the context. Right now, the particular context that we are interested in is the testing context.

When testing, mock versions of the global variables requiring interaction with external services, can be provided. These mock variables will immensely reduce the complexity and boiler-plate code required by our tests.

Let's take the following example from the code bundle of *Chapter 5, Human Readable Rules*:

```
global AuditService auditService;
rule "Send Suspicious Operation to Audit Service"
when
    $so: SuspiciousOperation()
then
    auditService.notifySuspiciousOperation($so);
end
```

The preceding rule uses a `global` to interact with an audit service and notify it about suspicious operations found in the session.

If, in the previous example, we had just instantiated a concrete `AuditService` instance on the right-hand side of the rule instead of using a global, it would have made the whole testing process more complicated.

Having this kind of **Contexts and Dependency Injection** (CDI) global variables makes our knowledge bases more test-friendly, we can always provide mock versions of them that facilitate the particular testing process that we are dealing with.

Debugging the left-hand side of a rule

From all the different components of a KIE Base (rules, functions, globals, and so on), the most difficult one to debug/troubleshoot is the left-hand side of a rule.

Unlike the right-hand side of a rule, the left-hand side translation to Java is not straightforward. As we will see in the next chapter, a first glance of this was already introduced in *Chapter 1, Rules Declarative Nature*—the left-hand side of all the rules in a KIE Base is compiled into a network of nodes (which is also known as the PHREAK network). Inside this network, the relation between a pattern, or even conditions inside a pattern, and the individual rule that it belongs to can't be determined most of the time. A single pattern or condition in the PHREAK network could potentially be related to multiple rules.

While this network of nodes dramatically improves the evaluation time of our rules, it also makes potential errors more obscure and difficult to troubleshoot. The following sections in this chapter will try to shed some light over this topic by providing some techniques and tips to make our work as testers easier.

Left-hand side troubleshooting

We have already stated that the left-hand side of a rule is probably one of the most difficult things to troubleshoot in Drools. Nevertheless, we still have some options to identify and fix problems in this area. This section is all about that.

However, before we can even start talking about fixing problems, we first need to identify them. There are typically three types of problems that we can find in the left-hand side of a rule in Drools:

- Compilation errors
- Runtime errors
- Rules not being triggered when they should

Let's go over these three problem types in greater detail.

Compilation errors

Compilation errors on the left-hand side of a rule are the easiest to identify. If compilation errors are present in a resource, the entire KIE Base where this resource is used will not be built.

 `KieContainer` will not complain about the compilation errors in the KIE bases that it contains, it will return an empty KIE Base (without rules, globals, and so on) when they are requested instead. This is the reason why it is so important to always verify the KIE Container before using it.

Typical cases for compilation errors are as follows:

- Syntax errors: The DRL itself is malformed
- Use of unregistered components: Such as custom accumulate functions or operators
- Errors related to the model: Non-existing classes, attributes, and so on
- Missing or wrong imports

No matter what type of compilation error we are dealing with, the error message generated when the corresponding KIE Container is verified will contain enough information for us to quickly identify its cause.

As an example, let's go back to the rule that we took from *Chapter 5, Human Readable Rules,* and introduce a compilation error to it, as follows:

```
rule "Send Suspicious Operation to Audit Service"
when
    $so: SuspiciousOperationXXX()
then
    auditService.notifySuspiciousOperation($so);
end
```

If you take a close look at the preceding rule, you will notice that now it refers to a non-existing class called SuspiciousOperationXXX. If we try to validate a KIE Container that includes this resource, we will receive the following error results:

```
[ERROR] - chapter05/globals-5/globals-5.drl[28,0]: Unable to resolve
ObjectType 'SuspiciousOperationXXX'
[ERROR] - chapter05/globals-5/globals-5.drl[26,0]: Rule Compilation
error $so cannot be resolved to a variable
```

> Take a look at the org.drools.devguide.BaseTest class to see how the error messages are formatted.

As we can see, the error results contain a descriptive message about what the specific error was, along with the failing resource name and the line and column of the error.

> Remember that when dealing with resources other than DRL (such as DSL, Decision tables, Rule Template, and so on), the line and column numbers of the error results will reference to the generated DRL resource and not to the concrete resource itself.

Let's now move to a more annoying type of errors: runtime errors.

Runtime errors

Similar to runtime errors in any application, these kinds of errors in Drools are usually painful to identify beforehand. The consequence of runtime errors in Drools is particularly risky as they may leave a KIE Session in an invalid state. Drools is not transactional (unless we use a persistent Drools session, which we will discuss in *Chapter 10, Integrating Rules and Processes*) in the sense that if the insertion / modification / deletion of a fact caused an error, the execution of this session will be halted at whatever point it is—leaving the offending fact in the session, and most likely, also leaving rules without being evaluated or executed.

This is the reason why testing our rules when using Drools is absolutely mandatory: the best way to mitigate and reduce the number of potential runtime errors is to have an extensive set of testing scenarios covering most (if not all) of the possible situations that our sessions could be exposed to.

The most common causes of runtime errors in Drools are as follows:

- Exceptions thrown by the model: Some of the getters or methods of the models classes invoked from the left-hand side of a rule may throw an exception

- Exceptions thrown by a component: Such as functions, custom accumulate functions, custom operators, and so on

- A bug in Drools: Well…yes, Drools may also have some bugs

Usually, the exceptions generated by runtime errors in Drools will provide a stack trace showing two important exceptions: the main exception will be related to Drools' internal classes where the exception occurred and the root exception that is related to the real cause of the problem.

Let's take the rule about suspicious operations detection from *Chapter 5, Understanding KIE Sessions*, as follows:

```
rule "Detect suspicious amount operations"
when
    $c: Customer()
    Number( doubleValue > amountThreshold ) from accumulate (
        Order ( state != OrderState.COMPLETED, $total: total)
            from orderService.getOrdersByCustomer($c.customerId),
        sum($total)
    )
then
    insert(new SuspiciousOperation(
            $c,
            SuspiciousOperation.Type.SUSPICIOUS_AMOUNT)
    );
end
```

Now, let's assume that the `getOrdersByCustomer` method in the `OrderService` implementation we are using may fail with `IllegalStateException` if there is no connection to the external host where the service is running. When this exception occurs, the following stack trace will be generated (the stack trace was shortened to make it easier to read), as follows:

```
[Error: orderService.getOrdersByCustomer($c.customerId): No connection
to host]
[Near : {... orderService.getOrdersByCustom ....}]
               ^
[Line: 1, Column: 1]
at o.m.o.i.r.ReflectiveAccessorOptimizer.compileGetChain(ReflectiveAcc
essorOptimizer.java:435)
… 55 more
Caused by: java.lang.reflect.InvocationTargetException
at sun.reflect.NativeMethodAccessorImpl.invoke0(Native Method)
... 61 more
Caused by: java.lang.IllegalStateException: No connection to host
at org.drools.devguide.chapter05.GlobalsTest$3.
getOrdersByCustomer(GlobalsTest.java:263)
... 62 more
```

In this case, the main exception provides some information about the problem and the region in the DRL where it occurred. The root exception (`IllegalStateException`) is then shown as the root exception at the end of the stack trace. This exception shows us exactly where the problem is: `GlobalsTest.java:263`.

Even if our rules compile without any problem and we have covered all of the possible scenarios with unit and integration tests to reduce the risk of runtime errors, there is still one problem that most of the Drools developers struggle with at some point: why is the rule not being triggered when it is supposed to?

Rules not being triggered

One of the most frustrating situations when working with Drools is to find that a rule that should be triggered is not. We are not talking about an error here; this is just the situation where we build our KIE Base, create a KIE Session, and insert some facts into it, but for some reason, the rule that we are expecting to be triggered is not.

Now, let's be clear here, 99% of the time, this situation is related to the following obvious cases:

- The rule is not written to do what we think it is. A common situation is to misinterpret the intention of a rule and make wrong assumptions about it.

- The facts that we are inserting in our KIE Session are different from what we think they are.

- The KIE Base that we are using doesn't contain the resources that we think it does. This may sound obvious, but it happens.

The other 1% may be related to a bug in Drools. So, when facing this situation where our rules are not being triggered, we first have to check, double-check, and triple-check the three previous bullet points. The following two subsections will present us some techniques to aid us in this process.

All of the preceding bullet points look pretty obvious, but the first one could sometimes be trickier than it looks. Inadvertently using the wrong attribute of a class or wrong operator in a comparison are things that, even when they could easily happen, are easy to detect and correct. There are some other situations though where things are not so obvious. Let's take an example of two situations where the **from** keyword is used in a way that may look correct but doesn't yield the expected behavior.

The *Chapter 4, Stepping up our Rule Game* introduced the **from** keyword as a way to write patterns about information that is not a part of the session. The sources of this information can be external services, global variables, bound variables, and so on. Contrary to what we may think, Drools doesn't perform any type check between the left-hand side and the right-hand side of a **from** keyword; actually, it does check the types, but it doesn't fail if a mismatch is found.

As an example, let's say we want to write a rule to mark orders having a discount greater than 90% as a suspicious operation. The rule could be written as follows:

```
rule "Detect suspicious discount operations"
when
    $c: Customer()
    $o: Order(customer == $c)
    Discount(percentage > 90.0) from $o.discount
then
    insert(new SuspiciousOperation(
        $c,
        SuspiciousOperation.Type.SUSPICIOUS_DISCOUNT)
    );
end
```

Let's say we make a mistake (maybe a copy and paste error) when writing the rule and we use `Item.id` instead of the `Discount.percentage` method:

```
rule "Detect suspicious discount operations"
when
    $c: Customer()
    $o: Order(customer == $c)
    Item(id > 90.0) from $o.discount
    then
    insert(new SuspiciousOperation(
        $c,
        SuspiciousOperation.Type.SUSPICIOUS_DISCOUNT)
    );
end
```

Our first impression is that Drools will fail when the previous rule is compiled, but that is not the case. Nevertheless, this should throw an exception during runtime, right? Well, no. What Drools is actually going to do is evaluate the entire pattern as false. After all, a `Discount` is not an `Item`. This behavior, which may look awkward to Drools' newcomers, is a design feature that allows, among other things, the usage of heterogeneous collections in the right-hand side of a **from** keyword without generating unnecessary errors.

Talking about collections, there is another not-so-obvious situation regarding the usage of collections in the right-hand side of a **from** keyword. Imagine that we want to write a rule to lower the category of a GOLD customers having more than three suspicious operations. Let's also assume that we have the following service that returns the collection of suspicious operations for a given customer:

```
public interface SuspiciousOperationService {
    public Collection<SuspiciousOperation>
            getSuspiciousOperationsByCustomer(Long customerId);
}
```

As we now know, there are several ways to write the required rule, but let's say that we come up with the following one:

```
rule "Low category of customers with suspicious operations"
when
    $c: Customer(category == Category.GOLD)
    Collection(size > 3) from suspiciousOperationService
            .getSuspiciousOperationsByCustomer($c.customerId)
    then
    modify($c){setCategory(Category.SILVER)};
end
```

Notice that the rule is using the global service called `suspiciousOperationService` to retrieve the collection of suspicious operations for a customer and is also checking whether the returned collection contains more than three elements.

Now, even if our `suspiciousOperationService` service is returning a collection containing more than three `SuspiciousOperations` for a particular customer, the rule will not fire.

The reason this rule is never going to be triggered is because of the way Drools treats collections on the right-hand side of a **from** keyword. Some of the examples introduced in the previous chapters already showed this behavior, but it was never discussed before. Whenever a `Collection` is found on the right-hand side of a **from** keyword, Drools will implicitly iterate over its elements and will evaluate the corresponding pattern for each of them.

In this particular case, the objects being evaluated on the left-hand side of the pattern containing the **from** keyword will be instances of `SuspiciousOperation` and not a collection. The pattern will be evaluated once for each of the elements of the collection on the right-hand side of the **from** keyword. Because we now know what happens when incompatible types are evaluated using a **from** keyword, we can deduce why the mentioned pattern will always evaluate to `false` in Drools (unless the service returns a `Collection` of `Collections` of `SuspiciousOperations`, of course).

The way to avoid the implicit loop in this rule is to collect all the `SuspiciousOperation` objects using a `from collect` pattern:

```
rule "Low category of GOLD customers with suspicious operations"
when
    $c: Customer(category == Category.GOLD)
    List(size > 3) from collect (
        SuspiciousOperation() from suspiciousOperationService
                .getSuspiciousOperationsByCustomer($c.customerId))
then
    modify($c){setCategory(Category.SILVER)};
end
```

Even if this implicit loop seems unnatural at first, once we get used to it, we will discover that it actually provides a very powerful, flexible, and compact way to iterate over collections, including heterogeneous ones. We can go back to the examples in *Chapter 5, Understanding KIE Sessions* to see how services returning a collection of elements are properly used in a rule.

We now know the things that could go wrong on the left-hand side of our rules. Compilation time and runtime errors are the less problematic of these situations. Having rules that are not activated when they are supposed to be is one of the biggest problems we face when authoring rules. Let's introduce some techniques we could use to understand, detect, and fix these complicated situations in the following subsections.

Event listeners

Event listeners have already been introduced in *Chapter 5, Understanding KIE Sessions*. Out of all the different types of event listeners Drools supports, there are two that are particularly helpful for identifying problematic situations in our rules: RuleRuntimeEventListener and AgendaEventListener.

The RuleRuntimeEventListener is more related to the right-hand side of the rules and can be used to notify whenever a fact is inserted, updated, or removed from the session. On the other hand, AgendaEventListener can be used to know when a match (a rule whose left-hand side evaluates to true) is created or cancelled and when the right-hand side of a rule is actually fired.

One of the situations that was not covered in the previous section when we talked about rules not being triggered was the possibility of conflicts between different rules in the same KIE Base.

Let's assume we have the following rule in our KIE Base to lower the category of a GOLD customer with more than three suspicious operations (this rule is similar to the one introduced in the previous section, but it doesn't use an external service to retrieve the suspicious operations of a customer anymore):

```
rule "Low category of GOLD customers with suspicious operations"
when
    $c: Customer(category == Category.GOLD)
    List(size > 3) from collect (SuspiciousOperation(customer == $c))
then
    modify($c){setCategory(Category.SILVER)};
end
```

As we now know, we have to provide strict tests for any rule we introduce in our system, so we go ahead and create some unit tests that prove that the rule works as expected. So far, so good. But remember that unit tests alone are never enough. Depending on the other rules present in the KIE Base where this rule is deployed, its behavior may appear to change. All of a sudden, the rule may no longer be triggered depending on some of the rules included in the KIE Base. What may be happening is that another rule in the KIE Base is interfering in some way with the rule we just created. As an example, let's say we also have the following rule in the same KIE Base:

```
rule "Categorize Customers between 22 and 30"
when
    $c: Customer(age > 21, age < 31, category != Category.BRONZE)
then
    modify($c){setCategory(Category.BRONZE)};
end
```

This rule sets the category of a customer according to their age. The question is: what happens if this rule fires before our previous rule? What if we have a 24-year-old GOLD Customer? In this situation, both rules will match, but depending on which rule gets executed first, chances are that the rule about suspicious operations never gets fired.

In large knowledge bases, conflicting rules could create more than a headache. Event listeners in Drools are one of the resources that we can use to identify where the problem is. Using a combination of a `RuleRuntimeEventListener` and an `AgendaEventListener`, we could determine when an activation (match) for a rule is created when a fact is inserted, modified, and more. This information is really useful when dealing with conflicting rules.

If we don't want to implement our own listeners, Drools already provides some predefined implementation that will log the information they receive into a `PrintStream`. The concrete implementations we are talking about are `org.kie.api.event.rule.DebugRuleRuntimeEventListener` and `org.kie.api.event.rule.DebugAgendaEventListener`. In *Chapter 5, Understanding KIE Sessions*, we already covered how we can register these listeners into a KIE Base. The default behavior of these implementations is to use `System.err` as the `PrintStream`. The concrete stream to be used can be modified using the corresponding constructor.

A simplified example of the output generated by these two event listeners in the example we have introduced is shown here:

 For the complete log, we can run the test in the `EventListenerTest` class that is included in the chapter's source bundle.

```
==>[ObjectInsertedEventImpl: [object: [Customer [id = 1, age=24,
category = GOLD]]]
==>[ObjectInsertedEventImpl: [object: [SuspiciousOperation
[customer=Customer [id = 1, age=24, category = GOLD], type=SUSPICIOUS_
AMOUNT]]]
==>[ObjectInsertedEventImpl: [object: [SuspiciousOperation
[customer=Customer [id = 1, age=24, category = GOLD], type=SUSPICIOUS_
AMOUNT]]]
==>[ObjectInsertedEventImpl: [object: [SuspiciousOperation
[customer=Customer [id = 1, age=24, category = GOLD], type=SUSPICIOUS_
AMOUNT]]]
==>[ObjectInsertedEventImpl: [object: [SuspiciousOperation
[customer=Customer [id = 1, age=24, category = GOLD], type=SUSPICIOUS_
AMOUNT]]]
==>[ObjectInsertedEventImpl: [object: [SuspiciousOperation
[customer=Customer [id = 1, age=24, category = GOLD], type=SUSPICIOUS_
AMOUNT]]]
==>[ActivationCreatedEvent: rule: [Categorize Customers between 22 and
30]]
==>[ObjectUpdatedEventImpl: [object: [Customer [id = 1, age=24,
category = BRONZE]]]
==>[AfterActivationFiredEvent: rule: [Categorize Customers between 22
and 30]]
```

The first line of the logs (each line starts with the ==> prefix) corresponds to the insertion of a Customer instance into the session. The following five lines correspond to the insertion of five SuspiciousOperation objects for the customer we have inserted before. After this point, the activation (match) of the Categorize Customers between 22 and 30 rule is created and executed. The execution of this rule results in the creation of an ObjectUpdatedEventImpl event, which indicates that a fact was updated in the session. In the logs, we don't see any activation or execution of the Low category of GOLD customers with suspicious operations rule. By analyzing the logs and rules, we can deduce that the execution of Categorize Customers between 22 and 30 results in the modification of the Customer object in a way that it no longer matches the conditions of Low category of GOLD customers with suspicious operations—the category of that customer is now BRONZE.

Drools logs

Drools internally uses **SLF4J** (http://www.slf4j.org/) as its logging framework. SLF4J is a facade for various logging frameworks, such as Logback (http://logback.qos.ch/), Log4j (http://logging.apache.org/log4j), and Apache Commons Logging (https://commons.apache.org/proper/commons-logging/). By providing a concrete binding to any of these frameworks for SLF4J, we can enable Drools log messages. The log level we want to use will depend on how much information we want to get. A good idea is to start with a **TRACE** level (the name may change according to the concrete implementation we are using) on the org. drools package and then narrow down the scope according to the output we get.

Drools internal logs are a very convenient and powerful way to get low-level information on what's going on inside the PHREAK algorithm and the framework in general.

Create simpler versions of a rule

Another good technique we could use when dealing with apparently inexplicable behavior in our rules is to create simpler versions of them just for testing purposes.

Let's say that we have a rule with 10 different patterns and some unit tests for it. Let's say that, for some reason, a particular test is failing: the rule is not being triggered. Let's now assume that after applying all the tips and techniques that we have covered so far, we were not able to find the cause of the problem. What can we do then?

Even if it may sound obvious, a widely-used technique is to create different versions of the problematic rule with fewer patterns or fewer conditions in the patterns. The idea behind this technique is to create a version of the rule that actually fires in order to find the pattern or condition in a pattern that is preventing the rule to be triggered.

Once the problem is identified, it will typically fall under one of the following points mentioned in the *Rules not being triggered* section in this chapter:

- The rule is not written to do what we think
- The facts we are inserting in our KIE Session are not the ones we think they are

Making our rules simple is not just something we want to do only for testing purposes. If we have a rule with too many patterns, it is a good practice to split it into multiple rules, each one inserting a specific object to mark the rule as fired. Later, another small rule can group those marked objects and trigger the main consequence of our really complex rule. This would not only allow us to increase the performance of the session when having many objects, but also to create warning rules, which check whether only some of the marked objects are present and not the rest and take compensatory actions, such as sending a warning or invoking some external service to retrieve more data from a global variable.

Debugging the right-hand side of a rule

As we already know, the right-hand side of a rule in Drools may contain a combination of the following elements:

- Java sentences: Any regular Java sentence that is allowed in a Java method can also be used on the right-hand side of a rule in Drools.

- MVEL expressions: If the dialect of the rule is set to `mvel`, MVEL expressions are enabled on the right-hand side of the rule in Drools.

- Predefined variables and methods: Variables such as `drools` and `kcontext` and methods such as `insert`, `update`, and `delete` are also allowed. The special `modify(){}` structure could also be used on the right-hand side of the rule in Drools.

In the previous section, we introduced the notion of how, when compiled, the left-hand side of all the rules in a KIE Base is converted into a network of nodes. For the right-hand side of the rules, the situation is different. When a KIE Base is compiled, the right-hand side of each of the rules that it contains is converted into a Java class. This Java class will basically define a single method containing all the code that was on the right-hand side of the source rule. Inside the PHREAK network, a reference to this class is then added as a terminal node (this will be covered in greater detail in the next chapter).

Even if there is a way to use breakpoints to debug the right-hand side of the rule in a traditional way, this is only possible under some strict circumstances; this is why having a useful set of good practices and techniques to make the right-hand side of a rule easier to debug becomes mandatory.

There is a Drools Eclipse plugin that can be used, among other things, to debug the right-hand side of the rules in a DRL resource. This capability is only enabled for Drools projects. The scope of this plugin is beyond this book. More information about how to set up this plugin in Eclipse can be found in the following Drools' documentation: `http://docs.jboss.org/drools/release/latestFinal/` `drools-docs/html/ch01.html#d0e368`

Right-hand side troubleshooting

The good news about the right-hand side of a rule being converted into a Java class is that the errors that we may experience will look much more familiar to us than the errors found on the left-hand side of it.

Just like with any piece of Java code, two types of errors might be found: compilation errors and runtime errors.

Compilation errors

Compilation errors are caused by invalid syntax or grammar on the right-hand side of a rule. Similar to the compilation errors on the left-hand side of a rule, compilation errors on the right-hand side will create an error containing information about what the error was and where in the corresponding resource it occurred. The same consideration for compilation errors on the left-hand side of a rule also applies here: Drools will not complain about compilation errors in a KIE Base by itself. The verification of a newly created KIE Container is mandatory.

As an example, let's go back to the rule that was used to send suspicious operations to an audit service introduced in *Chapter 5, Understanding KIE Sessions*:

```
rule "Send Suspicious Operation to Audit Service"
when
    $so: SuspiciousOperation()
then
    auditServiceXXX.notifySuspiciousOperation($so);
end
```

In the preceding rule, we have intentionally introduced a compilation error: the name of the global being used as a service was changed from `auditService` to `auditServiceXXX`.

When a KIE Container containing the erroneous rule is validated, the following error will be generated:

```
[ERROR] - chapter05/globals-5/globals-5.drl[26,0]: Rule Compilation
error auditServiceXXX cannot be resolved
```

Similar to the compilation errors on the left-hand side of a rule, the generated error will indicate what the error was (auditServiceXXX cannot be resolved) and resource where the error occurred (chapter05/globals-5/globals-5.drl). An estimated line (26) and column (0) for the error will also be generated.

Using all this information, the identification and resolution of compilation errors in the right-hand side of a rule is, most of the times, trivial.

Runtime errors

Runtime errors on the right-hand side of a rule are caused by unhandled exceptions in the code. This type of errors on the right-hand side of the rule are as potentially harmful as runtime errors on the left-hand side: they can leave a session in an inconsistent and irrecoverable state. Special attention is then required for this type of errors in our knowledge bases. Just like we stated before for runtime errors on the left-hand side of our rules, the best mechanism to mitigate this kind of errors is to provide an extensive set of test scenarios covering all the different situations that our sessions could be exposed to.

Using the same rule from the previous section, now let's see what happens if the audit service used by this rule throws an exception during runtime. In this scenario, IllegalStateException will be thrown if the audit service can't be contacted. The stack trace generated during runtime for this scenario will look similar to the following (the stack trace was shortened to make it easier to read):

```
Exception executing consequence for rule "Send Suspicious Operation to
Audit Service" in chapter05.globals5: java.lang.IllegalStateException:
Unable to contact Audit Service: No route to host.
    at o.d.c.r.r.i.DefaultConsequenceExceptionHandler.handleException(
DefaultConsequenceExceptionHandler.java:39)
    at o.d.c.c.DefaultAgenda.fireActivation(DefaultAgenda.java:1083)
... 37 more
Caused by: java.lang.IllegalStateException: Unable to contact Audit
Service: No route to host.
    at org.drools.devguide.chapter05.GlobalsTest$4.notifySuspiciousOpe
ration(GlobalsTest.java:286)
    at chapter05.globals5.Rule_Send_Suspicious_Operation_to_Audit_
Service1050594099.defaultConsequence(Rule_Send_Suspicious_Operation_
to_Audit_Service1050594099.java:7)
... 40 more
```

The preceding stack trace shows the `IllegalStateException` being thrown by the service, and where in our code, the exception actually takes place. There are two important things to notice in the stack trace, other than the concrete exception: one is where the exception actually occurred. In this case, the concrete implementation of the service being used is defined as an anonymous class (`GlobalsTest$4`) in `GlobalTest.java`. The second thing to notice is where in our rule is the exception thrown. In this case, the class where the exception is thrown is `Rule_Send_Suspicious_Operation_to_Audit_Service1050594099`. This is the class that Drools generated for the right-hand side of the rule when it was compiled. We will come back to these generated classes later in this chapter.

Right-hand side good practices

Some of the good practices regarding the right-hand side of the rules that were already covered in this chapter and some of the good practices regarding the left-hand side also apply here. The use of global variables to reference services, for example, makes our rules independent of the context. Different context (that is, production, testing, and so on) could use different implementations of these global variables to obtain different behaviors. Using event listeners, we can also be aware of when the right-hand side of a rule modifies the state of the session by inserting, updating, or deleting facts.

As debugging the right-hand side of the rules requires some extra steps (either the Drools Eclipse plug-in or the generation of the corresponding Java classes), creating simple right-hand sides, when possible, is always a good idea. For example, instead of having 10 lines of code in the action part of a rule, we could extract this into a regular Java class and invoke it from the rule. This simplification will allow us to easily debug our Java class and not worry about the rule itself.

Along with keeping the right-hand side of our rules simple, we must also avoid any unhandled exception to happen in it. We already talked about the problems that this kind of exceptions cause in Drools.

Another good practice that should sound obvious for any experienced developer is to use a logger framework. Remember that the right-hand side of our rules is just Java. We could, and should, use a logger in our rules to get a more detailed idea of what is going on in our knowledge bases.

Dumping the generated Java classes

As already mentioned earlier, the right-hand side of our rules is converted, on the fly, into Java classes by Drools. This conversion is, by default, invisible to the application using Drools: we never get to see these generated classes. When dealing with errors on the right-hand side of a rule it is, sometimes, useful to understand which exact Java code is being executed during runtime.

Thankfully, Drools allows us to dump the generated Java classes from our rules into a directory in the filesystem. These classes are not only useful to understand what is the concrete Java code that is being executed by Drools, but they can also be used to attach a debugger to them in order to debug the right-hand side of the rules as a regular class.

Drools provides two simple ways to enable the dump of the generated classes into a directory via a system property or declaratively in the `kmodule.xml` file.

Using the `drools.dump.dir` system variable, the directory where we want to dump the generated classes can be specified. For example, if we are using Maven to run our tests and want to dump any generated class, we can invoke the following command:

```
mvn test -Ddrools.dump.dir="/tmp/classes"
```

We could achieve the same result by adding the following property to our `<kmodule>` section in the `kmodule.xml` files:

```
<kmodule>
    <configuration>
        <property key="drools.dump.dir" value="/tmp/classes"/>
    </configuration>
    ...
</kmodule>
```

If we take a look at the `kmodule.xml` file present in the code bundle associated with this chapter, we will notice that it is actually using the property that was mentioned earlier.

To get a better understanding of how these classes look and how the code on the right-hand side of our rules is executed inside them, it is highly recommended to execute the tests associated with this chapter. To get an even better understanding, try to use the `drools.dump.dir` property in other examples of this book.

Reporting a bug in Drools

Despite being a mature framework, Drools is not immune to bugs of course. When a bug is found, the best thing we can do as a Drools' user is report it. Drools' issues are tracked in the following web application: `https://issues.jboss.org/projects/DROOLS`

Before reporting an issue, we should always do some research and check whether the issue is not already reported. If we are dealing with an unreported issue, the best way to make it attractive to the Drools' team—and probably increasing the chances to be resolved—is to provide a complete description of the problem along with a self-contained Maven project, exposing the issue in one or more unit tests. Self-contained tests can also be submitted via pull-requests to the Drools GitHub repository at `https://github.com/droolsjbpm/drools`.

Once the issue is created, we can keep a track of it either in the issue tracker application or by joining the **#drools** channel on `www.freenode.net` IRC and politely asking the team if they have any update.

Summary

After reading this chapter, you should have a better understanding of why debugging and testing our rules in Drools is, most of the time, not trivial. The declarative nature of Drools might be a double-edged sword—very powerful for knowledge declaration but not so easy to test. Errors in the rules were categorized according to their source and cause and a detailed explanation on how they can be prevented or mitigated was also included. The chapter also provided a list of good practices and techniques to make the whole process easier. The techniques that were covered involved the use of global variables, event listeners, loggers, and some other good practices to both simplify and enhance the overall testing experience in Drools.

This chapter also introduced some concepts such as the PHREAK network and its nodes that serve as a kick off for the next chapter. Let's move to the next chapter and start talking about Drools' internals.

9
Introduction to PHREAK

As we already know, the pattern matching algorithm behind Drools 6 is called PHREAK. This algorithm is an evolution of the one used in previous versions of Drools: the RETE (also known as RETEOO) algorithm.

Even if, from previous chapters, we already have some idea of what PHREAK is and how it works, understanding its internals in more detail will give us the opportunity to write better and more performant rules. Another advantage of knowing how Drools works internally is that it will considerably increase our options when troubleshooting our knowledge assets.

One of the major drawbacks of PHREAK (in contrast to RETE) is that the former is a brand new algorithm that was developed for Drools and by the Drools team itself. The disadvantages of this young algorithm are the lack of adoption and the scarce documentation it provides. But don't be alarmed! PHREAK has so far shown itself to be a production-quality algorithm, able to deal with the complexities of critical applications in a variety of scenarios.

The idea of this chapter is to provide an introduction to the PHREAK algorithm, its characteristics, and particularities. To better understand the algorithm, different concrete examples will be presented and explained throughout this chapter.

The topics covered in this chapter are:

- A PHREAK introduction
- PHREAK network and nodes
- Concrete examples of different PHREAK networks
- Queries and backward-chaining reasoning in the context of PHREAK

Given the finite space we have, the goal of this chapter is to serve as an introduction to Drools' PHREAK algorithm. Most of the concepts in this chapter are oversimplified to make them easier to explain and learn. After grasping the initial ideas behind PHREAK, you are recommended to head to Drools' documentation at: (`http://docs.jboss.org/drools/release/6.3.0.Final/drools-docs/html_single/#ReteOO`), if a deeper understanding is required.

Let's start with an introduction to the PHREAK algorithm and its components.

Introducing PHREAK

One of the first assumptions Drools' newcomers make is that rules in a DRL file are evaluated in the same order they are defined, as if each rule were some kind of `if` statement from an imperative language forming a sequential evaluation structure. But evaluating rule conditions in sequence is neither efficient nor scalable at all. Even worse, adding inference capabilities into this scenario would also be a nightmare.

In the mid-seventies, *Dr. Charles L. Forgy* introduced a new pattern matching algorithm to be used in production systems, called RETE (`https://en.wikipedia.org/wiki/Rete_algorithm`). The RETE algorithm sacrificed memory for increased speed, providing an improvement in several orders of magnitude over traditional pattern-matching algorithms. Ever since, multiple production rule systems have been using a derived or customized version of RETE as their pattern matching internal algorithm. This chapter is based on Drools' implementation of RETE and its latest evolution: PHREAK.

PHREAK shares most of the concepts present in RETE— especially with the object-oriented version of RETE implemented since Drools 2.0—and it is impossible to explain one without the other. We will first start with the common concepts between the two algorithms and then focus on the improvements of PHREAK over RETE.

Like RETE, PHREAK decomposes the patterns and constraints present in the left-hand side of the rules to create a directed network of nodes:

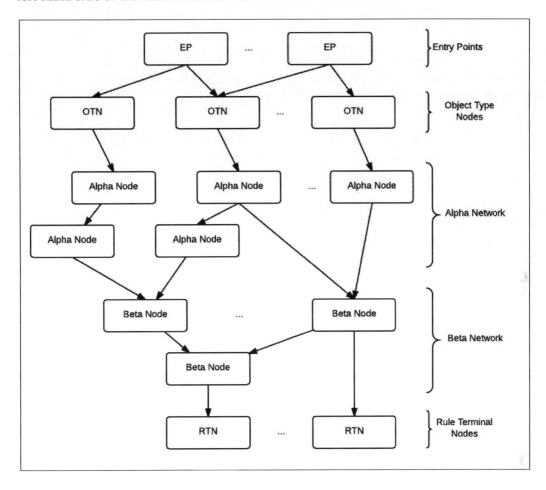

In PHREAK, the first level of nodes in the network is composed of **entry-point (EP)** nodes. Entry-points were introduced in *Chapter 6, Complex Event Processing*, as a way to partition the source of our facts. Each entry-point defined in a knowledge base will correspond to a node in the generated network.

Whenever a fact is inserted into a session, it will enter the PHREAK network through the corresponding entry-point node where the fact was inserted; if not specified, the default entry-point in Drools is called DEFAULT. The fact will then traverse each of the connected nodes in the network. Each node will perform some kind of evaluation on the fact that will determine whether it should be propagated or not to the next node.

The nodes in the PHREAK network are divided into three different categories, according to the type of evaluation they perform on the fact that is traversing it: **Object Type Nodes (OTN)**, Alpha Nodes, and Beta Nodes. Every possible path in the PHREAK network ends either in a **Rule Terminal Node** or a **Query Terminal Node (QTN)**. The former are in charge of the execution of the right-hand side logic of the rule they represent (in PHREAK there is one Rule Terminal Node for each of the rules in the knowledge base), and the latter are associated with the execution of the queries present in the knowledge base.

The following sections in this chapter are focused on the three types of evaluation nodes present in the PHREAK network: **Object Type Nodes**, **Alpha Nodes**, and **Beta Nodes**.

Object Type Nodes

Object Type Nodes perform a type evaluation on the fact being tested. This evaluation can be seen as an `instanceof` operation over the fact. Only when the current fact is an instance of the type (Java class) the node represents, will the fact be propagated to the next node/s in the network. The PHREAK network will contain as many Object Type Nodes as distinct classes used in the patterns of the rules it represents. This implies that rules using the same class in a pattern will share the same Object Type Node in the PHREAK network. So, when a particular Object Type Node is being evaluated, all the rules related to it are being evaluated at the same time.

It is important to note that a single fact may satisfy multiple Object Type Nodes in a network. For example, a fact of type `java.lang.String` will satisfy an `Object` Type Node of type `java.lang.String`, but it will also satisfy another node of type `java.lang.Object`.

As an example, let's analyze the PHREAK network generated by the following two rules:

```
rule "Sample Rule 1"
when
    $c: Customer()
then
    channels["customer-channel"].send($c);
end

rule "Sample Rule 2"
when
    $o: Order()
```

```
then
    channels["order-channel"].send($o);
end
```

The preceding rules each define a simple pattern. The patterns in this case are of two different classes: Customer and Order, which means that the generated PHREAK network will contain two different Object Type Nodes:

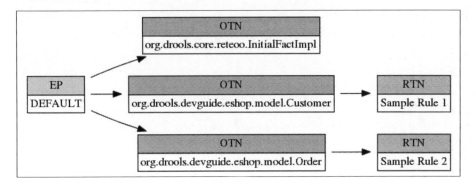

The preceding network is composed of a single **Entry-point Node (EP)**, three **Object Type Nodes (OTN)**, and two **Rule Terminal Nodes (RTN)**. The extra Object Type Node in the network—of type InitialFactImpl—is used to support some special patterns in Drools that will be covered later in this chapter.

When a fact is inserted through the only entry-point in the knowledge base, the three Object Type nodes will be evaluated. If the fact is of type Customer or Order, the corresponding Rule Terminal Node will be executed. It is important to remember at this point that Drools separates the rule evaluation phase from the rule execution phase. The execution of a Rule Terminal Node will not execute the right-hand side code from the corresponding rule; it will just notify the Drools Agenda that a new match for the corresponding rule is ready to be executed.

The code bundled with this book contains a module called phreak-inspector used to generate the PHREAK diagrams for this chapter. The code associated with this chapter shows how phreak-inspector can be used and how the diagrams in this chapter can be recreated.

The Object Type sub-network (composed of all the Object Type Nodes in the network) is always present in PHREAK and its depth is always 1: we will never find an Object Type Node followed by another Object Type Node.

Alpha Nodes

In Drools, a pattern may contain no or multiple constraints. Each individual constraint a pattern has is represented in the PHREAK network as an Alpha Node. This type of node is then in charge of the evaluation of the particular constraint it represents. If the constraint evaluates to `true`, the next node in the network will be evaluated:

```
rule "Sample Rule 1"
when
    $c: Customer(age > 30, category == Category.GOLD)
then
    channels["customer-channel"].send($c);
end
```

The preceding rule contains a single pattern with two constraints: one on the `age` attribute and another on the `category` attribute. Each of these constraints will be represented as an Alpha Node in the corresponding PHREAK network:

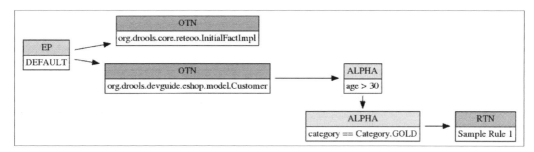

When a `Customer` fact is inserted in the network shown earlier, the first Alpha Node will be evaluated. If the age of the `Customer` is less than or equal to 30, the propagation will stop and the next Alpha Node in this path will not be evaluated at all. If the age of the `Customer` is indeed greater than 30, the next Alpha Node will be evaluated and, if it also evaluates to `true` (meaning that the `Customer`'s category is GOLD), a match will be created in the Agenda for the **Sample Rule 1** rule.

The order of the Alpha Nodes in the PHREAK network depends on the order in which the corresponding constraints are defined in DRL. If the age constraint precedes the category constraint in a rule, the age Alpha Node will precede the category Alpha Node in the generated network.

Alpha Node sharing

Just like with Object Type Nodes, Alpha Nodes can be shared among multiple rules (or patterns inside a rule) in a knowledge base. If the same constraint is used in more than one pattern, Drools will optimize the creation of the PHREAK network and a single Alpha Node will be used.

Let's assume the following two rules:

```
rule "Sample Rule 1"
when
    $c: Customer(age > 30, category == Category.GOLD)
then
    channels["gold-customer-channel"].send($c);
end

rule "Sample Rule 2"
when
    $c: Customer(age > 30, category == Category.SILVER)
then
    channels["silver-customer-channel"].send($c);
end
```

The earlier two rules have the same condition (age > 30) duplicated. The corresponding PHREAK network for these two rules will look like the following one:

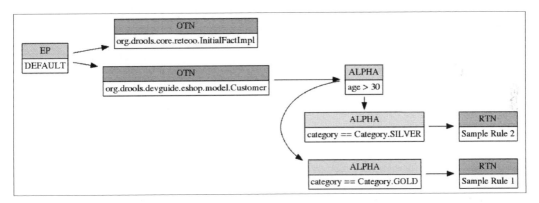

As we can see, the Alpha Node that corresponds to the duplicated constraint only appears once in the network. In addition to saving some memory, Alpha Node sharing reduces the evaluation time of a knowledge base because a condition that is present in multiple rules needs to be evaluated just once.

We have already mentioned that the order of the constraints in a pattern dictates the order of the corresponding Alpha Node in the PHREAK network. This concept is particularly important regarding Alpha Node sharing. For an Alpha Node to be shared, the order of the constraint must be the same in all the patterns. For example, the following two rules are semantically identical to the two rules introduced before, but the order of the constraints in the pattern in the second rule was altered:

```
rule "Sample Rule 1"
when
    $c: Customer(age > 30, category == Category.GOLD)
then
    channels["gold-customer-channel"].send($c);
end

rule "Sample Rule 2"
when
    $c: Customer(category == Category.SILVER, age > 30)
then
    channels["silver-customer-channel"].send($c);
end
```

If we analyze the PHREAK network generated by the new version of our rules, we will notice something interesting:

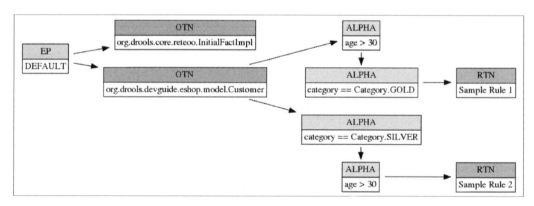

Because the order of the age constraint is not the same in the two rules, the corresponding PHREAK network will contain a duplicated alpha node. The major drawback here is that certain facts (for example, a SILVER Customer) will trigger the same evaluation over the same logical constraint multiple times.

Constraint JIT compilation

In order to evaluate the constraints of the rules in a knowledge base, Drools heavily relies on MVEL. MVEL, by default, uses an interpreter to evaluate the constraint expressions. This means that, most of the time, the evaluation of a constraint is not really happening at the Java bytecode level, which means that it is not as efficient as it could be.

Fortunately, Drools provides a way to compile an MVEL expression into Java bytecode. Because this compilation happens in runtime, it is usually referred as JIT (just-in-time) compilation. But of course, there is a catch. Otherwise, why does Drools not simply compile to bytecode all the constraints in a knowledge base? One of the major drawbacks of JIT compilation is that it could be memory-intensive and may create problems related to the permanent generation heap.

The way Drools deals with this drawback in JIT compilation is by using a threshold on the number of times a constraint is evaluated before it is compiled into bytecode. The assumption here is that, if a constraint is never evaluated, or is only evaluated a couple of times, it is more efficient to evaluate it in interpreted mode than to JIT-compile it. In Drools 6.3 the default threshold is 20 times.

There are two common ways in Drools to tune the default JIT threshold according to the specific needs of an application:

- By using the `drools.jittingThreshold` system property when running our application—that is, `-Ddrools.jittingThreshold=10` to reduce the threshold to 10 times

- By setting the desired threshold value in the KieBaseConfiguration object used to create our KIE Bases:

```
KieBaseConfiguration kbConfig = KieServices.Factory.get().
newKieBaseConfiguration();
kbCofig.setOption(ConstraintJittingThresholdOption.get(10);
```

The entire JIT compilation can be disabled by setting a negative threshold value.

Beta Nodes

The rules covered so far in this chapter were constrained to none or a single pattern. We know so far that the type of the pattern is converted by Drools into an Object Type Node and that each of the constraints they contain is translated into an Alpha Node. But what happens when a rule is composed of more than one pattern? The answer is simple: a Beta Node representing the `join` operation between each pair of patterns is created.

A Beta Node has two inputs and one or more outputs and it will wait until data is available in both inputs before moving to the next node/s in the network.

As an example, let's evaluate the PHREAK network generated by the following rule:

```
rule "Sample Rule 1"
when
    $p: Provider(rating > 50)
    $pr: ProviderRequest()
then
    channels["request-channel"].send($pr);
end
```

The rule is straightforward: for each `Provider` with a `rating` greater than `50` and the `ProviderRequest` fact, an activation of the rule will be placed in Drools Agenda. The corresponding PHREAK network for this rule will look like the following:

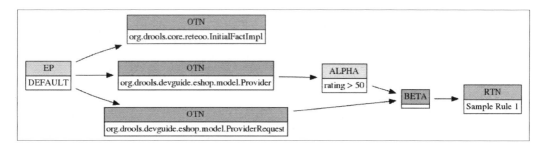

In the preceding PHREAK network, we can easily identify the two Object Type Nodes for our two patterns and the Alpha Node for the rating constraint. We can also see that the patterns in the network are joined by a Beta Node. Because there is no explicit relation between the `Provider` and the `ProviderRequest` in our sample rule, the Beta Node will create the Cartesian product of all the `Provider` and `ProviderRequest` facts it has in its inputs. Each of the generated tuples will be propagated to the next node. In this case, the Rule Terminal Node will determine that a new activation for the rule should be placed in the Agenda.

If we want to avoid the full Cartesian product of our facts, we can set a constraint on the `provider` attribute of the `ProviderRequest` pattern:

```
rule "Sample Rule 1"
when
    $p:  Provider(rating > 50)
    $pr: ProviderRequest(provider == $p)
then
    channels["request-channel"].send($pr);
end
```

Now, the rule is not interested in any `ProviderRequest`, but only in those who are related to the `Provider` matched in the previous pattern. When a constraint involves a variable that is bound to something that is external to the pattern where it is defined, the evaluation of the constraint doesn't happen inside an Alpha Node but instead inside the Beta Node performing the corresponding joining. In our sample, the PHREAK network will now look like the following:

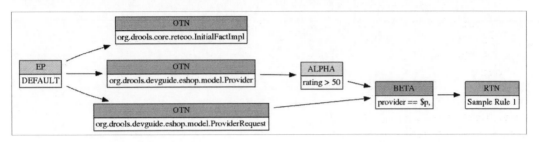

The Beta Node in the preceding network will not create the full Cartesian product of the facts coming from its inputs this time. Only those tuples matching the constraint in the Beta Node will be forwarded to the next node in the network.

Beta Node sharing

It shouldn't come as a surprise at this point that Beta Nodes can also be shared among multiple rules in the PHREAK network. As an example, let's see how Drools models the PHREAK network for the following two rules:

```
rule "Sample Rule 1"
when
    $p:  Provider(rating > 50)
    $pr: ProviderRequest()
then
    channels["provider-channel"].send($pr);
end

rule "Sample Rule 2"
when
    $p:  Provider(rating > 50)
    $pr: ProviderRequest()
    $o:  Order()
then
    channels["order-channel"].send($o);
end
```

The first two patterns in the preceding rules are identical. We already know that the Alpha Node belonging to the constraint on the first pattern will be shared among the rules. What we didn't know yet was that the Beta Node for the join between the `Provider` and `ProviderRequest` patterns will also be shared:

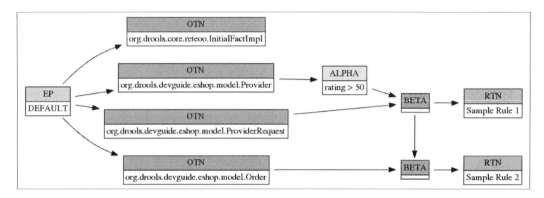

As we can see, the Beta Node at the top is shared among both rules.

It is important to note that, in order for a Beta Node to be shared, the order of the patterns in the rules matters. The concept is similar to the order of the constraints in a pattern when we were talking about Alpha Node sharing: if the order is not the same, Drools will not optimize it. For example, if we modify the second rule in our example by inverting the order of the first two patterns, the semantics of the rule doesn't change, but its underlying implementation in PHREAK does:

```
rule "Sample Rule 2"
when
    $pr: ProviderRequest()
    $p:  Provider(rating > 50)
    $o:  Order()
then
    channels["order-channel"].send($o);
end
```

The resulting PHREAK network in this case will look like the following:

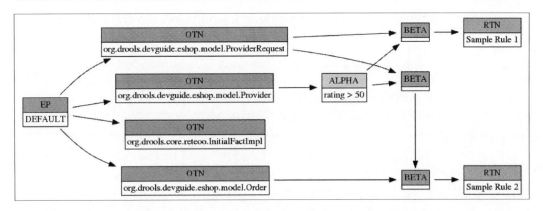

Because the order of the first two patterns in our rules is no longer the same, a new Beta Node now appears in the corresponding PHREAK network. But the order of the patterns is not the only thing that matters when it comes to Beta Node sharing: the nodes previous to a shared Beta Node must also be the same in order for Drools to optimize it. As an example, let's go back to our original rules, but let's change the `rating` constraint of the `Provider` in the second rule to `60`:

```
rule "Sample Rule 2"
when
    $p:  Provider(rating > 60)
    $pr: ProviderRequest()
    $o:  Order()
then
    channels["order-channel"].send($o);
end
```

What we have basically done is to break the shared Alpha Node both rules had. This means that our Beta Nodes for the first two patterns have different inputs now:

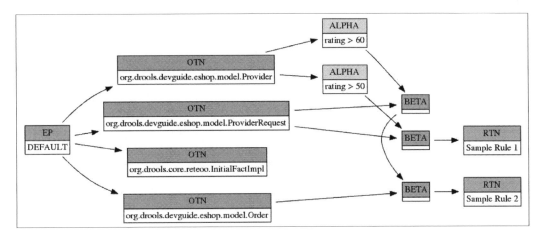

The preceding network now shows two different Alpha Nodes that result in two different Beta Nodes.

As we can see, Beta Node sharing is not particularly easy to achieve; when designing our rules, we must always try to keep the same order between patterns and constraints inside the patterns when they are reused among multiple rules. DSL, Templates, and Decision Tables are all good alternatives to ensure that this order is kept for large knowledge bases.

Or between patterns

A curious thing happens in the PHREAK network when the **or** conditional element is used between patterns. As a matter of fact, Drools doesn't really understand the **or** conditional element at all; what it does is to convert it into a semantically equivalent set of sub-rules inside the PHREAK network.

As an example, let's assume we have a rule to detect when a Customer that is not GOLD has a SuspiciousOperation or an Order bigger than $100,000. This rule can be written as follows:

```
rule "Sample Rule 1"
when
    $c: Customer(category != Category.GOLD)
    (
        Order(customer == $c, total > 10000) or
        SuspiciousOperation(customer == $c)
    )
then
    channels["suspicious-customer"].send($c);
end
```

Ideally, we should have used the conditional element exists to make sure we don't have multiple activations of this rule when multiple Orders or SuspiciousOperations for a customer exist. But, given that we haven't yet introduced the **exists** conditional element in this chapter, we will not use it.

The preceding rule will be converted by Drools into the following PHREAK network:

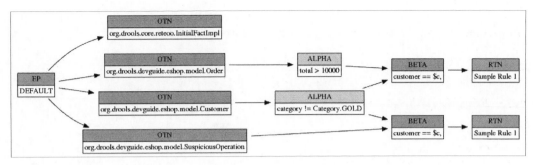

The network above shows the two sub-rules generated by Drools, evidenced by the presence of a duplicated Rule Terminal Node for the single rule we had. What Drools has basically done is to split the original rule into the following two rules:

```
rule "Sample Rule 1.1"
when
    $c: Customer(category != Category.GOLD)
    Order(customer == $c, total > 10000)
then
    channels["suspicious-customer"].send($c);
end

rule "Sample Rule 1.2"
when
    $c: Customer(category != Category.GOLD)
    SuspiciousOperation(customer == $c)
then
    channels["suspicious-customer"].send($c);
end
```

Each sub-rule in the PHREAK network is now independent: both of them can be independently activated and fired. This explains why there is no such thing as a short-circuit between patterns in Drools.

Special nodes in the network

So far we have covered the basic types of nodes present in PHREAK that allow us to create simple rules in Drools. But there are some others nodes with very specific behaviors that are used for some conditional elements we haven't discussed so far. This section will analyze the most commonly used of these conditional elements: **not**, **exists**, **accumulate**, and **from**.

The Not Node

The **not** conditional element is the non-existential quantifier in Drools that checks for the absence of one or more patterns in the working memory.

Drools provides a specialized version of a Beta Node to implement the necessary logic of the **not** conditional element.

As an example, let's use the following rule:

```
rule "Sample Rule 1"
when
    $c: Customer()
    not (SuspiciousOperation(customer == $c))
then
    channels["clean-customer-channel"].send($c);
end
```

This rule is activated when there is a Customer in the session without any SuspiciousOperation. With this example, we can tell that the **not** element must be some kind of Beta Node because it is actually performing a join operation between two patterns. But the join operation is not the one we have covered so far. For this particular node, the execution should only continue if the negated pattern is not present in the session:

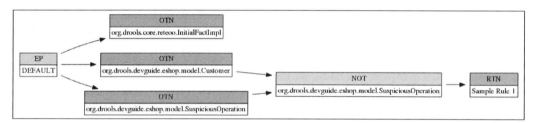

In the generated network, the Not Node looks like a regular Beta Node, but we now know that its behavior is not. If we first insert a Customer fact in our session, the Not Node will have data in one if its inputs (Customer OTN) but not in the other (SuspiciousOperation OTN). In this case, the execution will continue to the next node in the path.

If, before a Customer, we first insert a SuspiciousOperation fact, when the Not Node is evaluated it will have data in both of its inputs; the execution will then be terminated. If we then retract our SuspiciousOperation from the session, the Not Node will now evaluate to true and the next node in the path will be executed.

Let's now consider a situation where we want a rule to be executed when we don't have any `SuspiciousOperation` in our session regardless of the `Customer`. This rule could be written as follows:

```
rule "Sample Rule 1"
when
    not (SuspiciousOperation())
then
    channels["audit-channel"].send("OK");
end
```

We mentioned before that the Not Node is a specialized type of Beta Node. We also know that Beta Nodes require two inputs. But, in this scenario, there is no other pattern in our rule we can join to the Not Node. How does Drools solve this situation? In the previous version of this rule, the `Customer` pattern triggered the evaluation of the Not Node. In other words, when a `Customer` was inserted, the corresponding **OTN** was evaluated and then the Not Node was. But now we don't have any fact that could trigger our node:

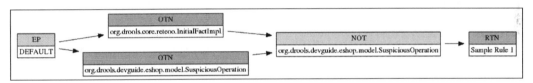

The answer to this problem is the `InitialFactImpl` fact. The `InitialFactImpl` fact is a special fact that is always present (but not always used) in a PHREAK network. Every time a new KIE Session is created, an `InitialFactImpl` is automatically inserted into it. This will allow patterns such as the **not** conditional element to be evaluated in situations such as the one we have described here.

The implication of the `InitialFactImpl` fact in our particular PHREAK network is that, as soon as a KIE Session is created from it, the **Sample Rule 1** rule will be activated.

The Exists Node

The **exists** conditional element is used to test the presence of one or more patterns in the working memory. No matter how often this pattern is present, the `exists` conditional element will only be triggered once. Just like the **not** conditional event, `exists` is also implemented in Drools by a specialized version of a Beta Node: the Exists Node.

To demonstrate how this node is implemented in Drools, let's take the opposite of the rule we introduced in the previous section: a rule that is activated when a Customer has one or more SuspiciousOperations:

```
rule "Sample Rule 1"
when
    $c: Customer()
    exists SuspiciousOperation(customer == $c)
then
    channels["dirty-customer-channel"].send($c);
end
```

Without the exists conditional element, this rule will be individually activated for each of the SuspiciousOperations a Customer may have. With the use of the exists conditional element, we are telling Drools that we only want this rule to be activated at most once per Customer. The PHREAK network generated by the preceding rule looks exactly like the one we had when using the **not** conditional element. The difference here is in the behavior of the Exists Node compared to the Not Node:

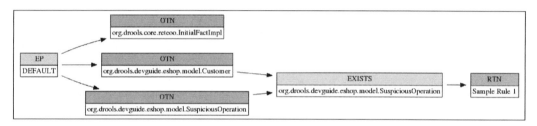

In this case, the Exists Node will keep track of the SuspiciousOperations facts and will only evaluate to true when it has at least one of them in the corresponding input. As soon as this input is empty, the Exists Node will evaluate to false.

It is also common in Drools to use an exists conditional element without any other pattern preceding it. For example, a rule that is activated when at least one SuspiciousOperations is present in our session could be written as follows:

```
rule "Sample Rule 1"
when
    exists SuspiciousOperation()
then
    channels["audit-channel"].send("FAIL");
end
```

In this case, like when we were using the **not** conditional element, we don't have any pattern (or node, in our PHREAK network) that causes the evaluation of our Exists Node. The solution here is similar to the one before: the InitialFactImpl fact.

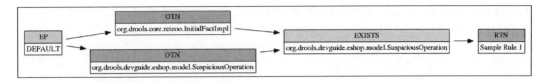

In this case, the `InitialFactImpl` fact is used as an aid: its corresponding input in the Exists Node will always contain a fact. This means that the only fact this node, in this particular situation, is interested in, is the `SuspiciousOperation` one.

The Accumulate Node

Another very useful conditional element in Drools is the **accumulate** element. This conditional element was introduced in *Chapter 4, Improving Our Rule Syntax*, as a way to execute `accumulate` functions over the facts in a KIE Session. In PHREAK, an `accumulate` conditional element is represented with a variation of a Beta Node, called an Accumulate Node. The Accumulate Node will execute the corresponding `accumulate` functions over the facts incoming from one of its inputs. After the functions are applied, the execution will always continue to the next node in the path.

To see how an `accumulate` conditional element is treated by Drools, let's analyze the following rule:

```
rule "Sample Rule 1"
when
    $c: Customer()
    accumulate( Order(customer == $c), $n: count(1))
then
    channels["audit-channel"].send($n);
end
```

Nothing new here. The rule is just counting all the `Orders` of each `Customer` we have in our session. Let's now see how the corresponding PHREAK network looks:

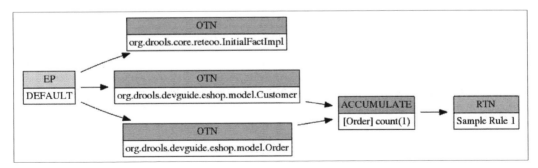

The first thing to notice in the network is the new Accumulate Node. In our scenario, the Accumulate Node will apply the `count` function to each of the incoming `Order` facts. Then, a tuple containing the result of the `accumulate` function and each of the Customers present in the other input will be propagated to the next node.

Another important thing to notice is that the constraints in the Order pattern (`customer == $c`) are not part of the network itself. The Accumulate Node will internally resolve any constraint before executing the corresponding `accumulate` function.

When an `accumulate` conditional element is used before any other pattern in a rule, the `InitialFactImpl` fact is again used as an aid. For example, the following rule could be used to count all the `Order` facts in a session:

```
rule "Sample Rule 1"
when
    accumulate( Order(), $n: count(1))
then
    channels["audit-channel"].send($n);
end
```

In this case, the generated PHREAK network will look like the following one:

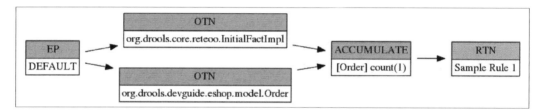

Once again, the `InitialFactImpl` fact comes to the rescue of Beta Nodes without two explicit input nodes.

The From Node

Chapter 4, Improving Our Rule Syntax also introduced a way to reason about objects that are not facts in our session through the use of the **from** conditional element. Because the PHREAK network is all about the evaluation of actual facts in a session, the implementation of the **from** conditional element in Drools is a bit obscure: the conditional element is represented in the PHREAK network as a single node, where both its right-hand side and left-hand side are executed and evaluated.

To illustrate how a **from** conditional element is represented in PHREAK, let's consider the following rule:

```
rule "Sample Rule 1"
when
    $o: Order()
    $ol: OrderLine(
item.category == Category.HIGH_RANGE,
quantity > 10) from $o.getOrderLines()
then
    channels["audit-channel"].send($ol);
end
```

The preceding rule is activated for each `OrderLine` in an `Order` fact containing more than 10 High Range items. In this case, the `OrderLines` themselves are not facts in the session: they are taken from each `Order` using a `from` conditional event. Now that we know how patterns and their constraints are represented in PHREAK, we would expect the generated network for this example to contain an `OrderLine` OTN followed by two Alpha Nodes: one for the `category` constraint and another for the `quantity` constraint:

To our surprise, the entire left-hand side of the `from` conditional element was not translated into PHREAK nodes. As mentioned before, the truth is that the `OrderLines` we are evaluating in our rule are not facts; that is why the evaluation path is not represented in PHREAK. When the From Node is executed in the preceding network, the right-hand side will be executed and the pattern on the left-hand side evaluated for each of the resulting objects.

Now that we have some understanding of how Drools evaluates the rules in our knowledge bases, let's move to another topic that was not covered so far in this book: backward-chaining reasoning.

Queries and backward-chaining

Queries were introduced in *Chapter 5, Understanding KIE Sessions,* as a way to retrieve information from a KIE Session. But queries are much more powerful than that in Drools. As a matter of fact, queries are the way Drools implements what is called **backward-chaining reasoning**. But before entering this new topic, and given that we were already talking about PHREAK, let's see how a regular query looks in the PHREAK network.

For this section of the book, we are going to introduce a new Java class that will be used to establish a whole-part relationship between `Item` objects. What this means it that an `Item` can now be composed of other `Items`:

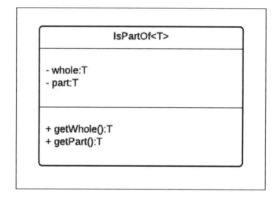

The whole-part relationship between `Items` is modeled as a generic class, called `IsPartOf`. This generic class allows us to define non-intrusive relationships, not just between `Items`, but also between any other types of object in our model. As an example, if we want to specify the relation between a `car`, an `engine`, and a `distributor` `Item`, we can do it with the following code snippet:

```
//The constructor arguments are: name, cost and sale price.
Item car = new Item("car", 15000D, 20000D);
Item engine = new Item("engine", 5000D, 7000D);
Item distributor = new Item("distributor", 200D, 280D);
//The constructor arguments are: whole and part
IsPartOf<Item> r1 = new IsPartOf<>(car, engine);
IsPartOf<Item> r2 = new IsPartOf<>(engine, distributor);
```

If all the `Item` and `IsPartOf` objects are facts in a knowledge base, we can write the following query to know whether an Item is part of another:

```
query isItemContainedIn(Item p, Item w)
    IsPartOf(whole == w,  part == p)
end
```

The preceding query has one major limitation: it doesn't expose the transitivity of the IsPartOf relationship. In other words, if we use this query to ask whether a distributor is part of a car, the answer will be no. We will take care of this limitation later; for now, let's see how the PHREAK representation of the preceding query looks:

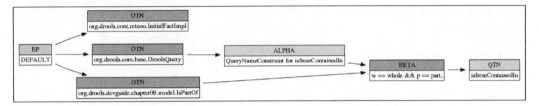

The first interesting thing to notice in the preceding PHREAK network is the presence of a DroolsQuery OTN. This class is used to represent every query in Drools, and it contains information such as the name and arguments of the query it represents. When a query is invoked in Drools, a new instance of this fact will be created with the corresponding name and arguments and inserted into the KIE Session as a fact.

The first node after the DroolsQuery OTN is the Alpha node that discriminates the name of the query. The Beta Node that follows joins the DroolsQuery and the IsPartOf patterns. This is indeed a Beta Node because the w and t variables used in the IsPartOf pattern are bound to the arguments of the DroolsQuery fact.

The last node in the network is a new type of node: a Query Terminal Node. This node will be in charge of the generation of the query result.

Unification

Drools supports argument unification in its patterns via the := symbol. This means that the same variable can be used in multiple places: the first occurrence of the variable will bind it to a value and any other occurrence will constrain to that same value.

Let's take the following rule from *Chapter 6, Complex Event Processing* and rewrite it using unification:

```
rule "More than 10 transactions in an hour from one client"
    when
        $t1: TransactionEvent($cId: customerId)
        Number(intValue >= 10) from accumulate(
            $t2: TransactionEvent(
                this != $t1,
```

```
            customerId == $cId,
            this meets[1h] $t1
        ),
        count($t2)
    )
    not (SuspiciousCustomerEvent(customerId == $cId, reason ==
"Many transactions"))
then
        insert(new SuspiciousCustomerEvent($cId, "Many
transactions"));
end
```

The variable $cId in the preceding rule is bound (defined) in the first pattern and then used in the following two. Using unification, this same rule could have been written as follows:

```
rule "More than 10 transactions in an hour from one client"
    when
        $t1: TransactionEvent($cId := customerId)
        Number(intValue >= 10) from accumulate(
            $t2: TransactionEvent(
                this != $t1,
                $cId := customerId,
                this meets[1h] $t1
            ),
            count($t2)
        )
        not (SuspiciousCustomerEvent($cId := customerId, reason ==
"Many transactions"))
    then
        insert(new SuspiciousCustomerEvent($cId, "Many
transactions"));
    end
```

When the variable $cId is first used in the first pattern, it is bound to the value of the customerId property of the TransactionEvent fact. Any other occurrence of this variable is then converted by Drools into an equals constraint.

For rules, the unification feature in Drools is mostly syntactic sugar. But when unification is used inside a query, things get interesting.

Going back to our `isItemContainedIn` query, let's assume that now we are also interested in knowing all the Items a specific Item is part of or what all the parts of a specified Item are. With our current knowledge, the new requirements introduce two new queries:

```
//Query to know if an Item is part of another
query isItemContainedIn(Item p, Item w)
    IsPartOf(whole == w,  part == p)
end

//Query to know all the parts of an Item
query getItemParts(Item w)
    IsPartOf(whole == w, $p: part)
end

//Query to know all the Items a specific Item is part of
query getItemsFromAPart(Item p)
    IsPartOf($w: whole, part == p)
end
```

The good news is that unification in queries gives us the possibility of having optional arguments. Using unification, the three previous queries can be rewritten as a single one:

```
query isItemContainedIn(Item p, Item w)
    IsPartOf(w := whole,  p := part)
end
```

When the query is executed, if both arguments are provided, the unification symbols in the `IsPartOf` pattern will be treated as constraints. For any argument that is not provided, the unification symbol will act as a binding. The results of this query according to its inputs are explained in the next table:

p	w	Resulting Pattern
bound	bound	IsPartOf (whole == w, part == p)
bound	not bound	IsPartOf (w: whole, part == p)
not bound	bound	IsPartOf (whole == w, p: part)
not bound	not bound	IsPartOf (w: whole, p: part)

Bound arguments in a query are referred to **input** argument and unbound ones as **output** arguments.

In Java, the way we have to use unbound arguments when executing a query is by using the special object `org.kie.api.runtime.rule.Variable.v` for the unbound arguments:

```
//engine and car are Item instances inserted as facts.
//Both arguments are bound
QueryResults qr1 = ksession.getQueryResults("isItemContainedIn",
engine, car);

//Argument 'p' is bound. Argument 'w' will be bound in the result of
the query to
//the corresponding values.
QueryResults qr2 = ksession.getQueryResults("isItemContainedIn",
engine, Variable.v);
```

The sources associated with this chapter contain different tests, showing how unification can be used in a query to allow the use of optional arguments. The `PhreakInspectorQueryTest` class is a good starting point.

Positional arguments

Positional arguments in Drools are a way to add equality constraints to fields of a fact without having to explicitly name them. The order of a positional argument in a pattern determines which field of the pattern's class it refers to. So, for example, the pattern `IsPartOf(w == whole,  p == part)` can be rewritten simply as `IsPartOf(w,  p;)`. Given that conditional arguments can be used along with regular constraints, a semicolon is used to indicate the end of the positional arguments section.

The map between the position of an argument in a pattern and the field it represents is explicitly stated using the `org.kie.api.definition.type.Position` annotation. This annotation, which can only be used at the field level of a class, will take an integer value that specifies its order. In order to be able to use positional arguments with our `IsPartOf` class, we then have to annotate its fields in the following way:

```
public class IsPartOf<T> {
    @Position(0)
    private final T whole;
    @Position(1)
    private final T part;
    ...
}
```

Fields in declared types can also be annotated with the @Position annotation but this is not required: by default the order in which the fields of a declared type are declared is used as its positional argument order.

Because the @Position annotation can be inherited by subclasses, possible conflicting values may appear. In these situations, the field in the superclasses will have precedence over the ones in the subclasses.

Another important feature about positional arguments is that they are always resolved using unification; if the variable used as an argument is not already bound, a new bind is created.

Backward reasoning in Drools

Now that we know some new tricks about queries in Drools, we are ready to introduce a new topic that will rely on them: backward reasoning (also known as backwards chaining).

Ever since its early development, Drools has always been a reactive forward-chaining engine: the rules react to the state of the session, and their action partintroduces or modify the available knowledge that can lead to the activation and execution of new rules. In this type of system, the available data is processed until a goal is reached.

The other side of the spectrum belongs to backward-chaining systems. Here, the starting point is the desired goal and the system works backward, checking whether the data in the session satisfies it or not. Both reasoning methods may involve the generation (inference) of new data in the process.

The way Drools implements a certain degree of backward reasoning is by using queries. In a backward-chaining world, queries can be seen as goals or sub-goals that need to be satisfied by the engine. But in an expert rule system, such as Drools, the individual conditions of a rule can also be seen as sub-goals. The way Drools came up with to bring both forward and backward reasoning together was by allowing queries to be used as conditions in a rule.

As an example, let's assume we have the following `Items` in our system and we know the **Is Part Of** relationship between them:

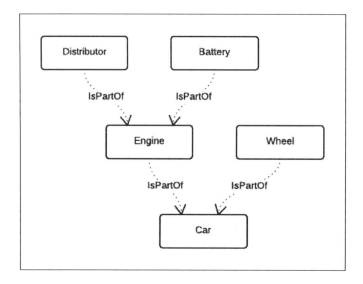

In code, the preceding diagram can be written as:

```
Item car = new Item("car", 15000D, 20000D);
Item engine = new Item("engine", 5000D, 7000D);
Item wheel = new Item("wheel", 50D, 75D);
Item battery = new Item("battery", 100D, 150D);
Item distributor = new Item("distributor", 200D, 280D);
IsPartOf<Item> r1 = new IsPartOf<>(car, engine));
IsPartOf<Item> r2 = ksession.insert(new IsPartOf<>(car, wheel));
IsPartOf<Item> r3 = ksession.insert(new IsPartOf<>(engine, battery));
IsPartOf<Item> r4 = ksession.insert(new IsPartOf<>(engine,
distributor));
```

Let's also assume that we want to apply a 5% discount to `Orders` containing related (via the `IsPartOf` relation) `Items`. So, an order containing, for example, an Engine and a Battery will get a discount, but an order containing a Wheel and a Distributor will not. In this case, one of the "sub-goals" to apply a discount is then whether an `IsPartOf` relation exists between two items in an order. In the previous section of this chapter, we have already worked on a query that will allow us to determine this relation between items. What we can do then is use the query we had already created in a new rule that will apply the corresponding discount:

```
rule "Apply discount to orders with related items"
no-loop true
when
```

```
$o: Order()
exists (
    OrderLine($item1 := item) from $o.orderLines and
    OrderLine($item2 := item) from $o.orderLines and
    isItemContainedIn($item1, $item2;)
)
then
    modify ($o){ increaseDiscount(0.05) };
end
```

The preceding rule can be read as: When there is an Order and it contains at least two items (that could be the same) where one is part of the other, then apply a 5% discount. The highlighted pattern in the rule is the invocation to the isItemContainedIn query. In this particular scenario, the query will be evaluated as soon as the $item1 and $item2 variables have a value. Drool will then try to see if both items satisfy the IsPartOf goal or not.

But remember that we know there is a major limitation in our query: an Order containing a Distributor and a Car will not get any discount, even if they are transitively related via the IsPartOf relationship. Now that we know that queries can be used as a pattern in Drools, there is an easy way to fix this:

```
query isItemContainedIn(Item p, Item w)
    IsPartOf(w, p;)
    or (IsPartOf(x, p;) and isItemContainedIn(x, w;))
end
```

The new version of our query now contains a recursive invocation that will deal with the transitive aspect of our relation.

When this query is invoked as isItemContainedIn(engine, car), its first pattern will match because we have an explicit relation between those two items. When it is invoked as isItemContainedIn(distributor, car) though, there is no explicit IsPartOf for those two items, so the first pattern of the query will not match. But we have now introduced a new path in our query; when the IsPartOf(x, p;) pattern is evaluated, x is an unbound variable that Drools will replace with the engine item (because we do have an IsPartOf fact for engine and distributor). Now that the x is bound, the query is recursively invoked now as isItemContainedIn(engine, car). The recursive call will indeed result in a match (we do have an IsPartOf fact for car and engine), meaning that the original query will also result in one.

The Query Element Node

The last remaining question regarding queries is, "How is a query invocation resolved in PHREAK?" The answer relies on a new type of node we haven't yet introduced: the Query Element Node.

In *Chapter 5, Understanding KIE Sessions* we learnt about live queries and how we can attach a `ViewChangedEventListener` to them in order to be notified in real-time when new information is available. This is pretty much how a reactive Query Element Node works. It registers itself as a `ViewChangedEventListener` to the corresponding query to react to new results or modifications in previously generated results.

The PHREAK network for a Knowledge Base containing the recursive version of the `isItemContainedIn` query and the `Apply discount to orders with related items` rule will then look like the following:

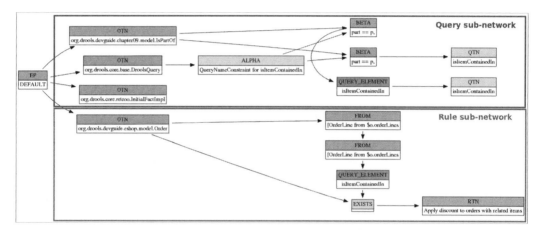

The network was visually split into two sections: one corresponding to the query and the other corresponding to the rule. Some interesting aspects of this network are:

- It contains two Query Terminal Nodes because of the `or` method we used in the query.

- It contains two Query Element Nodes: one for the recursive invocation inside the query itself and the other for the invocation of the query in the rule.

- There is no explicit relationship (no arrow) connecting any of the nodes from the query with a node of the rule. This relationship is not required because the communication between a query and any related Query Element Node is done using a `ViewChangedEventListener`.

PHREAK improvements over RETE

Most of the topics introduced so far in this chapter are not exclusive to the PHREAK algorithm. And this is not really a surprise; after all, the PHREAK algorithm is an evolution of the RETE algorithm implementation from previous versions of Drools (RETEOO). Even if both algorithms have a lot in common, PHREAK introduces some interesting modifications in the way the network of nodes is evaluated. Let's cover the most important improvements of PHREAK over RETEOO.

Delayed rule evaluation

When the PHREAK engine is started, all the rules are said to be **unlinked**. An unlinked rule is never going to be evaluated by Drools. When the **insert**, **update**, and/or **delete** actions modify the state of a KIE Session, the modification is only propagated up to the alpha sub-network and queued before it enters the beta sub-network. Unlike RETEOO, in PHREAK no Beta Node is then evaluated as a consequence of any of these operations. A heuristic determines which rule is the most likely to result in a match and thus imposes an evaluation order between them.

Only when all the nodes of a rule have data to be evaluated is the rule considered to be **linked**. But the nodes of a rule are not evaluated as soon as they become linked; all linked rules are added into a queue that is ordered according to the salience of each rule. Different Agenda Groups have different queues and only rules from the queue of the active Agenda Group are evaluated.

From an API perspective, there is no difference between RETEOO and PHREAK. But internally, PHREAK will delay the evaluation of the beta sub-network until the `fireAllRules()` method is invoked, and not until the `insert`, `update`, or `delete` operations are invoked.

Set-oriented propagation

In RETEOO, every time a fact was inserted/updated/deleted, the network was traversed from the top (the Entry Point) to the bottom (the Rule Terminal Node in the best-case scenario). Each node that was evaluated in the network created a tuple that was propagated to the next node in the path. This behavior was the one we used throughout this chapter to explain the basics of PHREAK. But, in reality, PHREAK doesn't work that way. All the `insert`/`update`/`delete` operations that were queued for a Beta Node are batch-processed and their results added to a set. This set is then forwarded to the next node in the path where all the queued actions are again evaluated and added into the same set. This set-oriented propagation provides performance advantages for certain rules and it leaves the door open for future optimizations regarding multi-threading evaluation of a network.

Network segmentation

The nodes that are shared among different rules in a KIE Base form segments. A rule is then seen by PHREAK as a path of segments rather than a path of nodes. A rule that doesn't share any of its nodes with any other rule is formed by a single segment. Each node inside a segment is assigned to a bit-mask offset. Each segment in a path is also assigned with a bit-mask offset. When a node contains enough data in its input to be evaluated, its bit is set to on. When all the nodes in a segment are on, the segment itself is set to on. A rule is then considered linked when all its segments are on. These bit-mask offsets are utilized by Drools to avoid the re-evaluation of already evaluated nodes and segments, providing more efficient evaluation of the PHREAK network.

 Drools 6.4 will introduce more interesting changes regarding how and when rules are evaluated in PHREAK. More information can be found in the following blog post: `http://blog.athico.com/2015/12/drools-detailed-description-of-internal.html`.

The goal of this section was to provide a simple and comprehensive list of the differences between RETEOO and PHREAK, but this list is by no means complete. For a better and deeper understanding of what PHREAK is and how it works, you are recommended to read Drools' documentation section for PHREAK: `http://docs.jboss.org/drools/release/6.3.0.Final/drools-docs/html/ch05.html#PHREAK`.

Phreak Inspector

Before moving to the next chapter in this book, it is important to introduce a utility class (from the source bundle associated with this book) that was extensively used for the creation of this chapter: `org.drools.devguide.phreakinspector.model.PhreakInspector`.

None of the PHREAK network graphs shown in this chapter were manually generated; on the contrary, all of them were automatically generated from a KIE Base containing the rules and/or queries we wanted to show. The `PhreakInspector` class in the **phreak-inspector** module was created for this purpose. This class is able to output a PHREAK network graph from a variety of resources, including:

- A manually built KIE Base
- A KIE Base defined in a `kmodule.xml` file
- A set of resources, such as DRL, DSL, Decision Table, and so on

In the source bundle associated with this chapter, you will find that most of the tests actually use the `PhreakInspector` class. In fact, you will find that all of the graphs displayed in this chapter can be recreated from the tests. The basic usage of the `PhreakInspector` class is:

```
KieBase kbase = //Obtain a KIE Base from somewhere.
PhreakInspector inspector = new PhreakInspector();
InputStream is = inspector.fromKieBase(kbase);
```

The resulting graph uses the DOT language (`https://en.wikipedia.org/wiki/DOT_(graph_description_language)`). DOT is a text-based format used to define graphs. There are several tools available to display DOT graphs, Graphviz (`http://graphviz.org/`) being one of the most popular.

Once we become familiar with the `PhreakInspector` class, we can use it to graph any of the Kie Bases, rules, and queries introduced in this book. We can even use this class in our own projects to get a better understanding of the internal representation of our KIE Bases in order to look for ways to improve them.

Summary

This chapter served as an introduction to the underlying pattern matching algorithm used by Drools. An explanation on how the rules and their internal patterns and constraints are decomposed into a network of nodes was provided. Some important tips on how to improve the performance of our KIE Bases was also included.

This chapter also covered a major topic in Drools: backward-chaining. We saw how, using queries, we can construct knowledge that follows the backward reasoning concept: start from a goal and try to fulfill it. The hybrid approach between forward and backward reasoning that Drools takes gives us a powerful and very expressive way to define our knowledge.

The main differences between RETEOO (the algorithm used in previous versions of Drools) and PHREAK were also explained in this chapter. Features such as delayed rule evaluation, set-oriented propagation, and network segmentation, not only make PHREAK a more efficient algorithm, but also facilitate real parallel evaluation and the execution of KIE Bases in Drools.

It is time to move on to a very different topic now. Rules are great at expressing business knowledge, but there is another—and complementary—way to define how a business works: business processes. The next chapter will introduce a business process framework that has achieved a lot of traction in the last couple of years and that is tightly integrated with Drools: jBPM.

10
Integrating Rules and Processes

By shortening the gap between Business Users and the IT Department, business processes help us to define in a declarative way how systems and people will collaborate to achieve meaningful goals.

This chapter is about why Drools and jBPM were designed together and how they can be used together. First, we will start with a short introduction about what jBPM is followed by a quick example. In the second half of the chapter, we will discuss more technical aspects of the Rules and Process engine integrations, such as how to start a business process from a Rule, how to use a rule from inside a process instance, persistence and transaction configurations for long-running business processes, and so on.

Other good books have already been published about jBPM 6, so you can consider this chapter as an introduction to jBPM plus a set of pointers and references that will get you started with this framework.

This chapter will cover the following topics:

- jBPM – The Process Engine
- Creating a simple process
- Drools and jBPM
- Integration patterns
- Persistence and transactions

jBPM – the process engine

jBPM is a lightweight and embeddable Business Process Engine. In the same way that Drools allows us to define declarative knowledge, jBPM allows us to define business process models that can be executed and automated. Luckily for us, Business Processes are more evolved than rules in the sense that they have a whole methodology defined around them. This methodology (also known as a discipline) is called **Business Process Management (BPM)** and it describes the whole life cycle of how to discover, formalize, execute, and monitor our business processes. You can find more about BPM here: `https://en.wikipedia.org/wiki/Business_process_management`.

Instead of using the DRL language, jBPM uses the standard notation called BPMN v2 (Business Process Modeling and Notation Version 2, defined by the OMG group) to define business process models. These models have a completely different nature from rules, in the sense that the former have a graphical representation (in contrast to the textual nature of the DRL and DSL languages). These graphical diagrams show the exact sequence of the activities that are going to be executed. When we introduce the concept of business processes to the uninitiated, the concepts and ideas sound generic and vague until we show them an example and then everything makes sense. So the following business process is an example extracted from our eShop use case:

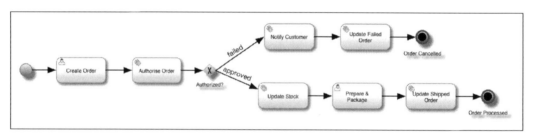

This business process represents how the eShop deals with customer orders. This process defines the activities that need to be performed by people inside and outside the eShop company to process an order from the moment that it is created in the customer portal until it is dispatched via a courier to its final destination. We enhanced the next diagram with all the external services and people surrounding the business process execution so it is clear who, and which systems/services, are involved:

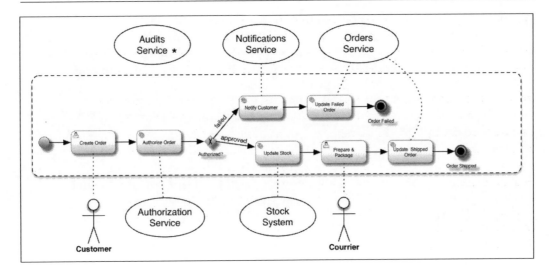

There are different types of activities in a business process. In this simple example, we can quickly identify two of them: User Tasks and Service Tasks. User Tasks will be performed by people inside or outside the company. In this simple example "Customer" and "Courier" represent groups of people. So anyone belonging to that group will be able to perform these activities. The **Create Order** activity will be triggered from the Customer User Interface when the Customer wants to checkout all the items in the shopping cart. Services Tasks are system-to-system interactions. For this example we have several systems and services involved; this is quite common in real-life scenarios. We can see that the **Authorize Order** activity will need to contact the **Authorization Service** in order to determine if the Order created by the customer is valid and if it can be processed further. Another thing to notice is that the **Audits Service** is not linked to any activity in the process and that's because it is in charge of keeping track of everything that the process engine does. Every time that we run one of these processes, we can record the process execution and the information that is created and used by the process, so we can analyze how things are working and how they can be improved.

Notice that the diagram represents what needs to be done in order to process an order and not *how* to process it. The diagram purposefully doesn't include too many technicalities. One of the main advantages of using the Business Process Management methodology is using these models to explain and train people in how the company works.

The graphical notation, and each of the icons and shapes in the diagram, have been specified in the BPMN2 specification and they not only have a standard graphical representation but also an execution semantic. In other words, these process models will be executed by the process engine following the BPMN2 specification.

As mentioned in the introduction to this chapter, there are several resources that we can use to learn more about jBPM and the BPMN2 specification. Starting from the specification itself that you can find here: `http://www.omg.org/spec/BPMN/`, there are a couple of books about jBPM6 (published by Packt) that we recommend:

- jPM6 Developer Guide (2014): `https://www.packtpub.com/networking-and-servers/jbpm-6-developer-guide`

- Mastering jBPM6 (2015): `https://www.packtpub.com/application-development/mastering-jbpm6`

The official documentation gives a lot more in-depth information and details of specific topics. You can find the up-to-date documentation here: `http://docs.jboss.org/jbpm/v6.3/userguide/`.

The next section shows how to create a very simple process with jBPM and introduces process-related methods inside the KEI APIs. While we look at the APIs, we will also learn about how our process behaves, deals with information, and how it interacts with people and external systems.

Simple business process example

Let's create the simplest process ever and see how we can execute it inside our Kie Containers. This section will give you a quick overview about how you can create a Process Instance based on a process model using the KEI APIs. As you can imagine, we cannot cover all the details about jBPM in just one chapter, so consider this as a very short introduction.

So let's get started by creating the following process:

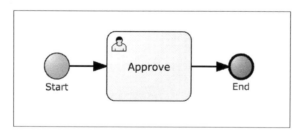

This process has just one User Task and two events, the Start Event and the End Event. We will start this process by submitting a value to be reviewed; the process engine will create an activity to a user so it can review the submitted value and approve or reject it.

The BPMN2 Specification also defines how these diagrams are stored and the XML schemas that are used to validate that our models are correct. So, at the end of the day, our process models will be stored in XML files that will need to be parsed by the Process Engine in order to be executed.

Most of the time, we will use a graphical tool to model our business processes, instead of manipulating the XML files. We strongly recommend you to take a look at KIE Workbench and Process Designer to model your business processes. You can find more about these projects here: `http://docs.jboss.org/drools/release/6.3.0.Final/drools-docs/html_single/index.html#d0e15772`.

You can also find it here:

`http://docs.jboss.org/jbpm/v6.3/userguide/ch12.html`

The following XML is a stripped down version of the XML generated by the Process Designer for this very simple example:

> Notice that the XML file tends to become huge, mostly because it stores all the graphical elements, their positions, colors, and everything needed to render the process diagram.

```xml
<bpmn2:definitions … >
  <bpmn2:process id="simple" name="simple" isExecutable="true">
    <bpmn2:property id="requested_amount"/>
    <bpmn2:property id="request_status" />
    <bpmn2:startEvent name="Start"></bpmn2:startEvent>
    <bpmn2:userTask name="Approve">
      <bpmn2:ioSpecification id="">
        <bpmn2:dataInput drools:dtype="Integer" name="amount"/>
        <bpmn2:dataOutput drools:dtype="Integer" name="status"/>
      </bpmn2:ioSpecification>
      <bpmn2:potentialOwner >
        <bpmn2:resourceAssignmentExpression >
          <bpmn2:formalExpression>manager</bpmn2:formalExpression>
        </bpmn2:resourceAssignmentExpression>
      </bpmn2:potentialOwner>
    </bpmn2:userTask>
    <bpmn2:endEvent name="End"> </bpmn2:endEvent>
    <bpmn2:sequenceFlow sourceRef="..." targetRef="..."/>
    <bpmn2:sequenceFlow sourceRef="..." targetRef="..."/>
  </bpmn2:process>
```

The complete XML file of this example can be found inside `chapter-10/chapter-10-kjar/src/main/resources/chapter10/simple.bpmn2`.

Highlighted in the XML snippet are the three tasks, the process variables (bpmn2: properties, information that the process will handle or generate), and sequence flows, which are the connection between the activities.

Using a similar parser to the one the rule engine uses to read DRL files, these XML files are parsed and compiled to become part of our Kie Basess. As soon as we have them inside our Kie Basess we can start using them by creating Process Instances. So let's take a look at the KIE API to interact with processes. In the same way that we used the Kie Session to interact with the Rule Engine to insert/update/retract facts and fire all the rules, we have a specific method to start process instances:

```
ProcessInstance pI = ksession.startProcess("simple", params);
```

The first argument is the process id that we specified in the `<bpmn2:process>` tag and the second argument is the initial information that we want to pass to the newly created Process Instance.

Some other methods to interact with our process instances are:

- We can abort instances that were previously created if they are no longer needed or if they don't make sense anymore:

  ```
  ksession.abortProcessInstance(processInstanceId);
  ```

- We can create Process Instances without starting them. Once we have created them, we can start them by using the generated Process Instance Id:

  ```
  ksession.createProcessInstance("simple", params);
  ```

- We can use this method if we have already created a process instance without starting it:

  ```
  ksession.startProcessInstance(id);
  ```

- We can use this method to get hold of all the process instances created inside a session:

  ```
  ksession.getProcessInstances(...);
  ```

- We can notify the Process Instances (or even all the processes inside a session) about an external event. The Process Instances might (or might not) react, based on the process definitions:

  ```
  ksession.signalEvent(...);
  ```

Kie Session advanced configurations

The following sections describe some of the most important methods on the Kie Session interface to configure our Process and Rule engine for specific needs.

Kie Session event listeners

Event listeners allow us to attach more functionality to the internal events generated by the Rule and Process engines while they are operating. The following event listener allow us to get hold of all the events internally generated by the process engine so we can get real-time information about our business processe executions:

```
ksession.addEventListener(new MyProcessEventListener());
```

We can attach to the Kie Session any number of the following: `org.kie.api.event. process.ProcessEventListener`. These listeners will let us know what the process engine is doing for every process that we run inside that session. Some of the events that are captured by the `ProcessEventListener` implementations are:

- before/after `ProcessStarted`
- before/after `ProcessCompleted`
- before/after `NodeTriggered`
- before/after `NodeLeft`
- before/after `VariableChanged`

We can create our own implementation to store the trace of the process execution in a separate database or storage to track progress, or for later analysis. This is an extension point provided by the engine for us to externalize the data that we might want to expose to the people interested in the execution of our processes.

Kie Session Work Items

Work Items provide our process with a way to interact with the outside world. In other words, Work Items represent any external work that needs to be performed by an external service or a person. We can define and register our own work item handlers to the Kie Session, so that, every time that we need to perform the same task, we can rely on the same implementation. Let's take a look at the `registerWorkItemHandler()` method and at a simple example:

```
ksession.getWorkItemManager().
registerWorkItemHandler("Human Task", new MyWorkItemHandler());
```

The `WorkItemHandlers` allows us to hook integration points with external entities. As you can see in this example, we are registering a new implementation of the `WorkItemHandler` interface to handle our Human Tasks inside the process. Human Tasks are represented by the User Task Activities inside the **BPMN2** specification. For the sake of the example, we are creating a Handler that will automatically complete the activity created.

Let's take a look at our first test scenario:

```
@Test
public void testSimpleBPMN2Rejected() {
    KieSession ksession = this.createDefaultSession();
    ksession.addEventListener(new SystemOutProcessEventListener());
    ksession.getWorkItemManager()
     .registerWorkItemHandler("Human Task",
     new ManagerApprovalSimpleWorkItemHandler());
    Map<String, Object> params = new HashMap<String, Object>();
    params.put("requested_amount", 1005);
    ProcessInstance processInstance =
    ksession.startProcess("simple", params);
    WorkflowProcessInstance wpi = (WorkflowProcessInstance)
    processInstance;
    assertThat(processInstance, notNullValue());
    assertThat(ProcessInstance.STATE_COMPLETED,
    is(processInstance.getState()));
    assertThat("rejected", is(wpi.getVariable("request_status")));
}
```

The source code of this test can be found in `chapter-10/chapter-10-tests/src/ test/java/org/drools/devguide/chapter10/SimpleProcessTest.java`.

The test starts by creating the default session that will include our `simple. bpmn2` file. Once we have the session for running our process instances, we register a new `ProcessEventListener`. We can find the implementation of the `SystemOutProcessEventListener` also in the project sources:

1. For this simple example the `SystemOutProcessEventListener` will just log to the console every activity executed by the process engine. If you execute the test you will see all the events that are being captured and printed out to the console.

2. We now register a new `WorkItemHandler` to deal with the User Tasks inside our process: `ManagerApprovalSimpleWorkItemHandler`. Now, for every User Task that we have in our processes running inside this session, this `WorkItemHandler` will be used.

Let's take a look at the implementation for this example:

```
private class ManagerApprovalSimpleWorkItemHandler
    implements WorkItemHandler {
  @Override
  public void executeWorkItem(WorkItem wi, WorkItemManager wim) {
    String actorId = (String) wi.getParameters().get("ActorId");
      if (actorId.equals("manager")) {
    Integer amount = (Integer) wi.getParameters().get("amount");
    Map<String, Object> results = new HashMap<String, Object>();
      if (amount >= 1000) {
        results.put("status", "rejected");
        wim.completeWorkItem(wi.getId(), results);
      } else {
    results.put("status", "approved");
        wim.completeWorkItem(wi.getId(), results);
      }
    }
  }
  @Override
  public void abortWorkItem(WorkItem wi, WorkItemManager wim) {}
}
```

The WorkItemHandler interface pushes us to implement two methods:

- This method will be called every time that an activity in our process is delegated to our WorkItemHandler implementation. This method gives us access to the WorkItem itself, which contains all the contextual information that we can use to interact with external systems or services. And it also allows us to execute operations using the WorkItemManager, such as completing or aborting the WorkItem:

  ```
  void executeWorkItem(WorkItem wi, WorkItemManager wim)
  ```

- For the sake of simplicity, in this example the abort WorkItem method is not executing any logic, but we should include here the logic to handle cases where the WorkItem is no longer needed and, for that reason, aborted:

  ```
  void abortWorkItem(WorkItem wi, WorkItemManager wim)
  ```

The logic inside the `ManagerApprovalSimpleWorkItemHandler` implementation works as follows:

1. Check that the activity is targeted to the `manager` user.

2. Get the initial `amount` value:

    ○ If the `amount` is greater than or equal to `1000` it will set the `status` variable to `rejected`

    ○ If the `amount` is less than `1000` it will set the status variable to `approved`

3. The last step is to complete the `WorkItem` by using the `WorkItemManager` and setting the results.

Now we are ready to start our process instances, and we can see that the test does exactly that after registering our `WorkItemHandler` implementation:

```
Map<String, Object> params = new HashMap<String, Object>();
params.put("requested_amount", 1005);
ProcessInstance processInstance = ksession.startProcess("simple",
params);
```

> Notice that we are only setting one of the two Process Variables defined in the process. We are starting the process with the `requested_amount` process variable set to `1005`. The other process variable will be filled by our `WorkItemHandler` implementation based on the evaluation of the `requested_amount` value.

In order to move information (process variables) from the Process Instance scope to the `WorkItems`, these variables will be copied so they can be manipulated. We can observe that, for each activity defined in the process definition, `DataInput`/ `DataOutput` associations are needed to define how data will be copied from the Process Variables to the `WorkItem` scope and the other way around (how the results created by the `WorkItem` execution will be copied back to the process variables). For this reason we will see that in the `WorkItemHandler` implementation we make reference to `amount` and `status` instead of using the names of the Process Variables.

Let's see the output of our test case called `testSimpleBPMN2Rejected`, which is starting a new Process Instance with the initial `requested_amount` set to `1005`.

```
###### Starting Simple BPMN2 ######
###### >>> Requesting $1005 ######
>>> BeforeVariableChanged: requested_amount new Value: 1005 - old
Value: null
>>> AfterVariableChanged: requested_amount new Value: 1005 - old
Value: null
```

```
>>> BeforeProcessStarted: simple
>>> BeforeNodeTriggered: Start
>>> BeforeNodeLeft: Start
>>> BeforeNodeTriggered: Approve
>>> Here the Manager reviewing requested amount
>>> Requested Amount: $1005
>>> But I can approve until $1000, so I'm rejecting the request
>>> BeforeVariableChanged: request_status new Value: rejected - old
Value: null
>>> AfterVariableChanged: request_status new Value: rejected - old
Value: null
>>> BeforeNodeLeft: Approve
>>> BeforeNodeTriggered: End
>>> BeforeNodeLeft: End
>>> BeforeProcessCompleted: simple
>>> AfterProcessCompleted: simple
>>> AfterNodeLeft: End
>>> AfterNodeTriggered: End
>>> AfterNodeLeft: Approve
>>> AfterNodeTriggered: Approve
>>> AfterNodeLeft: Start
>>> AfterNodeTriggered: Start
>>> AfterProcessStarted: simple
###### >>> Request Status rejected ######
###### Completed Simple BPMN2 ######
```

The output in the console shows all the steps internally executed by the
process engine; as we mentioned before, we have plugged in our own
`ProcessEventListener`, which is creating this output for us, but we can come up
with a much more interesting use of this information such as:

- Using this information for real-time monitoring in a dashboard-like interface
- Keeping track of unfinished processes or activities and meaningful send alerts
- If something fails, making sure that we know why
- Measuring activities—for example, their average time of completion
- Triggering new processes in the case of anomalies or unexpected situations

If we already have a Dashboard to monitor other applications or resources, we can
always create a `ProcessEventListener` then send information to it or to a database
of our choice.

Understanding our process execution

In the previous log, half of the entries seem to be linear as expected; we can follow the process graph jumping from one activity to the next one. But after the `AfterProcessCompleted` event, everything seems to go backwards. The next figure shows how the events are related to activity execution:

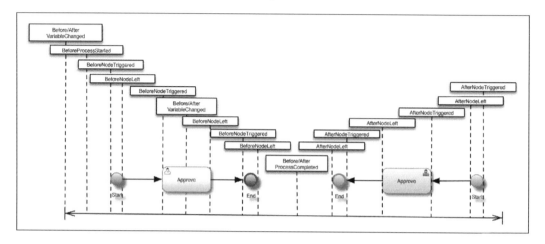

As we can see, the Process Engine nests the execution of the activities together and, from inside the Start Event, calls the Approve User Task; from inside the Approve User Task, it calls the End Event. When it reaches the end of the process, it needs to go back to the stack and this is where all the `AfterNodeLeft` and `AfterNodeTriggered` events are dispatched.

You can also take a look at the `testSimpleBPMN2Approved()` test, which shows how the requested amount is approved if it is under $1,000.

The last step in analyzing our very simple example is to simulate a more real-life scenario. If we have a User Task in our process, the execution will not go straight from Start to End in just one go. We will need to wait for external input and, as we know, human input is not always available. In reality, when we deal with people we need to wait for them; the same happens with some systems, so knowing how to deal with this waiting period is a must.

Let's jump to our last test called `testAsyncSimpleBPMN2Approved()`, which shows how to implement a `WorkItemHandler` that doesn't automatically complete the `WorkItem` after executing its internal logic.

This is the `executeWorkItem(...)` method of the
`AsyncManagerApprovalSimpleWorkItemHandler` implementation:

```java
@Override
public void executeWorkItem(WorkItem wi, WorkItemManager wim) {
    String actorId = (String) wi.getParameters().get("ActorId");
    if (actorId.equals("manager")) {
        Integer amount = (Integer) wi.getParameters().get("amount");
        if (amount >= 1000) {
            results.put("status", "rejected");
            results.put("workItemId", wi.getId());
        } else {
            results.put("status", "approved");
            results.put("workItemId", wi.getId());
        }
    }
}
```

We have two options while implementing an `Async WorkItemHandler`: we can do
some processing internally and then wait for external completion or we can just send
the contextual information needed to complete the activity and allow the external
system or person in charge of completing it to do the calculations. We will need to
choose what's best based on our domain and the information and systems that we
are trying to integrate together. As we can see here, we are keeping the `WorkItem` Id
inside the results map so that, from outside the `WorkItemHandler`, we know how to
complete it later on.

By having an `Async WorkItemHandler` we will see that the execution now changes
and it is clearly represented in the process logs:

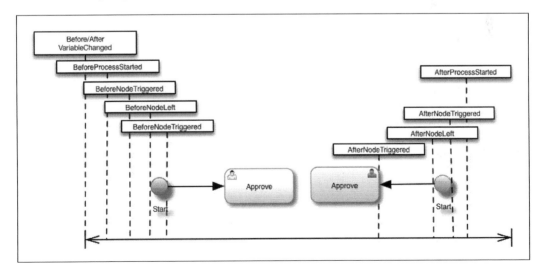

The process will run until there is nothing else to do, in this case after the logic inside the `WorkItemHandler` is executed, and it will return the control to the caller. In the test, the first thing that we do after getting the control back from the `startProcess(...)` method is to check the state of the process:

```
...
ProcessInstance processInstance =
    ksession.startProcess("simple", params);
assertThat(processInstance, notNullValue());
assertThat(ProcessInstance.STATE_ACTIVE,
    is(processInstance.getState()));
WorkflowProcessInstance wpi = (WorkflowProcessInstance)
    processInstance;
assertThat(null, is(wpi.getVariable("request_status")));
System.out.println(" ###### >>> Now I'm completing the WorkItem
    externally ###### ");
ksession.getWorkItemManager()
    .completeWorkItem((long)results.get("workItemId"),
        results);
assertThat(ProcessInstance.STATE_COMPLETED,
    is(processInstance.getState()));
```

Now the state of the process instance is Active, meaning that the process hasn't yet reached any End Event. We can also check the value of the process variable called `request_status` to see that it is in fact `null`. This is because, the `WorkItem` has not been completed yet; hence the process variable hasn't been updated. Next we can use the `ksession.getWorkItemManager().completeWorkItem()` call to complete the `WorkItem`, this time from outside the process engine scope. This simulates an external application or person completing the activity by using a form in a web application or a JMS message that is being picked up from a queue, for example. This will trigger the completion of the process instance by copying the results to the process variable and executing the End Event.

Look at a more advanced example in the test called `ProcessOrderTest`, which can be found here: `chapter-10/chapter-10-tests/src/test/java/org/drools/devguide/chapter10/ProcessOrderTest.java`.

This test executes the `process-order.bpmn2` file, which implements the process introduced at the beginning of the chapter:

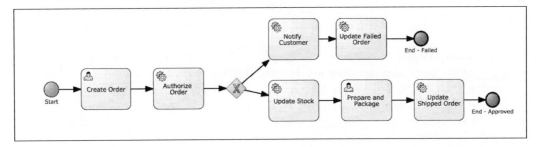

This process includes the use of Service Tasks and the Exclusive Gateway, which allows us to choose different paths from the process based on an expression that can evaluate Process Variables.

The tests are all using synchronous `WorkItemHandlers` for User Tasks and Java Bean Service calls for `ServiceTasks`. It is strongly recommended you take a look at the tests and play around with the idea of implementing Asynchronous interactions instead.

In the following sections, we will be reviewing some integration patterns that can be used to leverage processes while using rules and vice-versa. Again consider this as an introduction and not as an detailed guide.

Drools and jBPM: integration patterns

It is fundamental for us to understand why jBPM and Drools coexist under the KIE umbrella. The relationship between the two projects and the similarities they have make them share most tools and methodologies. These two projects complement each other, allowing end users to describe business knowledge using different paradigms and languages to model business scenarios. We will be able to choose the right tool for the job and then combine the power of the Rule world with the Process world.

This section will cover three of the most common patterns of rule and process integration. The main idea here is to open our mind to look for new alternatives to implement our business solutions.

We already learned in this chapter how to start new process instances by using the KIE APIs, but now we will see how we can interact with the process engine from within our rules.

In the next section we will learn how to interact with the Process engine from our rules. This will open the door for more advanced modeling techniques, giving us even more flexibility to implement our business scenarios.

Accessing the process engine from our rules

Using rules to start a process is one of the most common patterns that we can benefit from. The main idea is to use processes to deal with different scenarios that we might find difficult to perform by chaining rules.

One common scenario is Human Validation; as we saw before, the `simple.bpmn2` process's only mission was to request the input from an external actor to validate an amount. Most of the time, we will want to perform this kind of validation using rules, but we will find it difficult to cover all the possibilities, and sometimes there are sensible decisions and validations that must be performed by people. We can detect these situations by using rules and then delegate to a business process for further processing.

The following rule will create a new process instance via `OrderLine`, which we insert in our Kie Session:

```
rule "Validate OrderLine Item's cost"
    when
        $ol: OrderLine()
    then
        Map<String, Object> params = new HashMap<String, Oject>();
        params.put("requested_amount", $ol.getItem().getCost());
        kcontext.getKieRuntime().startProcess("simple", params);
    end
```

Once again, we are starting our `simple.bpmn2` process, but here we are binding the `OrderLine` item cost to the `requested_amount` process variable required by the process.

If we have too much procedural logic on the right-hand side of our rules, decoupling it as a business process can help us to have more maintainable rules and processes.

It is recommended that, if we want to interact with external systems or if we require human intervention, we just delegate that to a process, where we can easily make changes and plug different connectors. When human interventions are required, using a process engine allows us to automatically track their progress without needing to build all those mechanisms in our application.

By using the `kcontext.getKieRuntime()` we will be able to create, abort, and signal business processes. We can also access the `WorkItemManager` to complete `WorkItems` based on rules.

Process instances as facts

Another way to integrate processes and rules is to insert our Process Instances as facts in the Rule Engine; by doing this, we can start writing rules about our processes. We could even write rules about groups of processes that will enable us to enforce some business requirements.

We could manually insert our `ProcessInstances` objects into our Kie Session, but there is already a `ProcessEventListener` that does all the work for us. This listener is provided by jBPM and is called `RuleAwareProcessEventLister`. This listener will automatically insert our `ProcessInstances` and update them whenever a variable is changed.

The only catch with using this listener is that our processes need to include Async activities to be able to be evaluated by the Rule Engine. This is mostly because, if we run a simple process such as our `simple.bpmn2` example, the process will start and end inside the `startProcess` call, not allowing the Rule Engine to evaluate the `ProcessInstance` fact. This is usually not a big deal, due the fact that most of the processes end up containing multiple safe points to demarcate transactions, as we will see in the second half of this chapter. If we take a look at the `RuleAwareProcessEventLister` implementation, we will notice that the listener is in charge of inserting the `WorkflowProcessInstance` object as a fact and keeping it updated every time that a process variable is changed.

This allows us to start writing rules about those instances. A test class in the chapter source code called `ProcessInstancesAsFactsTest` shows a couple of example rules that evaluate our process instances as we create them.

Let's take a look at these rules. The first one will evaluate to `true` for every process instance that we start inside this Kie Session:

```
rule "There is a WorkflowProcessInstance fact"
    when
        $wi: WorkflowProcessInstance()
    then
    // There is a WorkflowProcessInstance fact: "+$wi
end
```

The next one will only evaluate to `true` for our "process-order" business process instances. For any other fact, we can filter our process instances by their field/ property values.

```
rule "There is a Process Order Instance"
    when
        $wi: WorkflowProcessInstance(processId == "process-order")
    then
        // There is a Process Order Instance: "+$wi
end
```

In the same way, we can get the value of the process variables. Notice that we need to check for null, due the fact that in the example process the Order process variable is set inside a User Task and not when we start the process. It is really useful to control what our process is doing. Remember that we can leverage all this power without doing much, besides adding the `RuleAwareProcessEventLister`.

```
rule "Process Order Instance with a big order"
    when
        $wi: WorkflowProcessInstance(
                        processId == "process-order",
                        $o: getVariable("order") != null &&
                    ((Order)getVariable("order")).getTotal() > 1000)
    then
        // We can abort or create another process instance
        //   to review this big orders here
end
```

Finally, it is important to understand that we can write rules to evaluate a set of Process Instances and mix that information with some other facts. The following rule, for example, checks how many Process Order instances are currently started. We can use this information to make decisions about whether the company can cope with a high number of concurrent orders. Notice that it is possible get a list of process instances and then execute operations on them, such as aborting them if they are not high-priority:

```
rule "Too many orders for just one Manager"
    when
      List($managersCount:size > 0) from collect(Manager())
      List(size > ($managersCount * 3)) from
         collect(WorkflowProcessInstance(processId == "process-
order"))
    then
        //There are more than 3 Process Order Flows per manager.
        //  Please hire more people :)
end
```

This rule will evaluate to `false` if the number of Managers inside the Kie Session is not enough to handle the orders.

BPMN2 Business Rule Tasks

Finally the BPMN2 specification proposes a specific type of task called a Business Rule Task. This task type proposes the most traditional integration between processes and Rules. Traditionally, a Rule Engine was seen as a stateless service that can be called with some data to get some results. As we saw in the rest of this book, Drools is much more than a simple stateless service, and for that reason using the Business Rule Task approach is, most of the time, a very limited approach. In this short section, we will see how the Business Rule Task can be used in a very simple example. In jBPM, the Business Rule Task is used in conjunction with a Rule Property called `ruleflow-group`. This rule property allows us to specify which rules can be fired when the Business Rule Task is executed as part of a process instance. We can have as many groups as we need, but we need to remember to set up the correct Rule Flow Group inside the Business Rule Task.

Note that rules inside a `ruleflow-group` are evaluated and activated as soon as data is available, but those rules will not be fired until the `ruleflow-group` where they belong is activated by a process instance triggering a Business Rule Task that corresponds with that `ruleflow-group`.

In the following example a process uses two Business Rule Tasks to validate and apply discounts to an Order:

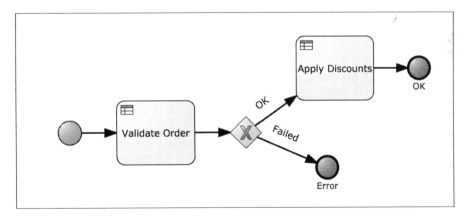

The Order is modeled as a process variable so our rules will pick up the `ProcessInstance` as a fact (as explained in the previous section) and it will analyze the Process Variable that contains the order. Two different `ruleflow-groups` are defined:

- Validation (`ruleflow-group Validation`):

  This `ruleflow-group` is in charge of validating different aspects of the order. Three simple rules validate that the order has a customer associated with it, that the order is not empty (at least one or more OrderLines), and that the state of the Order is pending.

- Discounts (`ruleflow-group Discounts`):

  This `ruleflow-group` can contain any number of rules to apply discounts based on the Order data. In this example two different rules were defined to evaluate the Order total and the Customer Category to apply different discounts.

These rules can be found here: `chapter-10/chapter-10-kjar/src/main/resources/chapter10/order-validation-rules.drl`.

Looking at the BPMN2 process file (here: `chapter-10/chapter-10-kjar/src/main/resources/chapter10/order-validation.bpmn2`), we can notice that each Business Rule Task has its correspondent `ruleflow-group` set:

```
<bpmn2:businessRuleTask id="..." drools:selectable="true" drools:ruleF
lowGroup="Validation" name="Validate Order">
```

Let's do this for `Discounts` as well:

```
<bpmn2:businessRuleTask id="..." drools:selectable="true" drools:ruleF
lowGroup="Discounts" name="Apply Discounts">
```

By adding this relationship with each `ruleflow-group` the engine will know which rules can be triggered at each point in our process instance.

Business Rule Tasks are just another way of defining when rules can be fired. We usually recommend creating a separate `WorkItemHandler` with a separate Kie Session to handle more complex rule sets. If you really want to interact with Drools in a stateless fashion, having a Rules Service and delegating to a `WorkItemHandler` implementation the interaction with this services is most of the time the best solution. We can take a look at what happens on the execution of this process looking at a test called: `BusinessRuleTasksTest` (chapter-10/chapter-10-tests/src/test/java/org/drools/devguide/chapter10/BusinessRuleTasksTest.java). This test class contains four unit tests that validate the correct behavior of our process and rules by inserting different orders as process variables.

These tests all use `RuleAwareProcessEventLister`, which will automatically add each `ProcessInstance` as a fact, and the `TriggerRulesEventListener`, which is in charge of firing our rules as soon as our `ruleflow-groups` get activated in our process instances.

Note that there is no strict rule for what the rules inside a `ruleflow-group` need to evaluate. For this example the rules are evaluating process instances as facts, but there is no restriction to adding any other Fact type on the conditional side of the rules. Because of this flexibility, you need to be careful how you write those rules; remember that they will evaluate all the data in the Kie Session and not only the data in your process instance.

We hope that these examples demonstrate how powerful these tools are when used together. The previous three patterns give us a wide range of possibilities to model complex scenarios. By mastering these three patterns, we should be able to simplify solutions that have been previously written based only on rules or processes into more natural and decoupled models. Instead of forcing rules to behave sequentially, we should be able to formalize a business process for the tasks that need to be performed in sequence. If we need to make decisions exclusively based on data, rules are the right tool for that job. Knowing when to choose rules over processes is a skill that we will learn by practicing and testing different approaches for implementing our business scenarios.

In the second half of this chapter, we will look at more advanced topics related to how we persist our processes and how to demarcate transaction boundaries. Both persistence and transaction mechanisms are shared by Drools and jBPM so we need to understand how these mechanisms impact the execution of our rules and processes.

Persistence and transactions

Drools is usually used in situations where persisting its contents is somewhat impractical. Either we want to execute rules as quickly as possible, and don't want the overhead of having to persist on a database, or we want to keep as much information as possible from the session in memory, so we can reuse it rapidly. The situation with jBPM is a bit different, because we are going to need to use the Kie Session to keep track of the immediate (automatic) steps of a process; then we might have long wait periods while a task is completed or until a signal is received. This scenario implies a sizable need to release resources when not being used; for that, the Kie Session provides persistence mechanisms.

In the following sub sections, we're going to see how Drools and jBPM provide a series of storing mechanisms to release resources from memory and place them into persistence. We will explore:

- Different persistence configurations we can use
- How transactions are managed and demarcated
- How we can use different strategies to customize how the data is persisted

How is state persisted?

As we have already seen, each process instance can interact with a lot of different things within a Kie Session: rules, other processes, external systems, and so on. The best way to keep Kie Session state properly persisted is to wrap every method we have in the Kie Session with a persistence mechanism. To do so, Drools relies on the command-pattern to create a command-based implementation of the Kie Session.

The command-pattern is a way of encapsulating a method call as a specific object; instead of doing multiple different method calls, you always end up doing the same call to the "execute" with a different command parameter, as introduced in *Chapter 5, Understanding KIE Sessions*. This means that, for each method of the Kie Session (insert, `fireAllRules`, and so on), there is an equivalent command object (`InsertObjectCommand`, `FireAllRulesCommand`, and so on) that will be passed to a single "execute" method.

The command-pattern's main purpose is to wrap the call of the execute method with anything we need. In our case, the execute method (being internally used for any operation done on the Kie session) will be preceded by a transaction initialization, and followed by a commit or a rollback depending on the success of the operation. The following diagram shows how the command-pattern is implemented for the Kie Session:

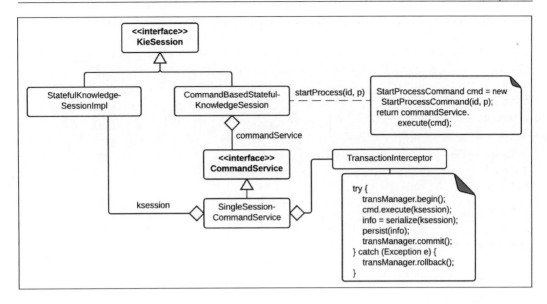

This class structure allows Drools to provide a way of wrapping every call in some extra operations, defined in the `SingleSessionComandService` class. We can see how they operate in the following sequence diagram:

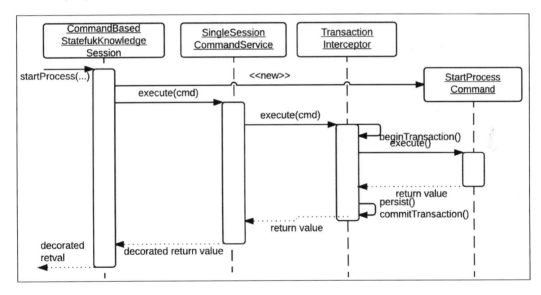

As you can see, instead of directly implementing a `startProcess` method, jBPM provides a `StartProcessCommand`, which does the same operation but lets the engine wrap the call in a transaction. In this same manner, each operation has its corresponding command in Drools.

After this pattern is implemented, the Kie Session will have a place to start and finish a transaction for each call done into it, but it will still need information about how to do it (which transaction manager to use, what type of persistence to use for persisting objects, and a few other configurations). Currently there are two persistence implementations available in Drools and jBPM off-the-shelf: JPA and Infinispan. Even though JPA is the recommended one to use because it is the most maintained of the two, we will explore each in some detail to understand the hookup points for Drools and jBPM persistence by comparison. Drools and jBPM also allow us to write our own persistence layer — for example, if we want to persist the state of the Kie Session using any other storage mechanism.

JPA implementation

This is the default suggested implementation for Drools persistence. It relies on the Java Persistence API to store all the content of the Kie Session, its Process instances, and extra info in tables in a relational database. It relies on a few configuration elements:

- A `persistence.xml` configuration file in the `META-INF` classpath folder
- Drools and jBPM persistence JPA dependencies in the class path
- An `EntityManagerFactory` (from JPA) passed to the Kie Session initialization

We can see the `persistence.xml` with minimal requirements in the `chapter-10-persistence-jpa` project in the source bundle. It contains all the initial classes needed to persist Kie Sessions and process instances. The main classes to pay attention to are `SessionInfo` (which persists the Kie Session data), `ProcessInstanceInfo` (which persists the process instance data), and `WorkItemInfo` (which persists the work items under execution). Each of these tables only persists information relevant to recreating the same state in a different thread depending only on the database, so most of the information is just binary data stored in a blob. Remember that every time we invoke a method on the Kie Session, every piece of data in it will be persisted, so performance is key to this operation.

Once we have the right `persistence.xml`, we need to add two important dependencies into the classpath by adding these two XML blocks into our `pom.xml`:

```
<dependency>
    <groupId>org.drools</groupId>
    <artifactId>drools-persistence-jpa</artifactId>
    <version>6.3.0.Final</version>
</dependency>
<dependency>
    <groupId>org.jbpm</groupId>
```

```
    <artifactId>jbpm-persistence-jpa</artifactId>
    <version>6.3.0.Final</version>
</dependency>
```

These dependencies will add the needed components in our application to start working with persistent Kie Sessions. Also, we will need to add all the relevant dependencies for the JPA implementation we want to use. Drools and jBPM Persistence modules don't enforce any specific JPA implementation to make it as adjustable as possible to the client's needs, though the JPA version targeted by the provided configuration examples is JPA 2.0. In our chapter-10-persistence-jpa/ pom.xml file, we have hibernate dependencies, a Bitronix Transaction Manager (org. codehaus.btm:btm:2.1.4), and an **H2** database (com.h2database:h2:1.3.168) we use for testing.

After we have these components, the next thing to do is get into our code. Most of the change is done to the way we obtain the Kie Session. After the Kie Session is created, we can use it like any other Kie Session object we've used before. In chapter-10-persistence-jpa, there is a test called PersistentProcessTest where we can see this initialization in detail. This test is based on the "process order" business process we've seen earlier, and relies on special database access methods to create and load Kie Sessions into and from the database, respectively. Let's see the block of code needed to create a new persistent Kie Session:

```
KieServices ks = KieServices.Factory.get();
KieBase kieBase = ...
KieSessionConfiguration kieSessionConf = ...
Environment env = EnvironmentFactory.
    newEnvironment();
EntityManagerFactory emf = Persistence.
    createEntityManagerFactory(
        "org.jbpm.persistence.jpa");
env.set(EnvironmentName.ENTITY_MANAGER_FACTORY, emf);
...
KieStoreServices kstore = ks.getStoreServices();
KieSession ksession = kstore.newKieSession(
    env, kSessionConf, kieBase);
```

The first few methods are used to create a Kie Base, an optional Kie Session configuration bean, and an environment variable. The environment variable will be a collection of elements needed to initialize the Kie Session. The one required element is this entity manager factory from JPA, which references the persistence unit defined in our persistence.xml file. It can also have other parameters; we will explore these in detail later on.

For loading an existing Kie Session, there is another method:

```
KieSession oldKieSession =
    Long id = oldKieSession.getIdentifier();
KieSession reloadedKieSession = kstore.
    loadKieSession(id, env, kSessionConf, kieBase);
```

The `loadKieSession` method lets us obtain an existing Kie Session from the database. The parameters are the same as for creating a Kie Session, plus an ID we can obtain from a persistent Kie Session. The Kie Base needs to be a parameter when we create or load the Kie Session because, in order to make serialization/deserialization of the Kie Session as fast as possible, only runtime data is stored in the database.

After we've restored our Kie Session, we can use it like any other Kie Session we have just created. We will be able to register listeners, work item handlers, globals, and channels. This will have to be done also to load the Kie Session, since listeners, work item managers, channels, and global variable references are not persisted in the database.

Infinispan implementation

Infinispan (`http://infinispan.org/`) is an open source data grid framework and platform. It provides a way to store information so that it is both distributed and easy to access, using a NoSQL (Not-Only-SQL) document structure. In a way that is very similar to how Drools and jBPM provide a persistence mechanism for JPA, it also provides a mechanism for working with Infinispan as storage for our Kie Sessions and process instances. This implementation, as with JPA, depends on three things:

- An `infinispan.xml` configuration file in the classpath
- Drools and jBPM persistence Infinispan dependencies in the class path
- A `DefaultCacheManager` (from Infinispan) passed to the Kie Session initialization

An example of the `infinispan.xml` is provided in the `chapter-10/chapter-10-persistence-inf` project in the code bundle. We won't go into too much detail about Infinispan configuration, but will just mention that the internal entity that will hold all the information for this storage is called `EntityHolder`. It will store Kie Sessions and process instance data in a `Base64`-encoded string representing the binary data of the serialized runtime.

As for the dependencies, we will need to add three main dependencies for our Infinispan persistence run:

```
<dependency>
    <groupId>org.kie</groupId>
    <artifactId>drools-infinispan-persistence</artifactId>
    <version>6.3.0.Final</version>
</dependency>
<dependency>
    <groupId>org.kie</groupId>
    <artifactId>jbpm-infinispan-persistence</artifactId>
    <version>6.3.0.Final</version>
</dependency>
<dependency>
    <groupId>org.kie</groupId>
    <artifactId>jbpm-infinispan-persistence</artifactId>
    <version>6.3.0.Final</version>
    <type>test-jar</type>
</dependency>
```

The third one is related to using **Bitronix** as the transaction manager, but it is not enforced by the implementation.

The code we will use for using our persistent Kie Session is very similar to the one we saw for JPA. We will have two calls we can make (one for creating a persistent Kie Session, and one for loading it back from the storage), but the calls will be done through a helper class called InfinispanKnowledgeService, and the environment variable will hold a DefaultCacheManager instead of an EntityManagerFactory. Let's examine an example of the code for the creation of a persistent Kie Session:

```
KieServices ks = KieServices.Factory.get();
KieBase kieBase =
    KieSessionConfiguration kieSessionConf =
    Environment env = EnvironmentFactory.
    newEnvironment();
DefaultCacheManager cm = new DefaultCacheManager(
    "infinispan.xml");
env.set(EnvironmentName.ENTITY_MANAGER_FACTORY, cm);
...
KieSession ksession = InifnispanKnowledgeService.
        newStatefulKnowledgeSession(
        env, kSessionConf, kieBase);
```

The previous code will register a `DefaultCacheManager` using the same key the JPA implementation used to register an entity manager factory. After that is provided, along with a Kie Base and an optional Kie Session configuration, we will use the `newStatefulKnowledgeSession` method of the helper class to obtain an Infinispan persisted Kie Session.

Here's the code for loading a persistent Kie Session:

```
KieSession oldKieSession =
    Long id = oldKieSession.getIdentifier();
KieSession reloadedKieSession =
    InfinispanKnowledgeService.
        loadStatefulKnowledgeSession(
            id, env, kSessionConf, kieBase);
```

The Infinispan implementation is a valid alternative to the JPA implementation, but it is relatively new and very few people are currently using it. Use it with caution, as it is not currently recommended for production environments.

Extending persisted data

Now that we've seen the different flavors of persistent Kie Sessions, and what information is stored, we should note a few important restrictions:

- Only binary data is stored, so querying from outside the engine would be difficult

- The model is somewhat fixed, so reusing possibly existing persistence mechanisms and relating them to our persistent Kie Session is complicated

To solve these issues, there are a few tricks and tools we can use. The first one we will discuss is event listeners.

Event listeners can be registered in the Kie Session to notify external components about changes in the agenda, the working memory, and the process instance state. When using a persistent Kie Session, the calls inside event listeners are executed inside the same transaction that wraps each operation of the Kie Session, so we can extend items that are persisted from the Kie Session in these methods.

Actually, this is something that the Kie Session already does out of the box. There is an `AuditLoggerFactory` class that we can use to build event listeners that can export more data to other tables (specifically, `ProcessInstanceLog`, `NodeInstanceLog`, and `VariableInstanceLog` tables). This audit logger can be found in the `jbpm-audit` dependency and can be added to our Kie Session with the following code:

```
ksession.addEventListener(AuditLoggerFactory.
    newJPAInstance(environment));
```

> When using persistent Kie Sessions, process instance information is only kept in memory while the processes are referenced and active. Using this audit logger is the only way to actually query for a completed process instance. Refer to the end of the test in `PersistentProcessTest` to see the audit log service for info retrieval.

The other type of persistence extension mechanism provided by the Kie Session is called object marshaling strategies. They give the Kie Session a special way to map certain types of objects in and out of the database.

By default, all entities inserted into the persistent Kie Session will be persisted serialized into the binary blob of data for the Kie Session. This is done in this way because the default object marshaling strategy used by the persistent Kie Session is prepared to take any object in the working memory and serialize/deserialize it on read or write operations from the database.

However, we can define more types of object marshaling strategy, and the Kie Session environment allows us to define more than one strategy at the same time. Let's take a look at how the environment variable can hold information about object marshaling strategies:

```
Environment env = EnvironmentFactory.newEnvironment();
env.set( EnvironmentName.OBJECT_MARSHALLING_STRATEGIES,
    new ObjectMarshallingStrategy[] {
    new JPAPlaceholderResolverStrategy(emf),
        new SerializablePlaceholderResolverStrategy(
            ClassObjectMarshallingStrategyAcceptor.DEFAULT)
});
```

In the previous code, we set two object marshaling strategies. As we can see, they are passed to the environment as an array of `ObjectMarshallingStrategy` objects. Each one of its elements will define an accept method (to decide if an object should be serialized or deserialized using this strategy). The engine will take this array of strategies and, for each one in the presented order, it will test whether it accepts each object that has to be written into/read from the database. If it doesn't, the engine will try with the next available strategy.

Specifically in this case, we're using two out of the box implementations of this type of strategy. The first strategy will try to read objects from a JPA-based entity. If an object is not a JPA entity, it will not accept it. For those cases, it will store the data entirely inside the binary blob of the `SessionInfo` table, by using the serialization strategy.

We can find a more detailed example of how these strategies interact with the Kie Session in the `OMSTest` file in the `chapter-10/chapter-10-persistence-jpa` project.

Transaction management

Transactions are managed internally by the Kie Session, to guarantee that, whenever we call an operation inside the Kie Session, we're inside one transaction. This means any call to persistence mechanisms inside event listeners, work item handlers, and any possible interaction component, should take into account joining an existing transaction when we implement them.

Transactions will be searched in the JNDI context of the application if not provided explicitly. This makes the configuration easy in most application servers. However, to create a test, if we want to specify a transaction manager, user transaction, or transaction synchronization registry, we can do so through the Environment bean we use to create or load the Kie Session:

```
Environment env = EnvironmentFactory.newEnvironment();
env.set(EnvironmentName.TRANSACTION, myUserTransaction);
env.set(EnvironmentName.TRANSACTION_MANAGER, transManager);
env.set(EnvironmentName.
    TRANSACTION_SYNCHRONIZATION_REGISTRY,
        transSynchronizationRegistry);
```

All of these components are optional. You can see an example of how this is used to configure a Bitronix Transaction Manager instance inside `PersistentProcessTest` in the `chapter-10-persistence-jpa` project.

Summary

In this chapter we have analyzed jBPM and how it can be used in conjunction with Drools. We analyzed the two most important patterns with regard to how rules can benefit from processes and vice-versa. In the second half of the chapter we reviewed how shared mechanisms such as persistence and transactions can be configured and used.

The next chapter is about how to integrate Drools (and jBPM) with our applications and services. We will be looking at the new Kie Server introduced in version 6.3, and how Drools and jBPM integrate with popular frameworks such as Apache Camel, Spring, and CDI.

11
Integrating Drools with our Apps

We have covered all the important aspects of using Drools as a rule engine. We've explored stateless and stateful Kie Sessions and interaction with business processes, and seen how complex event processing is managed. The last step we need to take is to understand the different ways Drools can interact with the rest of our application.

Drools is a framework; as such, it can interact with other frameworks in as many ways as we can imagine. In the next sections, we will discuss some of the most common design and architecture approaches to integrating Drools with the rest of our design, including some pros and cons for each approach. We will cover an in-detail explanation of:

- Types of Drools integration and architecture considerations
- How to integrate Drools with popular integration frameworks such as Spring and Camel
- Available examples of integrations, such as the Kie Server

Architecture considerations

The first thing we will need to address when designing how Drools should interact with the rest of our application components is how they will fit in the overall architecture; we will have specific requirements regarding how data will be fed into the rule engine, either from our own application or from external sources. Also, we must decide how information should be published back to our application from the rule engine, or how it should be exposed to external applications. We've already seen many mechanisms throughout previous chapters to communicate between Drools and the rest of the application (to name a few):

- We can use global variables to send and receive information outside the Kie Session, and to communicate with different systems. These global variables could represent any Java component, from simple lists, to database accessors, to web service client stubs, allowing the session to communicate with any part of our infrastructure.

- We can use entry points to identify different sources of information Drools will receive facts and events from. In our application, we could use each entry point in a different endpoint that communicates with our Kie Sessions.

- We can register channels to send new information inferred from the Drools runtime out to any other component. Registering listener-like classes, we can send information about specific domain situations.

- We can use any of the pluggable components to detect changes in the status of information inside the working memory (from event listeners to object marshalling strategies) to publish information about our Kie Session to any form of data source. Later on, other services can be built to query those data sources.

Also, we need to decide whether or not our rules should be running in a discrete or continuous fashion, based on the necessities of our domain logic. We will discuss this case in the next subsection.

Asynchronous versus Synchronous Design

As we discussed in *Chapter 6, Complex Event Processing*, we might have situations where the absence of input data on a Drools runtime might trigger a rule. For such cases, asynchronous management of rule execution is required. Even if this is not the case, we might still design our application as a set of asynchronous components connected through a common messaging bus, such as JMS, and still need to manage our rules in a way that accommodates asynchronous management.

If we need to execute our business rules in a synchronous manner, we can take a series of actions to simplify integrating our rule execution to our application, including:

- Using stateless Kie Sessions, if keeping state between rule executions is not something we need to worry about. If you do this, you can create as many Kie Sessions as potential service requests.

- Use global variables to store specific rule execution information. Since we will invoke `fireAllRules` after the insertion of new data, we can get the rule execution information that might modify a global variable, and expose it in the response.

If we need to execute our business rules in an asynchronous manner, we need to take care of a few other things:

- Kie Sessions may be shared between different threads, because some of them may insert new information and others might take care of firing rules (that is, using `fireUntilHalt`).

- If rule execution is delayed to a different thread, we need to think about our rules in such a way that they notify special cases to other parts of the application, also asynchronously. One way to accomplish this would be to register special listeners as global variables that take care of notifying other components about special situations detected by the rules, instead of using lists of data as global variables to store information deferred to after rule execution. This is mainly because rule execution will not cease for rule-firing threads.

- Entry points become a very useful component when multiple sources will be inserting information into a single Kie Session, since it lets the rules easily identify the source of the information.

These considerations will be affecting the full structure of our application, and not just the Drools runtime. The purpose of this discussion of common practices used in Drools asynchronous and synchronous uses is just to understand that we can adapt to any situation we design our applications to handle.

Once we take care of these considerations, we might start considering how the Drools runtime will be deployed along with the rest of our application.

Integrating with the rest of an application

Drools has been historically used (and will most likely continue to be used) to cover many different use cases. Since, as a framework, it acts as a behavior injection component, we can use it to inject all sorts of logic anywhere in our applications. Since we cannot cover all possible types of integration, we will try to cover the most common cases here, and discuss the natural evolution that is usually seen for Drools integration in diverse applications.

The first most common step for integrating Drools is usually embedding its dependencies and code inside our own application and using it as a library.

Embedding Drools into our application

This is usually the first scenario for integrating Drools with our own apps because it is the quickest way to start using Drools. We just need to add the right dependencies and start using the APIs directly in the locations we want. The following figure shows this integration as it happens in the first stage:

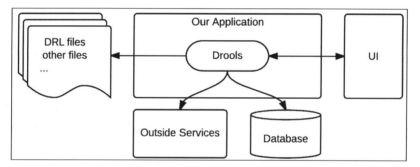

First stage: Drools embedded inside our application

The first rule projects we defined in this book followed this structure. As you can see, Drools can interact with any and all layers of our application, depending on what we expect to accomplish with it:

- It could interact with the UI to provide complex form validations
- It could interact with data sources to load persisted data when a rule evaluation determines it is needed
- It could interact with outside services, to either load complex information into the rules or send messages to outside services about the outcome of the rules execution

During this first stage in the development of rule-based projects, all the components needed to run our rules are usually included in our application, including the rules. This means we will have to redeploy our application if we want to change the business rules running in it.

The first thing we usually need to do in these situations is to start updating the business logic inside the rules at a faster rate than the rest of the application. This leads us to upgrade our architecture so as to move business rules as an outside dependency, defined as a **KJAR**. Components in our rule runtime can dynamically load these rules from outside repositories, as the following diagram shows:

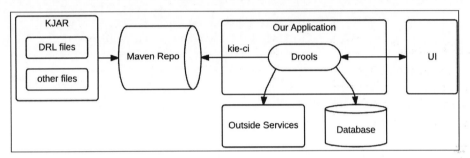

Second stage: Drools getting our rules from an external repository

In this structure, we moved the rules away from our application. Instead, we take them from an external JAR. This change is not just a project rearrangement, because the actual JAR with all the rules won't be a dependency at the moment of deploying our application. Instead, the Drools runtime will read the JAR directly from our Maven repository (local or remote) and load the rules whenever it needs to do it. The Drools runtime can do so by letting CDI directly inject our Kie-related objects with the appropriate version using a @KReleaseId annotation:

```
@Inject @KSession
@KReleaseId(groupId = "org.drools.devguide",
    artifactId = "chapter-11-kjar",
    version = "0.1-SNAPSHOT")
KieSession kSession;
```

Alternatively, we can directly build our Kie Container objects based on a specific version of our code. If done this way, we can use a KieScanner to let our runtime know it should monitor the repository for possible future changes, so that the runtime can change versions without even having to restart:

```
KieServices ks = KieServices.Factory.get();
KieContainer kContainer = ks.newKieContainer(
    ks.newReleaseId("org.drools.devguide",
        "chapter-11-kjar", "0.1-SNAPSHOT"));
```

```
KieScanner kScanner = ks.newKieScanner(kContainer);
kScanner.start(10_000);
KieSession kSession = kContainer.newKieSession();
```

We should mention at this stage that nowhere else in the project have we added a direct dependency to the specific JAR from which we want our Kie Session to be built. Dependency resolving is entirely managed by the runtime, by having `org.kie:kie-ci` as a dependency. You can see examples of these two cases in the `chapter-11/chapter-11-ci` project in the code bundle. Both examples are inside the `KieCITest` class.

 Note: In the previous code snippet, we use a specific Maven Release ID. But, just like in Maven, we can use ranges to define the version of the release on which we want to work. Also, the use of SNAPSHOT and LATEST can let the Maven components worry about the right version they should obtain, instead of returning a single specific version.

This is a necessary step toward having an independent development life cycle for our business rules. This independence will allow for the rules to be developed, deployed, and managed as many times as needed without having to redeploy our applications.

The main disadvantage at this stage of having Drools embedded in our application is the amount of dependencies needed to do all this. We started our case with only a few DRL files and about a dozen lightweight dependencies added to our classpath, but at this stage we will have a few other dependencies directly in our runtime that we might want to keep out of our classpath. This is the point where we start looking at exporting our rule runtime to external components, and we will discuss this in the next subsection.

Knowledge as a Service

Once our business rule requirements start growing—including dynamic rule reload, more and more calls, and interactions with external systems—we get to the point where multiple applications would need to replicate a lot of things in their own runtimes to reach the same behavior for what could be common business logic. The natural transition at this point is creating knowledge-based external services outside our application. Managing independent rule development life cycles becomes easier, as does the possibility of replicating the service environment for higher demands. The following diagram shows a common way to design such services:

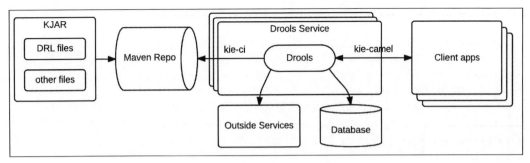

Third stage: Drools as a Service

In the previous diagram, we can notice two important aspects:

- As many client applications as desired can access the Drools runtime without adding big complexities to their own technology stack, because that complexity is entirely on the Drools Service side.

- All the rules are stored in a Maven repository. This allows for all environments to work with the same Business Rules if they share business logic, and for all of them to have the same versions of that knowledge updated at the same time, if rules are modified.

Creating this sort of component makes most sense when we want to add several custom configurations to our Drools runtime—for example, accessing external services in a legacy way, or when we want to provide custom responses to outside clients. We can use common integration tools, such as the Spring Framework (`http://projects.spring.io/spring-framework/`) and Apache Camel (`http://camel.apache.org/`), to integrate other components and environments with our Drools runtime. We will see how to configure these elements in further subsections.

However, when we need to use the Drools runtime internally (where the specific structure of the response can be adjusted later), and configurations are standard in terms of what Drools expects in a `kmodule.xml`, we might use a simpler approach. Drools provides a module called `kie-server`, which can be used to configure similar environments that are only responsible for running Drools rules and processes, taking the kJAR from outside sources, as the following diagram shows:

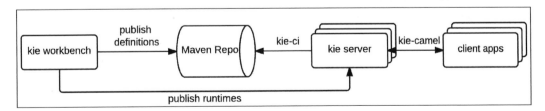

We will see how the `kie-server` is configured in a further section.

As you can see, there are multiple ways of integrating Drools, depending on our architecture, design, and performance-oriented decisions. Let's discuss some of the off-the-shelf integration tools available to make Drools interact with the rest of our components and applications.

CDI integration

One of the first integration frameworks we discussed in this book was the **Contexts and Dependency Injection (CDI)** standard. It lets us define how we should bind beans together depending on `@Inject` annotations, to avoid having to write code to `init` and bind all our beans together. If we are already using CDI in our application, we have already seen we can use injected Kie Sessions, Kie Containers, and Kie Bases in previous chapter. There is no other required change in our application, other than a CDI implementation dependency.

In our `chapter-11/chapter-11-ci` example, we use Weld (`http://weld.cdi-spec.org/`) as an implementation by adding this dependency into our POM file:

```
<dependency>
    <groupId>org.jboss.weld.se</groupId>
    <artifactId>weld-se-core</artifactId>
    <version>1.1.28.Final</version>
</dependency>
```

Also, we need to define an empty `beans.xml` file inside our project, in the `src/main/resources/META-INF` folder. Doing these two things lets our Java runtime understand it should start injecting beans, depending on our class annotations.

Spring integration

Another well known framework for dependency injection is the Spring Framework (`http://projects.spring.io/spring-framework/`). Drools can be easily integrated to other components in an application using Spring, and we have an example of this integration in the `chapter-11/chapter-11-spring` project of the code bundle.

Introducing Spring Framework

The Spring Framework is, in its core, an integration framework that allows binding of different Java components together using Inversion of Control. Through XML configuration files or injection annotations, it lets us tie together bean constructors and setters to initialize the runtime of our applications. Besides that base functionality, Spring has been in the market for several years now, and has a lot of adoption and pluggable libraries that allow us to bind all sorts of functionalities to our apps, including Data Access libraries, Aspect-oriented programming features, URL binding, and Transaction management.

Kie Spring Config example

Drools provides a module to integrate with the Spring framework called Kie Spring. It lets us define Kie Modules, Bases, Sessions, and set components on them and bind them together with the rest of our Spring configurations. To start using it, we first need to define this dependency inside our POM file:

```
<dependency>
    <groupId>org.kie</groupId>
    <artifactId>kie-spring</artifactId>
    <version>6.3.0.Final</version>
</dependency>
```

And after that, we define our Kie components inside our Spring context file. Here's a section of the `chapter-11-spring/src/main/resources/spring-context.xml` file that shows the configuration we need to use to define a Kie Session:

```
<kie:import releaseId-ref="kjarToUse" />
  <kie:releaseId id="kjarToUse"
                 groupId="org.drools.devguide"
                 artifactId="chapter-11-kjar"
                 version="0.1-SNAPSHOT" />
  <kie:kmodule id="kie-spring-sample">
    <kie:kbase name="kbase1">
      <kie:ksession name="ksession1"/>
    </kie:kbase>
  </kie:kmodule>
```

In the previous example, we defined a set of important components:

- **kie:import** and **kie:releaseId**: With these two tags, we announce the context we should dynamically load in a specific release of a Kie JAR, and load it into the classpath.

- **kie:module**, **kie:base**, and **kie:session**: These components are used in a very similar fashion to what we would define inside `kmodule.xml`. It will let us define Kie Bases and Sessions we can later on reference from other Spring managed components.

- The **kie:batch** tag: It lets us define a specific set of commands that needs to be executed to initialize our Kie Sessions; using kie:batch, we can set globals, insert initial facts, or anything specific we need to do to initialize our Kie Session, without having to write any code for it.

- We can run this example by running the `KieSpringTest` JUnit test in the `chapter-11-spring` project of the code bundle. If you want to see a full explanation of the types of tags available for configuring Kie Spring contexts, you can find it at: `http://docs.jboss.org/drools/release/latest/drools-docs/html/ch13.html`.

Camel integration

Spring and CDI are great frameworks for integrating Drools inside our own applications. In cases where we want to expose Drools functionality as a service to other applications, we need to start looking at frameworks that expose service endpoints. For this purpose, there is an integration component that allows us to expose Drools components through Apache Camel (`http://camel.apache.org/`) endpoints, called Kie Camel.

Integrating the Apache Camel framework

Apache Camel is an integration framework that lets us define routes that merge together different types of services and components, using a series of predefined and market accepted patterns called **Enterprise Integration Patterns** (**EIP**). Similarly to a design pattern, an EIP allows us to define reusable, easy to understand and extensible components. The main focus of EIP is to provide simple, reusable structures to define service endpoints.

Creating our Kie endpoints

In order to use Kie Camel, the first thing we need to do is add a dependency to our POM file:

```
<dependency>
    <groupId>org.jboss.integration.fuse</groupId>
    <artifactId>kie-camel</artifactId>
    <version>1.3.0-SNAPSHOT</version>
</dependency>
```

Note: the kie-camel component is managed as part of the JBoss integration tooling, outside the Drools projects, and that is why it uses a different versioning scheme from the rest of the Kie components. Version 1.3.0-SNAPSHOT is the current version, which uses Drools 6.3.0.Final dependencies internally.

This component will have all the dependencies as Camel core libraries, which will make it easier to define our endpoints. These endpoints will be defined using a Camel concept called routes; routes are specific Enterprise Integration Pattern implementations, where we configure how different endpoints interact with each other. We can define them using a Spring context file, and here's a short example of how to create a route that uses Drools:

```
<bean id="kPolicy" class="org.kie.camel.component.KiePolicy" />
<camelContext xmlns="http://camel.apache.org/schema/spring">
  <route>
    <from uri="direct://someOriginalRoute"/>
    <policy ref="kPolicy">
      <unmarshal ref="xstream" />
      <to uri="kie:ksession1" />
      <marshal ref="xstream" />
    </policy>
  </route>
</camelContext>
```

This simple piece of Spring context does a lot of things:

1. **It defines a KiePolicy bean**: This is done to expose Drools-related paths through a REST endpoint, in order to enable these paths to parse Kie commands that can be fed into a Kie Session.

2. **It defines a route**: The route contains three main steps: unmarshalling a message using the XStream framework, passing the unmarshalled object directly into a previously defined Kie Session "ksession1", and then marshalling the response back using XStream once again.

As we can imagine, there is a lot more that we can do with Apache Camel to expose different parts of this Kie Session to other beans. We could feed information from its listeners to other endpoints, perform previous validations to the data being introduced into the Kie Session, or anything else we can imagine.

When we expose the endpoint through a REST server (you can find the rest of this configuration in the chapter-11-camel/src/test/resources/cxf-rs-spring. xml file), we can invoke it by passing XML representations of a Drools Kie Session command, such as the following:

```
<batch-execution lookup="ksession1">
  <insert out-identifier="myItem">
      <org.drools.devguide.eshop.model.Item>
          <cost>119.0</cost>
          <category>NA</category>
      </org.drools.devguide.eshop.model.Item>
  </insert>
  <fire-all-rules/>
</batch-execution>
```

This will cause the command to be fed into the Kie Session, which will then insert the specified Item object into the working memory and fire all the rules. A full list of the XML commands which can be fed into a Kie Session in this manner can be found at http://docs.jboss.org/drools/release/6.3.0.Final/drools-docs/html/ ch11.html.

We can run this example by running the KieCamelTest JUnit test in the chapter-11-camel project in the code bundle. Apache Camel is a very large topic to be fully covered in this book, but for those who still find it useful and want to start looking into Camel, you can get started at http://camel.apache.org/manual.html.

Kie Execution Server

We've already discussed the possibility of having a specific Drools oriented service to run our rules in an isolated environment. The **Kie Execution Server** (or Kie Server for short) is an out of the box implementation of such a service. It is a modular, standalone server component that can be used to execute rules and processes, configured as a WAR file. It is currently available for web containers and JEE6 and JEE7 application containers.

The main purpose of the Kie Server is to be a runtime environment for Kie components, and one that uses as few resources as possible in order for it to be easily deployed in cloud environments. Each instance of the Kie Server can create and use many Kie Containers, and its functionality can be extended through the use of something called **Kie Server Extensions**.

Also, the Kie Server allows us to provide **Kie Server Controllers**. These are endpoints which will expose Kie Server functionalities. In a sense, they will be the front-end of our Kie Server.

Let's take a look at how we can configure these components inside our Kie Server instances.

Configuring Kie Server

Kie Server provides two default Kie Server Extensions: one for Drools and one for jBPM. Even though they are the only ones currently provided, Kie Server Extensions are thought to be something we can add to the Kie Server in as many flavors as we need. The way the Kie Server will load them is through the `ServiceLoader` standard: a set of files included in the `META-INF/services` folder of the application classpath with information about the different implementations of expected interfaces.

In our case, the expected interface is `KieServerExtension`, so we will need a `META-INF/services/org.kie.services.api.KieServerExtension` file, whose only contents will be the name of the implementations of that interface.

In this case, we have an example of such a configuration in the projects under the `chapter-11/chapter-11-kie-server` folder of our code bundle. This project adds an extra feature to the Kie Server by making sure all Kie Bases inside it have statistics published through JMX. We have a `CustomKieServerExtension` Java class that defines a series of methods:

- **init/destroy**: These let us define how to start/stop the associated server components related to providing a specific service in our Kie server. In our case, we're just making sure we have JMX enabled by asking for the MBean Server.

- **createContainer/disposeContainer**: For every Kie Container used in our Kie Server, we can define these methods to do special treatment for them. Since our functionalities will be targeted at Kie components mostly, this is the proper connection point for our special services targeted at created Kie components. In our case, we're registering the JMX beans using the special methods in the `DroolsManagementAgent` singleton class:

```
DroolsManagementAgent.getInstance().
        registerKnowledgeBase(kbase);
```

- **getAppComponents**: These methods will be used by other extensions to get information about the exposed services we started with in our extension (if any).

Once these have been deployed in an app server, we will need to create a user with the `kie-server` role in the aforementioned server, and we will be able to access our deployment through the `http://SERVER/CONTEXT/services/rest/server/` URL. The following is an example of an expected response:

```
<response type="SUCCESS" msg="Kie Server info">
  <kie-server-info>
    <capabilities>BRM</capabilities>
    <capabilities>Statistics</capabilities>
    <capabilities>KieServer</capabilities>
    <capabilities>BPM</capabilities>
    <location>
      http://localhost:8230/kie-server/services/rest/server
    </location>
    <name>KieServer@/kie-server</name>
    <id>15ad5bfa-7532-3eea-940a-abbbbc89f1e8</id>
    <version>6.3.0.Final</version>
  </kie-server-info>
</response>
```

Inside the capabilities, we can see `Statistics` is one of the exposed capabilities. That is the one extension we created. Any functionality can be exposed in this way, like a special protocol exposition to our other Kie Server Extensions (that is, through the Apache Mina - `https://mina.apache.org` - or RabbitMQ - `https://www.rabbitmq.com` - communication protocols).

Note: When we run this example inside our test, it will create a Wildfly App Server (`http://wildfly.org`) instance and deploy our customized Kie Server inside it. In order for it to work properly, we also create a few configuration files inside that server. You can review the assembly steps of the project inside the POM file of the `kie-server-tests` project for the Wildfly server. If you wish to configure it for any other App or Web Server, here's a detailed list of how to configure it for other environments: `https://docs.jboss.org/drools/release/6.3.0.Final/drools-docs/html/ch22.html#d0e21933`.

Default exposed Kie Server endpoints

As for the API exposition from the Kie Server, it comes in two main flavors: REST and JMS. These two endpoints work with the same commands for creating/disposing containers, and operating against Kie Sessions. These two endpoints are used in almost the same way if we use a client utility called `KieServiceClient`, available in the **org.kie.remote:kie-remote-client** Maven dependency. Internally, however, they work in very different ways.

REST exposes the functionality of Kie Containers through a REST API. It provides a very useful way to interact with any type of system, since any commercially used language now comes with APIs to invoke REST APIs. This is the best choice both for interacting with applications written in other languages and for the initial use of the API. A full description of the REST API exposed through the Kie Server can be found here: `https://docs.jboss.org/drools/release/6.3.0.Final/drools-docs/html/ch22.html#d0e22326`.

JMS exposes the functionality of Kie Containers through three specific JMS queues, called `Kie.SERVER.REQUEST` (for handling incoming Command requests), `Kie.SERVER.RESPONSE` (to send back a response), and `Kie.SERVER.EXECUTOR` (for asynchronous calls, mostly used by BPM components). Since JMS is naturally asynchronous, it makes it the best choice when creating distributed environments; Each of the Kie Servers available at any time can compete to take messages from these queues, so high availability and performance are naturally managed with the growth of requests.

There are two examples in the code bundle of using these APIs. Both can be found in the `chapter-11/chapter-11-kie-server/kie-server-test` folder, under the names **RESTClientExampleTest** and **JMSClientExampleTest**, for REST and JMS respectively. They are extremely similar, with the exception of how the `KieServicesClient` class is initialized:

```
KieServicesConfiguration config =
KieServicesFactory.newRestConfiguration(
    "http://localhost:8080/kie-server/services/rest/server",
"testuser", "test", 60000);
KieServicesClient client = KieServicesFactory.
    newKieServicesClient(config);
```

In the previous code, we see the initialization block for a Kie Server Client that uses REST as an endpoint configuration for a Kie Server running in `http://localhost:8080`.

Besides performing these deployment managements through code, the Kie projects provide a set of usable workbench tools that allow us to create, build, and deploy rule definitions in any Kie Server without having to write any code. These tools are referred to as Workbenches, and we'll see an introduction to how they work in the next section.

Kie Workbench

There is one more component we have briefly mentioned before, **Kie Workbench**. Kie Workbench is a web environment where we can create and test all sorts of Kie assets, such as rules, processes, and data models. It is a very useful tool to include business people with little technical knowledge of the specifics of implementation into the development cycle, because it provides a user-friendly environment for rule writing. Go to `chapter-11-workbench-tests`, compile it, and run the standalone script from the `target/wildfly.8.1.0.Final/bin/` folder to start the environment. After it starts, go to `http://localhost:8080/kie-wb` on your machine and log in using the "`testuser`" username and `test` password to get to the following page:

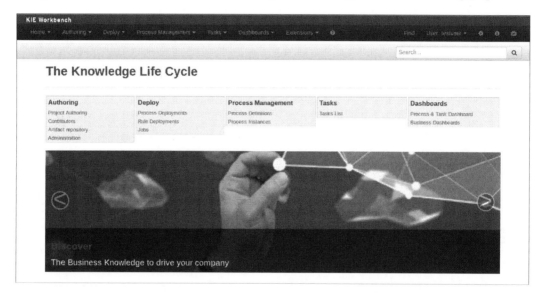

 Note: it will take a few minutes to start, so if you get a 404 from the URL, just give it a few more minutes to load

Once it loads, we will be able to see the options involving authoring Kie Assets if we go to the **Authoring | Project Authoring** option in the top menu:

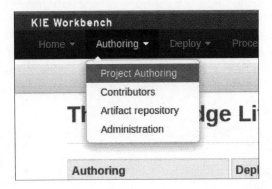

From the opening perspective, we will have a lot of screens available, where we will be able to create rules, processes, data models, and many more elements using the **New Item** option. We can also create new projects to group these assets, and they will be internally managed as Maven projects versioned inside (also internally) a Git repository. We have a few predefined projects to start playing with.

We will open the mortgages project editor. To do so, we'll click on the **uf-playground** option next to the demo organizational unit (in the Project Explorer screen on the left), and then on the **mortgages** option in the list next to it. Once that is open, click on the button that appears over the listboxes, called **Open Project Editor**. Then, on the opening editor we can see to the right, we will see a set of options on the top. Clicking on the **Build** option will display the **Build & Deploy** option, and clicking on it will deploy the project in an internal Maven repository:

We will use this deployed project to test a Kie Execution Server. There is a very large set of tools we could use inside the Kie Workbench, but unfortunately we cannot explain them all within this book. There is a very good set of training sessions for using the Workbench features available online, created by *Eric D. Schabell*. You can find them at the following URL: `http://bpmworkshop-onthe.rhcloud.com/ brms6_1/lab01.html`.

We will concentrate on the specific components of the Kie Workbench that bind it to the Kie Server we just discussed. Once we have built and deployed a project, it will be available inside the Maven repository exposed by the workbench (for the mortgages project, it can be found at `http://localhost:8080/kie-wb/maven2/ mortgages/mortgages/0.0.1/mortgages-0.0.1.jar`). This JAR will be available with the same credentials used by the Kie Workbench. From there, we can perform deploys through the UI to any Kie Execution Server we have available. To do so, we must go to the top menu option **Deploy | Rule Deployments**, and click on the **Register** button:

We've already deployed a Kie Execution Server inside the same environment, using the customized WAR we created in the previous section. In order to be able to deploy to it, we must register it with the proper data. The **Identifier** property must have the base REST endpoint of the Kie Server. For our environment, it will be `http://localhost:8080/kie-server/services/rest/server`. For the **Name** property, we will just write some identifying text, such as **devguide-server**.

Once the Kie Server is created in the **Rule Deployments** view of the Kie Workbench, we can select it and click on the plus sign visible on the right of the devguide-server line. By clicking on that button, we can see a window with a form to deploy a specific container in the given Kie Server. We will use it to deploy the **mortgages** project, as shown in the following screenshot:

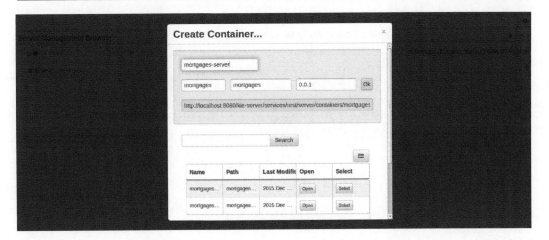

After we deploy the container, we can see its details by clicking on the small arrow to the right of the created container (it will appear right below the plus sign button we clicked before). We can also select it by clicking on the radio button to the left of the created container, and clicking on the **Start** button on the top left of the Rule Deployment screen. After you deploy and start the container, it can start resolving requests with the rules and processes defined in the given project.

Using these tools can allow non-technical people to write, deploy, and execute rules, without having to write a single line of code in a conventional IDE setup. Everything can be done through the tool. This allows business specialists to be more easily introduced to the realm of rules, and can be a great tool to help them collaborate in the development process of Drools-based projects.

Drools and beyond: extending our functionality

We've seen in this chapter, and throughout the whole book, a lot of different ways to use Drools. Whether we use it as an embedded library, a service, or a closed product, the main goal is to enable our applications to grow in a manageable way. We must consider our design, inside and around business rules, to achieve this. We will try to cover a few tricks that have facilitated growing our Business Rule-enabled applications in the past.

One of the first extensions of functionality we've seen for Drools components has been global variables. If we define them as interfaces or abstract classes, we can define them by using different classes for different runtime components (that is, test cases, local versus QA, or production environments, and so on). They are a very simple way of providing ease of extensibility because of their pluggable nature.

Global variables also provide a very useful feature that sometimes gets overused; because we can keep a reference to the global variables we set, and we can store information from our rule executions into it, we end up storing a lot of information in global variables that is clutter our rule consequences—for example, a log of rules is triggered:

```
global List rulesExecuted;

rule "example of bad action"
    when
        //our conditions
    Then
        //our actions
        rulesExecuted.add("example of bad action");
end

KieSession ksession = ...;
List rulesExecuted = new ArrayList();
ksession.setGlobal("rulesExecuted", rulesExecuted);
...
ksession.fireAllRules();
System.out.println(rulesExecuted.size());
```

In the previous example, we can see a common point where we start abusing global variables. Global variables, if used to record information about our rule execution, should be used to store specific business-related information. If we just want to store which rules were triggered (or a sub-group of them) or anything common to all our Drools executions, we are better off using Event Listeners. Event Listeners are the best choice when we want to audit our execution, rather than obtaining specific information about our domain. We need to keep the difference in mind when we design our runtime.

Another important aspect of rule-related application design is to make our runtime code as agnostic as possible about which specific rules are triggered. If you couple your execution to the firing of specific rules, it will be very hard to extend your application. This is also true when it comes to designing our rules. Like we said before, rules should be independent of each other, and that extends to the application that runs them; all we should care about in the execution of our rules is the final decisions made by them. Otherwise, any change or add-on in our rules will need to be impacted into our runtime as well.

This applies to creating tests for our rules. We should try to avoid validating that specific rules have fired, and rather verify that the consequences of the rule execution have been followed. For example, when testing the execution of our online shop case, we should strive to test whether the final outcome of the rules has been followed (items have been catalogued, discounts have been applied, and so on), and not just whether one specific rule or another has been tested. To put it more simply, we should let the rule engine do its job.

Summary

Business Rules adoption is a very rewarding task once we get past the first learning curve. Once we reach a point where rule stakeholders have control over the rules used in their environment (and the tools to do so), the speed of development and deployment increases enormously. Also, Business Rules become an easy way to break down requirements and leave them registered in a traceable, understandable way. This helps intercommunication between technical groups and domain experts, thanks to this common language. No organization has ever regretted learning Drools, much less adopting it in their everyday activities.

We have learnt in this chapter about the many different tricks and tools to use Drools with common designs and architectures, and an introduction to the tools provided by the Kie Workbench and the Kie Server; we have also learned how to access them. It is up to the end user to determine the best way to make use of these components to link Drools to their existing enterprise infrastructure, but it is our honest hope that now you will have all the tools to make the best decision for your needs.

Index

A

accumulate keyword 87
action 3
Agenda 8
Alpha Nodes
  about 220
  constraint JIT compilation 223
  sharing 221, 222
Apache Camel framework
  integrating 290
  reference link 287-292
Apache Commons Logging
  URL 207
Apache Mina
  URL 294
Apache Open Web Beans
  URL 30
application
  Drools, embedding into 284-286
  Drools, integrating with 284

B

backward-chaining reasoning 236, 237
Beta Nodes
  about 224, 225
  or between patterns 228, 229
  sharing 225-228
Bitronix 275
Boolean operations 82, 83
business process example
  about 252-254
  Kie Session advanced configurations 255
Business Process Management (BPM)
  about 72

URL 250
Business Rule Management Systems
  (BRMS) 12

C

Camel integration
  about 290
  Kie endpoints, creating 290, 291
CDI integration 288
CEP-based Rules, declaring
  about 141
  events, semantics 142
  temporal operators 144
  time-based-events, declaring 143, 144
CEP-based Scenarios
  about 153
  continuous versus discrete
    rule firing 154, 155
  limitations 156, 158
  session clock, testing 155, 156
  stream processing, configuring 153, 154
channels 118-120
collect from objects 86
collection operations 83, 84
command pattern
  URL 108
complex event 140
complex event processing (CEP)
  about 139
  CEP-based Rules, declaring 141
  events and complex events 140, 141
Complex Systems 14
condition 3
conditional
  named consequences 102, 103

conditional elements 91
consequence 3
Context & Dependency Injection (CDI)
  about 28, 29, 30
  global variables 196
  URL 28
Contexts and Dependency
      Injection (CDI) 288
customer classification decision tree
      example
  about 188, 189
  DataDictionary 189
  header 189
  model 190
CustomKieServerExtension Java class
  createContainer/disposeContainer
      method 293
  init/destroy method 293

D

Data Access Object 62
data, in working memory
  delete/retract keywords 65
  insert keyword 63
  insert memory 63
  modify and update keywords 64
Data Mining Group
  URL 185, 186
decision tables
  about 167, 168
  enhanced decision tables 176, 177
  RuleSet section 169, 170
  RuleTable section 171, 172
  scenario 173-175
  structure 168
  troubleshooting 175
Declarative Programming 3
declared types 78, 79
default exposed Kie Server
      endpoints 294, 295
delete/retract keywords 65, 66
dictionary file, DSL
  about 160, 161
  constraints, adding to pattern 162, 163
Domain Specific Languages
  about 160

dictionary file 160, 161
rules file 163, 164
simple scenario 165, 166
troubleshooting 164, 165
don keyword 97
DOT language
  URL 247
DRL constructs
  URL 35
Drools
  about 1, 160, 281
  architecture considerations 282
  asynchronous, versus synchronous
      design 282, 283
  backward reasoning 241-243
  bugs, reporting 213
  embedding, into application 284-286
  functionality, extending 299, 301
  inline casts 95
  integrating, with application 284
  issues, URL 213
  nested accessors 94
  null-safe operators 95
  persistence 270
  positional arguments 240, 241
  Query Element Node 244
  unification 237-239
Drools CEP 139
Drools DSL 160
Drools Eclipse plugin 209
Drools Fusion 139
Drools GitHub repository
  URL 213
Drools project
  creating 21-24
Drools Rule Language (DRL)
  about 30, 61
  loosely coupled DRLs, creating 194
Drools runtime instances 41

E

elements
  deviations 100, 101
  logical insertion 98
end template 179
Enterprise Integration Patterns (EIP) 290

entry-point (EP) nodes 217-219
environment
    setting up 20, 21
event-driven architecture (EDA)
    about 148, 149
    Event Channels 149
    Event Consumer 148
    Event Processing Agents 149
    Event Producer 148
    sliding windows 150
    split event sources, with entry
        points 149, 150
event listeners
    about 123-125
    Kie Bases 123
    Kie Sessions 123
events, semantics
    about 142
    interval events 142
    punctual events 142
EXISTS keyword 92-94
exists node 231, 232
external interactions
    adding, with global variables 61, 62

F

FORALL keyword 92-94
from clause 84-86
from keyword 201-203

G

Git
    URL 20
globals
    about 110, 111
    benefits 195, 196
    information, collecting from
        session 116, 117
    interacting with external systems,
        in RHS 117, 118
    new information, introducing
        in LHS 114-116
    pattern condition, parameterizing 111-114
global variables
    external interactions, adding 61, 62

Graphviz
    URL 247

H

H2 database 273

I

Imperative programming
    versus Declarative implementation 3, 4
inferences 6
Infinispan
    implementing 274, 275
    URL 274
inline casts 95
insert keyword 63
integration patterns
    about 263
    BPMN2 Business Rule Tasks 267-269
    process engine, accessing from rules 264
    process instances, as facts 265, 266

J

Java Message Service (JMS) queue 149
jBPM 72 250-252, 263
jBPM6
    books, URL 252
JMSClientExampleTest 295
JPA
    implementing 272, 273
JProfiler
    URL 157

K

kcontext 160
kie-api artifact 181
kie:base component 290
Kie Base components
    about 123-125
    custom accumulate functions 134-138
    custom operators 127-134
    functions 125-127
KieBases 49
kie:batch tag 290
Kie Camel 290

KieContainer classpath
  about 44, 45
  KieHelper, preferring over 194, 195
Kie endpoints
  creating 290, 291
Kie Execution Server 292
KieHelper
  over KieContainer classpath 195
  preferring, over KieContainer classpath 194
kie:import tag 289
KieModule
  about 43, 44
  and KieContainer 44
  configurations 49-52
  KieModule A 44
  KieModule B 44
  KieModule Parent 44
  rules, loading from classpath 45-47
  rules loading, Maven artifacts
    (Kie-CI) used 48
kie:module component 290
KieModules 44, 45
kie:releaseId tag 289
Kie runtime components
  about 110
  channels 118, 119
  event listeners 123-125
  globals 110, 111
  queries 120, 121
KieScanner
  about 53, 54
  Artifacts version resolution 54-56
  unexpected issues and errors,
    dealing with 57-59
Kie Server
  configuring 293, 294
  default exposed KIE Server
    endpoints 294, 295
Kie Server Controllers 292
Kie Server Extensions 292
KieServices (ks) 46
KieSession
  about 49, 123
  advanced configurations 255
  event listeners 255
  work items 255-259
kie:session component 290

Kie Spring Config example 289, 290
Kie Workbench
  about 296-299
  and Process Designer, URL 253
KJAR 285
kmodule.xml file
  URL 52
Knime
  URL 185
Knowledge Artifacts 48
Knowledge as a Service 286-288
knowledge base (KB) 193
Knowledge is Everything (KIE) 42

L

left-hand side, troubleshooting
  about 197
  compilation errors 197, 198
  runtime errors 198-200
  untriggered rules 200-204
Log4j
  URL 207
Logback
  URL 207
loops
  controlling 75
  model properties, execution control 77, 78
  property reactive beans 79-81

M

matches operators 83
Maven project
  URL 20
Maven versions
  URL 56
modify keywords 64

N

nested accessors 94
network, special nodes
  about 229
  accumulate node 233, 234
  exists node 231, 232
  from node 234, 235
  not node 230, 231

no-loop attribute 173
non matches operators 83
NOT keyword 92
not node 230, 231
null-safe operators 95
numeric operations 82, 83

O

objects
  in memory, decorating 95-97
Object Type Nodes (OTN) 218, 219
operations
  about 81
  Boolean operations 82
  collection operations 83
  numeric operations 82
  regex operations 83
org.kie.remote:kie-remote-client 294

P

persisted data
  extending 276, 277
PHREAK
  about 13, 216-218
  Alpha Nodes 220
  Beta Nodes 223
  improvements, over RETE 245
  Inspector 246
  Object Type Nodes 218, 219
  URL 246
PHREAK, improvements over RETE
  about 245
  delayed rule evaluation 245
  network segmentation 246
  set-oriented propagation 245
phreak-inspector module 246
Predictive Model Markup Language
    (PMML)
  about 185, 186
  customer classification decision
      tree example 188, 189
  in Drools 186, 187
  limitations 191, 192
  troubleshooting 191
process execution 260-263

Q

projects
  organizing 35-40

queries
  about 120, 121
  live 122
  on-demand queries 121, 122
Query Element Node 244

R

RabbitMQ
  reference link 294
regex operations 83
REST API, Kie Server
  reference link 295
RESTClientExampleTest 295
RETE 216
RETEOO 215
right-hand side, troubleshooting
  about 209
  compilation errors 209
  runtime errors 210, 211
R language
  URL 185
rule atomicity 7
rule attributes
  about 66
  example 67-72
  rule dates, management 73, 74
  rule groups, types 72
rule engine
  about 12, 41
  algorithm 13
  bootstrapping, CDI used 28-30
  uses 17, 18
rule execution, life cycle
  about 8, 9
  collaboration, with rules 9-11
  people involvement with rules,
      BRMS used 11
rule inheritance 102
rule, left-hand side
  debugging 196
  Drools logs 207
  event listeners 204-206

rule, simpler versions 207
troubleshooting 197
rule, right-hand side
about 208
compilation errors 209
generated Java classes, dumping 212
good practices 211
runtime errors 211
troubleshooting 209
rules
about 2, 5
atomicity of rules 7
basic structure 2, 3
complex applications, examples 15
Complex Systems 14
date, management 73, 74
Declarative Programming 3
deviations, handling 99
eShop system, example 16, 17
ever-changing scenarios 15
executing 24-27
execution chaining 6
groups, types 72
independence 5
language 30-35
loops, controlling 74, 75
ordering rules 7
uses 14
writing 24-27
rules file, DSL 163, 164
rule templates
about 178
array data source 182
objects data source 183, 184
spreadsheet data source 181, 182
SQL result set data source 184, 185
structure 178, 179
template header 179
working with 180, 181
Rule Terminal Nodes (RTN) 218, 219

S

shed keyword 97
single template section 179
SLF4J
URL 207

sliding windows, event-driven architecture
declared 152
length-based 150
time-based 151
Spring Framework
about 289
reference link 287, 288
Spring integration
about 288
Kie Spring Config example 289
state
persistence 270, 272
Stateful Kie Sessions 106, 109
Stateless Kie Sessions 49-52, 106-108
Subject Matter Experts (SME) 159

T

tags, for Kie Spring contexts configuration
reference link 290
template 179
temporal operators
about 144-148
URL 146
time-based-events
declaring 143, 144
TRACE level 207
transactions
managing 278

U

update keywords 64

W

Web Service 62
Weld
URL 30, 288
Wildfly App Server
reference link 294
WildFly AS
URL 29

X

XML commands, Kie Session
reference link 292